ADVANCES IN SOFTWARE SCIENCE AND TECHNOLOGY

VOLUME 3

JAPAN SOCIETY FOR SOFTWARE SCIENCE AND TECHNOLOGY
World Trade Center Building 7F, 2-4-1 Hamamatsu-cho
Minato-ku, Tokyo, 105 Japan

ADVANCES IN SOFTWARE SCIENCE AND TECHNOLOGY
VOLUME 3

JAPAN SOCIETY FOR SOFTWARE SCIENCE AND TECHNOLOGY

ACADEMIC PRESS, INC.

Harcourt Brace Jovanovich, Publishers

Boston San Diego New York
London Sydney Tokyo Toronto

Co-published for
Japan Society for Software Science and Technology
by Academic Press, Inc.
and
Iwanami Shoten, Publishers

This book is printed on acid-free paper. ∞

ACADEMIC PRESS, INC.
1250 Sixth Avenue, San Diego, CA 92101

United Kingdom Edition published by
ACADEMIC PRESS LIMITED
24–28 Oval Road, London NW1 7DX

Library of Congress Catal Card Number: 90–660056

ISBN 0–12–037103–0
ISSN 1044–7997

AP Exclusive Sales Territory: United States, its territories and dependencies, Canada, and Europe.
Iwanami Shoten Exclusive Sales Territory: Japan.
Nonexclusive sales rights throughout the rest of the world.

Printed in the United States of America

91 92 93 9 8 7 6 5 4 3 2 1

Contributors

Numbers in parentheses refer to the pages on which the authors' contribution begin.

Kokichi Futatsugi (127), Electrotechnical Laboratory, 1–1–4 Umezono, Tsukuba, Ibaraki, 305 Japan

Shigeki Goto (71), NTT Basic Research Laboratories, 3–9–11 Midori-cho, Musashino-shi, Tokyo, 180 Japan

Takashi Hattori (53), Research Institute for Mathematical Sciences, Kyoto University, Kita-Shirakawa Oiwake-cho, Sakyo-ku, Kyoto, 606 Japan

Junji Hinami (1), Department of Computer Science and Communication Engineering, Faculty of Engineering, Kyushu University, 6–10–1 Hakozaki, Higashi-ku, Fukuoka, 812 Japan

Hiroshi Horiguchi (151), Department of Mathematics, Tokyo Denki University, 2–2 Nishiki-cho Kanda, Chiyoda-ku, Tokyo, 101 Japan

Yutaka Ishikawa (127), Electrotechnical Laboratory, 1–1–4 Umezono, Tsukuba, Ibaraki, 305 Japan

Takuya Katayama(13), Department of Computer Science, Tokyo Institute of Technology, 2–12–1 Ookayama, Meguro-ku, Tokyo, 152 Japan

Yasushi Kuno (109), Graduate School of Systems Management, Univ. of Tsukuba, Tokyo, 3–29–1, Otsuka, Bunkyo-ku, Tokyo, 112 Japan

Hiroshi Maruyama (157), IBM Research, Tokyo Research Laboratory, IBM Japan, 5–11 Sambancho, Chiyoda-ku, Tokyo, 102 Japan

Ken-ichiro Murakami (37), NTT Software Laboratories, 3–9–11 Midori-cho, Musashino-shi, Tokyo, 180 Japan

Reiji Nakajima (53), Research Institute for Mathematical Sciences, Kyoto University, Kita-Shirakawa Oiwake-cho, Sakyo-ku, Kyoto, 606 Japan

Ikuo Nakata (93), Institute of Information Sciences and Electronics, University of Tsukuba, Tsukuba, Ibaraki, 305 Japan

Naoyuki Niide (53), Research Institute for Mathematical Sciences, Kyoto University, Kita-Shirakawa Oiwake-cho, Sakyo-ku, Kyoto, 606 Japan

Takashi Sakuragawa (53), Research Institute for Mathematical Sciences, Kyoto University, Kita-Shirakawa Oiwake-cho, Sakyo-ku, Kyoto, 606 Japan

Masataka Sassa (93), Institute of Information Sciences and Electronics, University of Tsukuba, Tsukuba, Ibaraki, 305 Japan

Toshihisa Takagi (1), Educational Center for Information Processing, Kyushu University, 6–10–1 Hakozaki, Higashi-ku, Fukuoka, 812 Japan

Shin Takakura(13), Advanced Software Development, IBM Japan Ltd., 1623–14 Shimo Tsuruma, Yamato, 242 Japan

Kazuki Takenaka (53), Control & OR Department, Sumitomo Metal Industries, 1–3 Nishi-Nagasu-Hondori, Amagasaki, 660 Japan

Naoyoshi Tamura(13), Department of Electrical and Computer Engineering, Yokohama National University, 156 Tokiwadai, Hodogaya-ku, Yokohama, 240 Japan

Tsutomu Tayama (151), Department of Mathematics, Tokyo Denki University, 2–2 Nishiki-cho Kanda, Chiyoda-ku, Tokyo, 101 Japan

Satoru Tomura (127), Electrotechnical Laboratory, 1–1–4 Umezono, Tsukuba, Ibaraki, 305 Japan

Kazuo Ushijima (1), Department of Computer Science and Communication Engineering, Faculty of Engineering, Kyushu University, 6–10–1 Hakozaki, Higashi-ku, Fukuoka, 812 Japan

Jeehee Yoon (1), Department of Computer Science and Communication Engineering, Faculty of Engineering, Kyushu University, 6–10–1 Hakozaki, Higashi-ku, Fukuoka, 812 Japan

Contents

Society News

Editor's Message

Ikuo Nakata
Editor-in-Chief

This is the third issue of *Advances in Software Science and Technology*, an annual journal published by the Japan Society for Software Science and Technology (JSSST). The Society was founded in 1983 as a professional society dedicated to the advancement of the science and technology of computer software.

Unparalleled progress in hardware technology has been a driving force in modern computer technology. It has dramatically improved the performance and reliability, increased the level of complexity and sophistication, and created numerous new applications for computer systems. Progress in software technology, on the other hand, has been much more conservative. By and large, the volume and the quality of current software production depend on the skills and dedicated craftsmanship of programmers. With ever-increasing demand for software production, our ability to build and use computer systems is now limited mainly by our ability to produce software.

Advancing software technology requires active research effors toward scientific understanding of software systems, organized efforts to improve the current practice of software production, and drastic improvement of software education and training programs. The JSSST was founded to provide leadership, to promote and exchange ideas and experience, and to develop and organize concerted efforts in this direction.

The society has published a domestic bimonthly journal, *Computer Software*, since 1984. This contains original technical contributions that are refereed by the normal scientific review process. In addition, it contains survey papers, tutorials, conference reports, and miscellaneous articles. The journal covers a broad range of computer software. Topics featured in recent issues include algorithms, theory of programs, programming languages and methodology, operating systems, computer architecture, software engineering, artificial intelligence, and natural language processing.

Advances in Software Science and Technology is the second journal published by the JSSST. It is an annual publication with the same scope as *Computer Software*, and is intended to give international exposure to the activities of JSSST and to promote exchange of ideas and information among professionals and the public world-wide. Each issue of the journal contains original technical contributions as well as contributions that have appeared in previous issues of *Computer Software* in Japanese. The JSSST forms a special editorial committee for each issue of this journal; members of the committee for the third issue are listed in the front page together with those of *Computer Software*.

Like the previous issue of the journal, this issue describes a variety of activities, primarily in Japan. Software problems, however, are something we must all face today; and international collaboration and exchange are absolutely necessary. We very much look forward to publishing contributions from a wide variety of authors in future issues.

CONTENTS OF PREVIOUS VOLUMES

VOLUME 1

Research Contributions

Tutorial

VOLUME 2

Research Contributions

Tutorial

Software Critique

Prototyping a System of Writing Tools for Japanese Documents

Kazuo Ushijima Junji Hinami Jeehee Yoon Toshihisa Takagi

Summary. We have developed a system of writing tools called SUIKOU that analyzes a machine-readable Japanese document textually and provides the writers with useful information for polishing it. The development methods for writing tools for English could not be applied to the development of tools for a Japanese document because of their features. A prototyping method was adopted to develop SUIKOU. SUIKOU was developed through the following four phases: (1) groping, (2) addition and determination of functions, (3) improvement of efficiency, and (4) modification of the user interface. This paper evaluates the prototyping method by describing the development process, functions, and user interface of SUIKOU.

1 Introduction

The rapid progress in computer technologies has produced inexpensive word processors for Japanese. Many Japanese documents are now being written with them. However, they are used only for inputting, editing, storing, and outputting of documents; they do not support polishing these documents.

We have developed a system of writing tools called SUIKOU that analyzes a machine-readable Japanese document textually and provides the writer with useful information for polishing it. SUIKOU is a Japanese word that means the polishing of writing.

Writing tools for English documents such as IBM's CRITIQUE [4, 5] and UNIX™ Writer's Workbench [2, 3] are well known. The design goals of these tools might be expected to be useful for designing and implementing Japanese writing tools. But the functional specifications of those tools could not easily be applied to SUIKOU because Japanese documents have some features that differ from English documents. For example, Japanese has a large character set and in Japanese sentences there are no spaces between words. We were not able to give the precise specification of SUIKOU beforehand. Since it was difficult to develop it using conventional methods based on the life-cycle model of software development, we applied the prototyping method [6] to develop SUIKOU.

SUIKOU was eventually developed through the following four phases:
(1) groping, (2) addition and determination of functions, (3) improvement of efficiency, and (4) modification of the user interface.

In this paper, we evaluate the prototyping method by describing the development process, functions, and user interface of SUIKOU. Section 2 introduces briefly

ISBN 0-12-037103-0

1　はじめに

日本語文章推敲支援ツール［推敲］［１２，１３］　は機械可読な形で存在する日本語文章を解析してその推敲に役立つ情報を提供することを目的としたシステムである。その開発に際して，仕様をあらかじめ明確に与えることができないため，最近注目されているプロトタイピングの手法を採用した［１１］。

プロトタイピングは使い捨て型と改良発展型の２種類に大別できる［８］。どちらかといえば，前者は従来の要求仕様定義の代わりに用いられることが多く，後者は研究的色彩が強いソフトウェアの開発に利用されることが多い。［推敲］におけるプロトタイピングは仕様の確定という観点からは前者とみなせるが結果的には後者に属するものであり，徐々に改良して実用システムに近づけるという方式によりシステムを開発した。このような手法を使ってソフトウェアの設計や開発を行った事例は既にいくつか報告されているけれども［８］　，今回，我々が行った［推敲］のプロトタイピングでは従来あまり指摘されなかった過程を経験した。そこで，本論文ではプロトタイピングの観点から［推敲］の開発経過を順を追って述べることにより，プロトタイピング手法の意義とその問題点を明らかにする。

Fig. 1 An example of a Japanese document.

the textual features of Japanese documents. Section 3 describes the policy adopted at the start of the development. Sections 4 and 5 give some functions of the first and second versions of SUIKOU by using examples. Sections 6 and 7 describe the improvement of efficiency and the modification of the user interface brought about by the improvement. Section 8 presents the environment of the implementation. Section 9 discusses the effectiveness of our policy and method.

2 Features of Japanese Documents

There are many differences between Japanese and European languages such as English. In this section, we point out principal features of Japanese documents from the viewpoint of designing and implementing SUIKOU.

(1) Japanese has a large character set:
More than 2,000 characters are needed just for daily use. Therefore, at least two bytes are needed to encode a Japanese character. Although for a Japanese document file, coding methods and file formats differ from one computer system to another, a Japanese document is generally composed of a free mixture of passages in two kinds of character sets: One is a set of traditional alphabetic characters coded in one byte, and the other consists of *Kanji*, *Hiragana*, *Katakana*, and other Japanese characters that are coded in two bytes. To solve the coexistence problem of these two character sets, several methods are proposed: some of them use shift codes, and the others use special coding methods to distinguish them.

(2) A Japanese sentence is composed of a nonsegmented sequence of characters:
That is, Japanese sentences have no spaces between words as English does. Therefore, it is much harder to recognize words and analyze a document morphologically in Japanese than in English. Figure 1 shows an example of a Japanese document. KUTEN, a small circle, is ordinarily used as the end mark of a sentence. In some documents "." is used instead of KUTEN.

3 Development Policy

We adopted the following policy while developing SUIKOU.

(1) SUIKOU processes an ordinary complete scientific or technical paper.
We aimed to develop writing tools that can process an ordinary complete technical paper within a reasonable time. The size of a Japanese complete paper including figures and tables, which is printed in seven to eight pages of a technical journal, is usually about 10,000 Japanese characters (that is, about 20,000 bytes). Our tools must handle a paper of this size within a short response time of, say, a few seconds.

(2) SUIKOU analyzes a document only textually.
It is generally regarded as natural that writing tools analyze sentences both grammatically and semantically and then provide the writer with useful information for rethinking them. This means that writing tools are required to have natural language processing facilities. Actually, IBM's CRITIQUE [5] uses them to analyze an English document. But natural language processing is a time-consuming task, and the result of analysis may have ambiguities. To introduce natural language processing techniques would probably violate the development policy (1). Thus, we only adopted a textual analysis method that extracts information from a Japanese document with no machine dictionaries or grammatical analyses.

(3) It is not a computer but, rather, the writer who polishes sentences.
This policy means that SUIKOU itself does not improve a Japanese document. It only extracts information from a document so that the information can help the writer find the sentences and words whose usage is improper. The information extracted by SUIKOU may contain unrequested information. But SUIKOU must not miss requested information, because a user tends to examine only the information provided by SUIKOU. For example, when finding sentences in the passive voice, SUIKOU may extract nonpassive voice sentences, but must not miss any passive voice sentences. The user can decide whether or not the information is useful.

4 First Version of SUIKOU

To begin with, we tried to make some prototypes of writing tools intended to be useful. At first we developed these prototype on a mainframe FACOM M382, whose architecture is compatible with that of the IBM370 and whose performance is almost equivalent to that of the IBM 3090-200. These prototypes were written in SNOBOL4 with Japanese text processing facilities, since SNOBOL4 is suitable for developing prototypes of programs for text processing [8].

The first version of SUIKOU consists of the following four tools:

(1) SENTENCE
This tool analyzes a Japanese document, separates it into sentences by textually searching occurrences of KUTEN, "。", or carriage return code, and displays the head part, end part, and length of each sentence in a line in the order of occurrence. The end part of a Japanese sentence is important, because most Japanese sentences end with a predicate. This tool is useful for discovering the monotonicity of the end parts of sentences and indicating sentences that are too long.

```
□□□　日本語文章推敲支援ツール：ＳＥＮＴＥＮＣＥ　□□□
◎　データセット名　◎　：　SUIKOU.JEF

NO. レコード              文頭                       文末              文長
 1 01029000  1　はじめに                               はじめに：
 2 01030000  　日本語文章推敲支援ツー--的としたシステムである。：＊＊＊＋
 3 01030000  その開発に際して，仕様を--手法を採用した［１１］。：＊＊＊
 4 01032000  　プロトタイピングは使い--類に大別できる［８］　。：＊＋
 5 01032000  どちらかといい得ば，前者は--に利用されることが多い。：＊＊＊
 6 01032000  「推敲」におけるプロトタ--よりシステムを開発した。：＊＊＊＊＋
 7 01033000  このような手法を使ってソ--なかった過程を経験した。：＊＊＊＊＋
 8 01034000  そこで，本論文ではプロト--の問題点を明らかにする。：＊＊＊＋
 9 01036000  ２　「推敲」              --          ２　「推敲」：
10 01037000  ２．１　開発動機          --        ２．１　開発動機：
11 01038000  　日本語ワードプロセッサ--作成が容易になってきた。：＊＋
12 01038000  これの主な仕事は文章の入--的に助けるわけではない。：＊＊＋
13 01038000  ワードプロセッサでつくら--読な形で蓄えられている。：＊＋
14 01039000  それにもかかわらず清書出--というのではつまらない。：＊＋
15 01039000  計算機でその中に何とかふ--いう動機で開発を始めた。：＊＊
16 01040000  ２．２　プロトタイピング--２．２　プロトタイピング：＋
17 01041000  　推敲に役立つ情報とは何--されているわけではない。：＊＊＊＊
18 01041000  すなわち推敲を支援するソ--様が明確になっていない。：＊＊
19 01042000  また，推敲作業のためには--当であるのか分からない。：＊＊
20 01043000  　日本語文章の推敲支援ツ--４］　などが参考になる。：＊＊＊＊
```

Fig. 2 An example of an output of SENTENCE.

Figure 2 is an example of an output of SENTENCE. In this figure, "*" and "+" mean 20 and 10 characters, respectively. For example, "***+" indicates that the length of the sentence is 70.

(2) KWIC

This tool makes KWIC (Key Word In Context) lists. As mentioned in Section 2, written Japanese consists of three kinds of characters: *Kanji*, *Katakana*, and *Hiragana*. This tool recognizes a keyword as a string of the same kind characters. A KWIC list is useful for detecting misspelled words. Figure 3 shows an example of an output of KWIC for *Katakana* strings. This tool supports checking the uniformity of the expressions in *Katakana* character standing for words of foreign origin. *Katakana* strings are mainly used for expressing words of foreign origin. Since it is impossible to write pronunciation of foreign words exactly in *Katakana*, we use several *Katakana* strings to express one foreign word. It is not desirable to use multiple expressions for one foreign word in the same document.

(3) XREF

This tool cross-references keywords and the record numbers where they appear.

(4) PAREN

This tool points out the correspondence of parentheses and multi-nested parentheses.

5 Addition and Determination of Functions

The first version of SUIKOU revealed that some prototypes of writing tools provide a writer with useful information for improving a document by analyzing it only textually, although these prototypes have some drawbacks. For example, the tools KWIC and XREF produce a lot of output, making it hard for users to find the

```
□□□　日本語文章推敲支援ツール：ＫＷＩＣ　□□□
◎　データセット名　◎　：　SUIKOU.JEF
　　種類：カタカナ列

NO. 1  って，もし機能や：アルゴリズム　　　　：の変更などがあれ  01097000
NO. 2  元のプログラムの：アルゴリズム　　　　：には必ずしもとら  01108000
NO. 3  のよい文字列照合：アルゴリズム　　　　：が開発されている  01110000
NO. 4  が多いため，この：アルゴリズム　　　　：をそのまま適用す  01111000
NO. 5  る高速文字列照合：アルゴリズム　　　　：［１］　を採用す  01111000
NO. 6  ４　プログラムの：アルゴリズム　　　　：をそのまま利用し  01115000
NO. 7  より文字列の照合：アルゴリズム　　　　：を全く気にせずプ  02024000
NO. 8  作業は文字列照合：アルゴリズム　　　　：の習得期間を除け  02034000
NO. 9  たように，中には：アルゴリズム　　　　：を変更したプログ  02036000
NO. 10 インタフェースや：アルゴリズム　　　　：を全く変更せずに  02036000
NO. 11 の評価，人間との：インタフェース　　　：の評価などがある  02018000
NO. 12 　のＦＤＭＳ和文：エディタ　　　　　　：で作成された文章  01056000
NO. 13 降，ＦＤＭＳ和文：エディタ　　　　　　：で作成したファイ  01057000
NO. 14 　字種別（漢字，：カタカナ　　　　　　：，ひらがな，英字  01067000
NO. 15 できる，とくに，：カタカナ　　　　　　：列は表記のゆれの  01067000
NO. 16 図２にＫＷＩＣ（：カタカナ　　　　　　：列）出力例の一部  01067000
NO. 17 漢字，ひらがな，：カタカナ　　　　　　：等の文字集合を表  02028000
NO. 18 スト処理に便利な：キーワード　　　　　：の追加　　　日本  02028000
NO. 19 文字集合を表わす：キーワード　　　　　：を用意している。  02028000
```

Fig. 3 An example of an output of KWIC for *Katakana* strings.

information that they want.

We then iteratively evaluated the first version of the prototypes and enhanced them. Through this work, we were able to determine the functions and user interface of SUIKOU.

The second version of SUIKOU consists of 26 tools. In this section, we show three that are often used.

(1) KOSOA

This tool searches for words that point to other objects as demonstrative pronouns in a document and makes their occurrences conspicuous. Frequently, readers cannot understand what object a demonstrative pronoun points to. KOSOA makes a writer confirm what these words point to. Figure 4 is an example of an output of this tool. The halftone parts show their occurrences. KOSOA is named after the demonstrative pronouns "<u>ko</u>re ," "<u>so</u>re," and "<u>a</u>re ," which correspond respectively to "this," "it," and "that" in English.

(2) PASSIVE

Strunk and White recommend the use of active voices in English [7]. In Japanese documents, passive sentences are also liable to be long and ambiguous. A writer should avoid using too many passive sentences. This tool indicates the positions of the occurrences of the candidates for passive voice in a document. Figure 5 shows an example of an output of PASSIVE. In order to extract textually candidates for passive voice, we developed a textual analyzing method using five simple conditions [9]. In this paper, we omit the description of the method for the sake of space.

(3) LENGTH

This tool searches for keywords whose lengths are included in a range indicated by the user. For example, this tool helps in searching long *Hiragana* strings. The readability of Japanese documents depends on the balance of occurrences of *Kanji*

１　はじめに

日本語文章推敲支援ツール［推敲］［１２，１３］　は機械可読な形で存在する日本語文章を解析してその推敲に役立つ情報を提供することを目的としたシステムである。その開発に際して，仕様をあらかじめ明確に与えることができないため，最近注目されているプロトタイピングの手法を採用した［１１］。

プロトタイピングは使い捨て型と改良発展型の２種類に大別できる［８］。どちらかといえば，前者は従来の要求仕様定義の代わりに用いられることが多く，後者は研究的色彩が強いソフトウェアの開発に利用されることが多い。［推敲］におけるプロトタイピングは仕様の確定という観点からは前者とみなせるが結果的には後者に属するものであり，徐々に改良して実用システムに近づけるという方式によりシステムを開発した。このような手法を使ってソフトウェアの設計や開発を行った事例は既にいくつか報告されているけれども［８］　，今回，我々が行った［推敲］のプロトタイピングでは従来あまり指摘されなかった過程を経験した。そこで，本論文ではプロトタイピングの観点から［推敲］の開発経過を順を追って述べることにより，プロトタイピング手法の意義とその問題点を明らかにする。

Fig. 4　An example of an output of KOSOA.

□□□　日本語文章推敲支援ツール：ＰＡＳＳＩＶＥ　□□□

◎　データセット名　◎　：　SUIKOU.JEF

NO. 1	とができないため，最近注目	されて	いるプロトタイピングの手法	01031000
NO. 2	要求仕様定義の代わりに用い	られる	ことが多く，公社は研究的色	01032000
NO. 3	いソフトウェアの開発に利用	される	ことが多い。［推敲］におけ	01032000
NO. 4	った事例は既にいくつか報告	されて	いるけれども［８］　，今回	01034000
NO. 5	イピングでは従来あまり指摘	されな	かった過程を経験した。そこ	01034000
NO. 6	い。ワードプロセッサでつく	られた	文書は機械可読な形で蓄えら	01038000
NO. 7	た文書は機械可読な形で蓄え	られて	いる。それにもかかわらず清	01038000
NO. 8	清書出力と保存とにしか利用	されな	いというのではつまらない。	01039000
NO. 9	のか，など必ずしも明らかに	されて	いるわけではない。すなわち	01041000
NO. 10	日本語文章には，分かち書き	されて	いないので，辞書なしに文節	01044000
NO. 11	階である。推敲に役立つと思	われる	機能をとりあえず実現して試	01048000
NO. 12	行うことが有効な方法と考え	られる	。実際，ＥＰＩＳＴＬＥ　で	01051000
NO. 13	間がかかりすぎることが予想	される	［１９］。そこで，辞書を使	01052000
NO. 14	日本語文章は分かち書き	されて	いないので，辞書なしに文節	01054000
NO. 15	ＦＤＭＳ和文エディタで作成	された	文章を解析対象とする。解析	01056000
NO. 16	あえず，九大センターに設置	されて	いる日本語ラインプリンタに	01057000
NO. 17	いこと　等が問題点として挙げ	られた	。しかし，そのような問題点	01076000
NO. 18	外に，推敲作業に必要と考え	られる	機能を実現の容易なものから	01080000
NO. 19	文献［１２，１３］　を参照	された	い。　図３はＫＯＳＯＡ　の	01081000
NO. 20	わかった。文字種毎に切り出	された	文字列を処理対象とするプロ	01089000
NO. 21	日本語ＳＮＯＢＯＬ４　で書	かれた	プログラムをＦＯＲＴＲＡＮ	01105000
NO. 22	ルゴリズムには必ずしもとら	われな	いことにした。　具体的には	01108000
NO. 23	キスト上の文字列照合に費や	されて	いる。しかし，日本語文章テ	01110000
NO. 24	字列照合アルゴリズムが開発	されて	いるわけではない。そこでと	01111000
NO. 25	キスト上でその有効性が確認	されて	いる高速文字列照合アルゴリ	01111000
NO. 26	ンドの処理時間が大幅に短縮	され，	［推敲］は実用システムのレ	01120000
NO. 27	ルを処理するコマンドが追加	された	ので（図６参照），利用者は	01124000
NO. 28	，利用者は日本語文章の格納	されて	いるソーステキストファイルに	02001000
NO. 29	７（ａ）のメニュ画面が表示	され，	利用者はその中のコマンドに	02009000
NO. 30	の作業の経過及びそれから得	られた	知見を以下にまとめる。（１	02014000
NO. 31	報告［８］　ではあまり指摘	されて	いない点である。　一般にプ	02017000
NO. 32	作っていったことによると思	われる	。プロトタイプの性能で満足	02019000
NO. 33	のファイルの仕様は明らかに	されて	おらず，他言語でこのファイ	02026000
NO. 34	Ｉ／Ｏ　プリミティブが設計	された	［１７］。これは，日本語Ｓ	02038000
NO. 35	ンドが書き換えにより高速化	された	ことによって，［推敲］はよ	02041000

Fig. 5　An example of an output of PASSIVE.

```
□□□　日本語文章推敲支援ツール：ＬＥＮＧＴＨ　□□□
◎　データセット名　◎　：　SUIKOU.JEF
　　　　種類：ひらがな列
キーワード長：１１文字～１５文字

NO. 1  らかじめ明確に与：えることができないた－め，最近注目され  01030000
NO. 2  保存とにしか利用：されないというのでは－つまらない。計算  01039000
NO. 3  ，など必ずしも明：らかにされているわけ－ではない。すなわ  01041000
NO. 4  あればそれを指摘：することができればよ－い。推敲するのは  01049000
NO. 5  ７］　を一応想定：しているけれどもそれ－に限るものではな  01050000
NO. 6  に違う文字列を書：いてしまうことがある－けれども，これら  01068000
NO. 7  ンプリンタに出力：するようにしていたた－め出力結果を取り  01076000
NO. 8  力結果を取りに行：くのがわずらわしいこ－と等が問題点とし  01076000
NO. 9  りに長いと読み易：さをそこなうおそれが－ある。ＬＥＮＧＴ  01086000
NO. 10 部分に実行が集中：していることがわかっ－た。文字種毎に切  01088000
NO. 11 ルゴリズムには必：ずしもとらわれないこ－とにした。　　具  01108000
NO. 12 ルゴリズムが開発：されているわけではな－い。そこでとりあ  01111000
NO. 13 各コマンドを実行：できるようになってい－る。図７（ｂ），  02009000
NO. 14 供しうるように作：っていったことによる－と思われる。プロ  02019000
NO. 15 に区別せず取り扱：うことができるように－している。　　（  02026000
NO. 16 　コマンドを発行：できるようになってい－たので特にプロト  02030000
NO. 17 らも容易に呼び出：しができるようになっ－ている。Ｉ／Ｏ　  02038000
```

Fig. 6 An example of an output of LENGTH.

characters and *Hiragana* characters. A Japanese sentence is composed of a non-segmented sequence of characters. A long *Hiragana* string may contain many words, so the readability of a document may be decreased by sentences having long *Hiragana* strings. Figure 6 shows an example of an output of LENGTH. In this example, *Hiragana* strings whose lengths are in the range of 11 to 15 characters are displayed.

6 Improvement of Efficiency

Through the development of the second version, we were able to determine the functions and user interface of SUIKOU. But the execution speed of the second version written in SNOBOL4 was slow, because the processor of SNOBOL4 is not a compiler, but an interpreter.

Table 1 gives the processing time of some commands of the second version. This table shows that most tools of the second version satisfy the development policy (1). But some tools such as the KWIC command require much time for processing a long document. For example, the KWIC command for *Kanji* strings needs about 50 seconds for processing the document D of about 37,000 Japanese characters. Thus, we rewrote the second version using Fortran77 instead of SNOBOL4.

During rewriting, we also devised pattern-matching techniques suitable for Japanese documents. The KOSOA command finds 11 demonstrative pronouns such as "kore," "sore," and "are" in a document. In the SENTENCE command, three patterns of KUTEN, ".", and carriage return code must be searched. We can reduce these searching processes to a string-matching problem for multiple patterns. As an algorithm that is appropriate for multiple patterns, the Aho-Corasick algorithm [1] is well known for use with Roman alphabetic texts. We modified this algorithm to be suitable for Japanese texts [11, 12] and used it in implementing

Table 1 Processing times of commands of the second version (ms)

Document (number of characters)	SENTENCE	KOSOA	KWIC (*Kanji*)	KWIC (*Hiragana*)	INDEX (*Kanji*)
A(5007)	1,039	395	5,845	5,610	1,722
B(9842)	1,866	654	9,790	10,752	2,726
C(23583)	5,991	1,535	39,425	64,496	11,701
D(36605)	17,741	2,598	46,484	94,253	11,735

Table 2 Processing times of commands of the third version (ms)

Document (number of characters)	SENTENCE	KOSOA	KWIC (*Kanji*)	KWIC (*Hiragana*)	INDEX (*Kanji*)
A(5007)	58	107	193	205	55
B(9842)	74	122	317	354	66
C(23583)	167	196	793	943	118
D(36605)	272	278	887	1,042	128

some tools.

The execution speed of SUIKOU was remarkably improved. For example, the KOSOA command of the third version processes document D 10 times faster than that of the second version. Table 2 shows the processing time of the commands of the third version.

7 Modification of User Interface

The restriction of inefficiency of the second version necessitated a user managing some intermediate files. That is, in the second version, a user was not able to obtain a KWIC list directly from a source document, but only from an intermediate file, called a *string file*. This file contains a set of strings cut out from the source document, because the cutting process written in SNOBOL4 was a time consuming task. Some other commands such as LENGTH also got the result of the command from the string file as efficiently as the KWIC command did. Figure 7 shows the relationship between commands and intermediate files in the second version. This figure shows that the result of the FREQUENCY command can be obtained only via three intermediate files: string, kwic, and index. Thus, in the second version, a user was requested to manage those intermediate files.

The improvement of efficiency led us to look at the user interface of SUIKOU again. In the fourth version, we reconstructed the configuration of commands and improved the user interface of the third version by hiding the intermediate files from users. This could be done because we were able to obtain directly the result of all commands without intermediate files by developing the efficient third version. In the fourth version, a user may manage only a source document file.

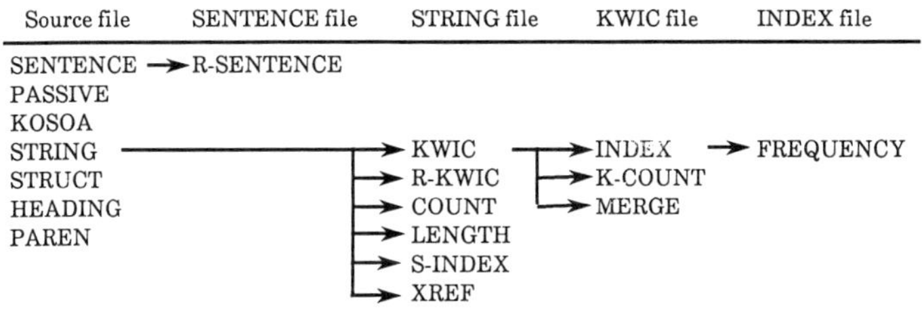

Fig. 7 The relationship between commands and intermediate files in the second version.

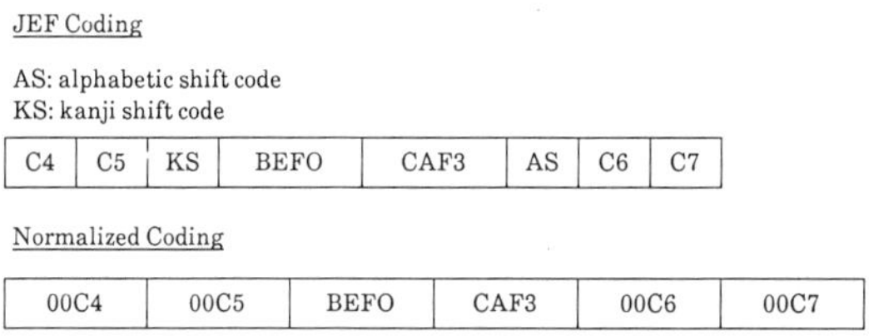

Fig. 8 Internal representation of a Japanese document.

8 Environment and Coding Method

As mentioned in Section 4, SUIKOU was implemented on the FACOM M382 system at the Computer Center of Kyushu University. The operating system is FACOM OS IV/F4 with JEF (Japanese Extended Features). The FACOM M382 is a mainframe computer whose architecture is compatible with that of the IBM370, and OS IV/F4 is basically equivalent to IBM MVS without JEF.

In the JEF environment, shift codes are used to distinguish alphabetic and Japanese character sets. If we handle a document using this coding method directly, the pattern matching processing necessary for textual analysis could be complex. Thus, we adopted a method for transforming an original document into the document using another coding method called the normalization coding and then analyze it.

The normalization coding [8], proposed by one of the authors, represents all alphabetic characters in two bytes by adding the padding in front. Figure 8 gives two internal representations of a Japanese document using the JEF and normalization coding methods respectively.

9 Discussion

The development and use of SUIKOU have made the following issues clear.

(1) Generally speaking, there are two types of prototype programs.
One is thrown away after the specification is determined; the other is gradually

enhanced and becomes a final product for practical use. The throwaway prototypes are usually made instead of a requirement specification in the life-cycle model. On the other hand, the gradually enhanced prototypes are used for developing research oriented software. We started the SUIKOU project as a throwaway-type prototyping, and subsequently, SUIKOU was iteratively enhanced and resulted in the current and practical system. Though the process of ordinary prototyping ends at the phase corresponding to "(3) Improvement of efficiency" described in Section 6, we experienced another phase of prototyping, as stated previously. This fact suggests that the efficiency of prototypes should be taken into account when evaluating the user interface of prototypes.

(2) We were easily able to rewrite prototypes in Fortran 77 within a short time since the functions and user interface of SUIKOU had already been determined. This development process of SUIKOU reveals that the prototyping method is effective for developing software such as SUIKOU.

(3) Problem-oriented languages such as SNOBOL4 and the environment for the Japanese text processing have important roles in prototyping. We were able to develop most tools of the first and second versions within a few days by using SNOBOL4 with Japanese text-processing facilities.

(4) According to our experience in using SUIKOU, it can be put to practical use. Actually, it provides useful information for improving a document, although it analyzes a document only textually. SENTENCE, KOSOA, PASSIVE, and KWIC are particularly useful.

(5) The processing speed of the fourth version of SUIKOU on the FACOM M382 system satisfies the development policy (1) mentioned in Section 3. For example, the running CPU times of SENTENCE, KOSOA, and PASSIVE for a Japanese document about 10,000 characters in length are about 100 ms, including the time for reading a document file, displaying it, etc.

(6) The two preceding facts mean that the development policy, our coding method for Japanese characters, and our pattern-matching techniques developed for Japanese documents are suitable.

10 Conclusions

Most of the problems in Japanese document processing will occur in other languages that have a large character set and nonsegmented sentences, such as Chinese. We suppose that some techniques adopted in developing SUIKOU could be useful for processing documents written in these languages.

Recently, many Japanese documents are being produced by using word processing software on personal computers. We transferred SUIKOU to a NEC PC-9800 system, the most popular personal computer in Japan [10]. It processes a Japanese document composed of 10,000 characters within a few seconds. We improved the user interface of SUIKOU by adopting a multiwindow system when transferring SUIKOU to the personal computers.

References

[1] Aho, A. V. and Corasick, M. J. : Efficient String Matching — An Aid to Bibliographic Search, *Comm. ACM*, Vol. 18, No. 6 (1975), pp. 333–340.

[2] Cherry, L. : Writing Tools, *IEEE Trans. Comput.*, Vol. COM-30, No. 1 (1982), pp. 100–104.

[3] Gingrich, P. S. : The UNIX Writer's Workbench Software — Result of a Field Study, *ibid.*, pp. 1909–1921.

[4] Heidorn, G. E., Jensen, L. T., Miller, L. A., Byrd, R. J. and Chodorow, M. S. : The EPISTLE Text-Critiquing System, *IBM Syst. J.*, Vol. 21, No. 3 (1982), pp. 305–326.

[5] Richardson, S. D. : Enhanced Text Critiquing using a Natural Language Parser, *IBM Research Report*, #51041 (1985).

[6] Special Issue on Rapid Prototyping, *ACM SIGSOFT Software Engineering Notes*, Vol. 7, No. 5 (1982).

[7] Strunk, W. and White, E. B. : *The Elements of Style*, Macmillan Publishing Co., New York, p. 92, 1979.

[8] Ushijima, K., Kurosaka, T. and Yoshida, K. : SNOBOL4 with Japanese Text Processing Facility, *Proc. ICTP'83* (1983), pp. 235–240.

[9] Ushijima, K., Ishida, M., Yoon, J. and Takagi, T. : A Simple Method to Extract Passive Voice in the Writing Tools for Japanese Documents, *Trans. Inf. Proc. Soc. Japan*, Vol. 28, No. 8 (1987), pp. 894–897 (in Japanese).

[10] Ushijima, K., Kurata, M., Takagi, T. and Suganuma, A. : Development of Writing Tools for Japanese Documents on a Personal Computer, *Proc. CCPCOL* (1988), pp. 576–580.

[11] Yoon, J., Takagi, T. and Ushijima, K. : Comparison and Improvement of String Matching Algorithms for Texts with a Large Character Set, *Proc. PCCS'85* (1985), pp. 400–402.

[12] Yoon, J., Takagi, T. and Ushijima, K. : An Experimental Study of String Matching Algorithms for Japanese Texts, *Proc. ICCC'86* (1986), pp. 297–304.

Initially published in "Computer Software", Vol. 3, No. 1, in Japanese.

Kazuo Ushijima
Department of Computer Science and Communication Engineering
Faculty of Engineering
Kyushu University
6–10–1 Hakozaki, Higashi-ku, Fukuoka
812 Japan

Junji Hinami
Department of Computer Science and Communication Engineering
Faculty of Engineering
Kyushu University
6–10–1 Hakozaki, Higashi-ku, Fukuoka
812 Japan
Current Address: Second Office Automation Division
NEC Corporation
10, Nisshin-cho 1-chome, Fuchu, Tokyo
183 Japan

Jeehee Yoon
Department of Computer Science and Communication Engineering
Faculty of Engineering
Kyushu University
6–10–1 Hakozaki, Higashi-ku, Fukuoka
812 Japan
Current Address:Department of Computer Science
Hallym University
1 Ockchun-Dong, Chuncheon, Kangwon-do
200–010 Korea

Toshihisa Takagi
Educational Center for Information Processing
Kyushu University
6–10–1 Hakozaki, Higashi-ku, Fukuoka
812 Japan

Attribute Grammar Evaluation System for Natural-Language Processing

Naoyoshi Tamura Shin Takakura Takuya Katayama

Summary.

This paper presents conditioned attribute grammars (CAGs) and a system for evaluating them that can be applied to natural-language processing. In an attribute grammar (AG), a grammar rule consists of syntax and semantic rules, so a semantic description of a programming language can be formally expressed. We attempt to apply CAGs, an extended version of AGs capable of controlling the application of rules, to natural-language processing. We have also implemented a CAG evaluation system. This is based on an LR-parser with simultaneous attribute evaluation, so even if there are ambiguities in the input sentences, efficient analysis can be done by using rule applicability conditions. We will also demonstrate the efficiency and practicality of our system.

1 Introduction

We present *conditioned attribute grammars* (CAGs) and a system for evaluating them that can be applied to natural-language processing.

In natural-language models or processing systems, rules are sometimes collected in the form of grammars, such as CFGs. It is, however, extremely difficult to describe universal laws by using simple grammar rules. Grammars are therefore sometimes augmented by additional information, such as precise controls of the applicability for each grammar rule. We took this approach, and we are aiming to construct a language model in which the additional information is represented as naturally as possible.

We are currently studying attribute grammars (AGs) [8]. In AGs, a grammar rule consists of syntax rules and semantic rules, so a semantic description of a programming language can be formally expressed. AGs have had some influence on recent research on compiler generators. We tried to apply AGs and other parsing methods used in programming languages to natural-language processing.

(1) Both a natural-language processor and a compiler of some programming language make outputs of the meaning of input sentences according to the predefined specification for the input sentences.

Natural-language processing systems can be classified according to the ways in which they represent syntax rules [10]. In such ways, especially in systems based on the rewriting by rules of a context-free grammar, the correspondence between

ISBN 0-12-037103-0

natural-language processing systems and compilers is more apparent, and further correspondences can be listed:

(2) Every syntax rule is related to its semantic description.

(3) Both processing systems usually have mechanisms of lexical analysis, syntactical analysis, and semantic analysis.

There are also the following differences between the systems, which we study in this paper:

(4) The number of rules. The number of syntax rules in a programming language is determined according to the specification of the language, whereas such a specification cannot be made for a natural language, and a sufficient number of rules is practically required for various patterns of sentences.

(5) Ambiguity. There is too much ambiguity in natural language, so a mechanism for clarification is necessary.

(6) Lexical analysis. Symbols other than operators, numbers, or punctuations are identifiers; however, there are an infinite number of words in natural languages, and a dictionary is required to categorize words before the actual parsing. A morphological analysis method is sometimes attached to the system.

We present some related studies on AGs, methods of evaluating them, and natural-language processing systems.

(1) We extend AGs by attaching an applicability condition to each (AG) production rule; we call these extensions conditioned attribute grammars (CAGs). A similar idea was introduced by [19], in which the conditions were used primarily to distinguish between rules with the same syntactical descriptions but different semantic descriptions.

(2) The following three attribute evaluation methods are typical:

   (a) attribute evaluation while performing several traversals on a constructed parse tree [1];

   (b) function calls where every *synthesized attribute* is returned by a function whose arguments are parse tree and *inherited attribute* values [5], [6], [19];

   (c) simultaneous attribute evaluation in LR parsing [4], [12], [14] .

   Our CAG evaluation method belongs to the third category, which is especially efficient for languages with fewer ambiguities. Although natural languages have many ambiguities, efficient parsing and attribute evaluation can be done by using *applicability conditions.*

(3) Our system uses bottom-up syntactical analysis. LINGOL [13], Extended LINGOL [17], and BUP [9] are similar to our system, because they use bottom-up syntactical analysis based on rewriting the rules of context-free grammars, and semantic information flows around the parse tree in semantic

analysis. This information flow can be defined by attribute definitions in our system.

2 Informal Description of CAGs

In this chapter we present conditioned attribute grammars (CAGs). Analysis of a sentence contains a kind of semantic operation in both formal languages and natural languages. In attribute grammars, this operation is formally described as a set of equations between attributes of grammar symbols. Moreover, for a system in which attributes are evaluated as a step of syntactical analysis, grammars with syntactical ambiguity can be semantically augmented by the relations between attributes. CAGs are versions of attribute grammars that are extended by introducing the applicability condition for every rule, not only to eliminate syntactical ambiguities, but also to check the validity of the analysis. In these respects our formalism is similar to the rule splitting of Watt [19] and the attribute grammar of Kastens [5]. However, we named it *Conditioned Attribute Grammars.*

2.1 The Outline of CAG

First, we illustrate a CAG with the simple example in Fig. 1. This grammar consists of six CAG rules, and if only the syntax parts of those rules are considered, the following four sentences can be generated:

(a) *I am happy.* (b) **I are happy.*
(c) **You am happy.* (d) *You are happy.*

In this example, (a) and (d) are correct English sentences, whereas (b) and (c) are incorrect because of subject-verb disagreement. Now we take attributes into account.

An attribute is a kind of variable attached to each grammar symbol. There are two types of attributes:

1. *Inherited attributes*: Information is carried in the direction from the root to the leaves of the parse tree, that is, left- and right-sensitive information flows to a subtree through inherited attributes of the nonterminal symbol, which corresponds to the root of the subtree.

2. *Synthesized attributes*: Information is carried in the opposite direction to that of inherited attributes, that is, information of a subtree flows to other parts of the parse tree through synthesized attributes of the nonterminal symbol, which corresponds to the root of the subtree.

Now let us introduce an attribute *psn* for the person of the noun phrase and the verb phrase. When CAG rules (3) and (5) are applied, the value of the attribute *psn* of terminal N and that of terminal V are both equal to 2 (hereafter we represent such values as *psn.N*, *psn.V*); that is, the applicability condition of CAG rule (1) holds. Therefore, sentence (d) is generated. On the other hand, when CAG rules (2) and (5) are applied, the applicability condition of CAG rule (1) does not hold, so sentence (b) is not generated. Thus, with this attribute, only sentences (a) and (d) are generated.

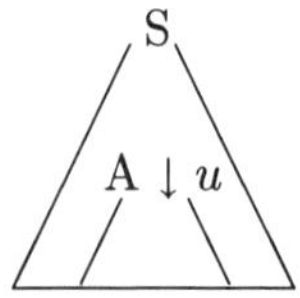

inherited attribute u

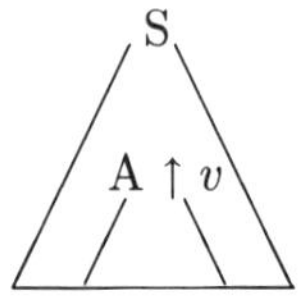

synthesized attribute v

Attribute p in Fig. 1 gives the parse of the input sentence. The semantic description of CAG rule (1) indicates that the parse of the input sentence is evaluated by concatenation (using operator $||$ in Fig. 1) of subparses $p.N$, $p.V$ and $p.C$, which are directly given in the other CAG rules.

2.2 Formal Definition of a CAG

For a grammar written in a CAG, a sentence in this language is evaluated by the CAG evaluator described in the next chapter. First of all, we define the CAG and the derivation in CAG.

Definition 1: CAG.
A conditioned attribute grammar CAG is formally defined by the following 6-tuple:

$$CAG =< G, At, Val, E, C, D >,$$

where

(1) $G =< V, \Sigma, P, S >$ is a *context-free grammar.* V is a finite set of *grammar symbols* (*symbols* for short), Σ is a finite set of *terminal symbols*, N is a finite set of *nonterminal symbols* (i.e., $V = N \cup \Sigma$), P is a finite set of *production rules*, i.e., $P \in N \times V^*$, and S is the *start symbol.* G is called the *underlying grammar* of the CAG.

(2) At is a set of *inherited* and *synthesized attributes* of symbols (terminal symbols and the start symbol have no inherited attribute). Every symbol $X \in V$ has a subset $At[X]$ of At. Let $INH[X]$ be the inherited attribute set, and $SYN[X]$ the synthesized attribute set of X. Then,

$$At[X] = INH[X] \cup SYN[X],$$

and

$$INH[X] \cap SYN[X] = \phi.$$

(3) Val is a set of values of all attributes.

(4) E is a set of *semantic rules* (*attribute definitions*). In a production rule $p : X_0 \rightarrow X_1 \cdots X_n \in P$, $a.X_k$ is called an *attribute occurrence*, where $a \in At[X_n]$, $0 \leq k \leq n$. For all synthesized attributes $a.X_0$ ($a \in SYN[X_0]$) and for all inherited attributes $b.X_k$ ($b \in INH[X_k], 1 \leq k \leq n$), there exists an attribute definition $E_{p,v}$ such that

$$E_{p,v} : v = f_{p,v}(v_1, \cdots, v_m),$$

Symbol	Inherited Attributes	Synthesized Attributes
S	ϕ	p
N	ϕ	psn,p
V	ϕ	psn,p
C	ϕ	p

(p, psn stand for the parse and the person)

(1) $S \longrightarrow N\ V\ C$
when $psn.N = psn.V$
with $p.S = 1 \parallel p.N \parallel p.V \parallel p.C$
(2) $N \longrightarrow$ 'I'
when *true*
with $psn = 1$
$p = 2$
(3) $N \longrightarrow$ 'You'
when *true*
with $psn = 2$
$p = 3$
(4) $N \longrightarrow$ 'am'
when *true*
with $psn = 1$
$p = 4$
(5) $V \longrightarrow$ 'are'
when *true*
with $psn = 2$
$p = 5$

Fig. 1 Simple example of a CAG.

where

$$v = a.X_0, \quad a \in SYN[X_0],$$

or

$$v = b.X_k, \quad b \in INH[X_k], \quad 1 \leq k \leq n.$$

Furthermore,

$$v_i = c.X_j, c \in INH[X_0] \cup SYN[X_1] \cup \cdots \cup SYN[X_n],$$
$$1 \leq i \leq m, \quad 0 \leq j \leq n$$

(v_i is an attribute occurrence of production rule p and is essential to the attribute evaluation of attribute v).
E is a finite set of attribute definitions $E_{p,v}$, which describe how to evaluate inherited attributes of the left-hand-side symbol (LSYM) in a CAG rule and synthesized attributes of right-hand-side symbols (RSYMs).

$$E = \bigcup_{p,v} E_{p,v} \,.$$

(5) C is a finite set of *applicability conditions* for each CAG rule. Every applicability condition is described with inherited attributes $v_1, \ldots, v_m$ of the LSYM and synthesized attributes of RSYMs of CAG rule p. Thus, if we let

$$C_p = Q_p(v_1, \cdots, v_m),$$
$$v_i = c.X_k, \quad (1 \leq i \leq m, 0 \leq k \leq n),$$
$$c \in INH[X_0] \cup SYN[X_1] \cup \cdots \cup SYN[X_n],$$

then

$$C = \bigcup_p C_p\ .$$

(6) D is a dictionary function

$$D : \Sigma \to Ps(Val)$$

which maps a terminal symbol b to a set of inherited attribute values of the terminal symbol, where $Ps(V)$ is the power set of set V.

Syntactical analysis and related attribute evaluation in the CAG are defined by the following two kinds of derivation:

Definition 2: Attributed and Conditioned Rightmost Derivation.
In $CAG =< G, At, Val, E, C, D >$ with $G =< V, \Sigma, P, S >$,
suppose $A \in N, \alpha, \beta \in V^*, w, x \in \Sigma^*$, and $A \to \beta \in P$.
Also assume

$$\pi : S \overset{*}{\underset{R}{\Longrightarrow}} \alpha A w \overset{*}{\underset{R}{\Longrightarrow}} \alpha\beta w \overset{*}{\underset{R}{\Longrightarrow}} x \qquad \cdots (a)$$

to be an ordinary *rightmost derivation.*

(1)

$$\underline{\alpha A w} \overset{*}{\underset{VR}{\Longrightarrow}} \underline{\alpha\beta w}$$

indicates that rule $p : A \to \beta$ has been applied to the rightmost nonterminal A in $\alpha A w$, and that attribute occurrences of A have values calculated from attribute values of A and β according to the semantic rules (attribute definitions) of rule p. $\underline{A}$, $\underline{\alpha}$, $\underline{\beta}$, and $\underline{w}$ in the above formula represent symbols with their inherited and synthesized attribute values. $\overset{*}{\underset{VR}{\Longrightarrow}}$ represents the transitive reflective closure of derivation, $\underset{VR}{\Longrightarrow}$.
For a rightmost derivation (a),

$$\pi : \underline{S} \overset{*}{\underset{VR}{\Longrightarrow}} \underline{\alpha A w} \overset{*}{\underset{VR}{\Longrightarrow}} \underline{\alpha\beta w} \overset{*}{\underset{VR}{\Longrightarrow}} \underline{x} \qquad \cdots (b)$$

is called an *attributed rightmost derivation.*

(2) In an attributed rightmost derivation (b), if every applicability condition holds, then the attributed rightmost derivation is also called the *conditioned rightmost derivation* and is represented as follows:

$$\pi : \underline{S} \overset{*}{\underset{VR}{\Longrightarrow}} \underline{\alpha A w} \overset{*}{\underset{CVR}{\Longrightarrow}} \underline{\alpha\beta w} \overset{*}{\underset{VR}{\Longrightarrow}} \underline{x} \qquad \cdots (c)$$

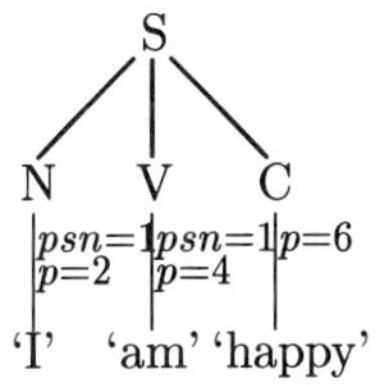

Fig. 2(a) Example of parse tree.

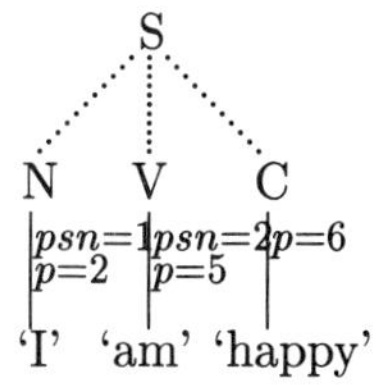

Fig. 2(b) Example of illegal parse tree.

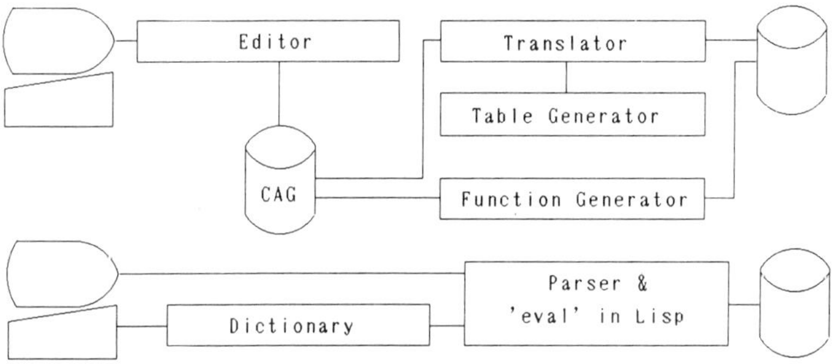

Fig. 3 CAG evaluation system.

3 Principles of the CAG Evaluator

In this chapter, we present the principles of the *CAG evaluator*. The evaluator is efficient and is made general so that it can be applied to practical natural-language processing. Figure 3 shows the structure of the CAG system.

3.1 Outline of Evaluation Principles

First, we outline the principles of CAG evaluation. In bottom-up parsing, where the parser constructs parse trees from the leaves to the root, it is difficult to evaluate inherited attributes that are used to pass information in the direction of the root. Evaluation is divided into two phases:

(1) *Parse tree construction*: The evaluator analyzes input sentences syntactically and generates parse trees. In this phase, synthesized attributes that can be evaluated independently of the values of inherited attributes are calculated. The evaluator also evaluates applicability conditions, using synthesized attribute values to eliminate as many improper parse trees as possible. The attribute evaluations and the management of the synthesized attribute values are done on a stack in this phase.

(2) *Attribute evaluation*: The evaluator evaluates all the attributes of symbols in the parse tree returned in phase (1) by attribute evaluating functions, and outputs synthesized attributes of the root node of the parse tree. Unevaluated applicability conditions in phase (1) and inherited attributes are also evaluated in this phase.

The parser in our CAG evaluator is basically a kind of *LR parser*; that is, it consists of a stack, an LR(k) action and a goto table constructed from the underlying grammar of CAG rules (in practice the table is an LALR (1) table), a look-ahead mechanism, and a simple attribute evaluation mechanism. An action of the parser, which may be a shift, reduce, accept, or error action, is determined by the parsing state (at the top of the stack) and k look-aheads, as long as the grammar is unambiguous. In a reduce action, attributes in a rule associated with the reduction are evaluated by using values of the synthesized attributes on the stack. The applicability condition of the rule is evaluated if this is possible. If the condition does not hold, an error action is called (i.e., backtracking). Almost all natural-language grammar is essentially ambiguous, and this ambiguity is detected by doubly defined actions (called *shift/reduce* or *reduce/reduce conflict*) in the action table of the grammar. Thus, our parser has the mechanism of pseudo-parallelism, which is implemented through backtracking.

The attribute evaluation functions corresponding to all the synthesized attributes of nonterminals have parse trees and values of inherited attributes as input parameters and are generated from given CAG rules before parsing [6], [7] . In practical attribute evaluation, the evaluator gives the parse tree to the attribute evaluation functions of the start symbol, which corresponds to the root of the parse tree. Then, attribute evaluating functions corresponding to synthesized attributes are called recursively. Finally, the values of synthesized attributes of the start symbol are returned as the values of the evaluation function.

In the following section we discuss the treatment of applicability conditions, the extraction of synthesized attributes independent of inherited attributes, syntactical analysis, and generation of attribute evaluation functions.

3.2 Treatment of Applicability Conditions

Predicates of applicability conditions can be described not only with synthesized attribute occurrences of RSYMs but also with inherited attribute occurrences of the LSYM. Because the values of inherited attributes flow in the direction of the leaves, in bottom-up parsing, where the parse tree is constructed upward from the leaves, the values of inherited attributes of the LSYM are not defined when a reduce action occurs. In the CAG evaluator, which uses αCAG (defined below) instead of the original CAG, syntactical analysis proceeds as if the applicability condition held. In αCAG every applicability condition holds, but a new attribute *cond* is attached. The attribute occurrence *cond*.X indicates whether a subtree with X as its root is generated by proper syntactical analysis. Therefore the applicability condition can be regarded as a synthesized attribute, and only a derivation for which the synthesized attribute *cond* of the start symbol is true is accepted.

Definition 3: Transformation α.
For every rule

$$p : X_0 \rightarrow X_1 \ldots X_n$$
$$\textbf{when } C_p$$
$$\textbf{with } E$$

in $CAG =< G, At, Val, E, C, D >$,
the set of

$$p : X_0 \rightarrow X_1 \ldots X_n$$
$$\textbf{when } true$$
$$\textbf{with } cond.X_0 = C_p \text{ and } cond.X_1 \text{ and } \cdots \text{ and } cond.X_n$$
$$E$$

(if X_i $(1 \leq i \leq n)$ is a terminal, $cond.X_i$=$true$.) is called αCAG, and the transformation from CAG to αCAG is called *transformation* α.

The value of attribute *cond* of the start symbol is the concatenation of the applicability conditions of all applied CAG rules. Therefore, if an applicability condition is evaluated as false in the syntactical analysis, an error action can be executed immediately.

3.3 Extraction of Computable Attribute Definition

In a CAG with no inherited attributes, attribute evaluation has little influence on syntactical analysis. Because attribute values are managed on a stack rather than in a parse tree, if there is a reduce action, quick references to synthesized attribute values are possible in the evaluation of attributes of the LSYM (see Section 3.4). Algorithm 1 excludes attributes affected by values of inherited attributes from given CAG rules and returns another set of CAG rules (which we will call βCAG) including only attributes that can be evaluated.

Algorithm 1: Extraction of Computable Attribute Definition.
Input : αCAG
Output: CAG with no inherited attributes (βCAG)

(1) $$C \leftarrow \alpha CAG \, ;$$
$$DELSET \leftarrow \phi \, .$$

($DELSET$: a set of attribute occurrences influenced by inherited attributes)

(2) For every CAG rule in C, let the set of inherited attributes of LSYM and RSYM X be empty (i.e., $INH[X] = \phi$).
Delete all attribute definitions of inherited attributes of RSYMs.
For all synthesized attribute definitions of the LSYM, if a definition has an inherited attribute occurrence of the LSYM, then delete this definition and add this attribute occurrence of the left-hand side of the definition to $DELSET$.

(3) For every CAG rule in C, if an attribute occurrence in the right-hand side of an attribute definition of the LSYM is a member of $DELSET$, then add this attribute occurrence of the left-hand side of this definition to $DELSET$ and delete this definition.

(4) Repeat the above steps as long as new synthesized attribute occurence are added to $DELSET$.

3.4 Syntax Analysis

This section describes the syntactical analysis in the CAG evaluator. Syntactical analysis is executed in the *LR-parsing* style, and the parser consists of the following:

(1) stack for storing symbols, attribute values, and parsing states;

(2) LR(k) action and goto table;

(3) look-ahead facility (input mechanism and reference mechanism for the dictionary);

(4) backtracking mechanism (for pseudo-parallelism).

The actual backtracking mechanism is implemented as the depth-first search for the space of parsing states. The parser executes one of the following actions according to the parsing state and input string (lookahead):

(1) *shift* (store input string and its synthesized attribute values on the stack);

(2) *reduce* (reduce and evaluate attributes);

(3) *terminate* (output the results and start backtracking for another solution);

(4) *conflict* (select one action and back up other actions and the stack);

(5) *error* (start backtracking).

First we define the functions *action* and *goto*, which the parser uses to determine the next action and the parsing state. The function *goto* is equivalent to the ordinary LR(k) goto function, but the function *action* is an LR(k) action function whose region is the set of possible actions. Because of the ambiguity of language, the ordinary LR(k) action function for a language sometimes has doubly defined actions on some entries. This is called *shift/reduce conflict* or *reduce/reduce conflict.* The function *action* has

$$Ps(\{reduce\ \pi | \pi \in P\} \cup \{shift\})$$

as its region in order to represent multiple action. Note that an error action is defined as the empty set $\{\ \}$.

Definition 4: Functions *action* and *goto.*
For $\beta CAG = < G, At, Val, E, C, D >$ with $G = < V, \Sigma, P, S >$, the functions *action* and *goto* are defined as follows:

$$action : Q_G \times \Sigma^k \rightarrow Ps(\{reduce\ \pi | \pi \in P\} \cup \{shift\});$$
$$goto\ : Q_G \times V \rightarrow Q_G \cup \{error\},$$

where Q_G is a set of states of the parser.

Next, we define the instantaneous description for representation in every evaluation state.

Definition 5: ID (Instantaneous Description).

(1) The *instantaneous description* ID of the parser is represented by

$$(\gamma T, z, \rho),$$

where

(a) $\gamma T \in \{T_0\} \times (V \times L \times Q_G)^*$ is a push-down stack, in which the rightmost element of γT is on the top of the stack, $L \subset Val$ is a set of synthesized attributes values, and T_0 is the initial state (T_m, used later, is the terminating state).

(b) $z \in \Sigma^*$ represents unevaluated input strings.

(c) $\rho \in P^*$ is a sequence of CAG rules (parse).

(2) The initial ID of the CAG parser is

$$(T_0, x, \Lambda),$$

where x represents the initial input string and Λ a null sequence. There are two special IDs, *error* and *terminate.*

The parsing action is uniquely defined for deterministic languages. However, for languages with ambiguity, such as natural languages, the parsing action is not deterministic. This is why the transition of parsing states is represented as a binary relation $\vdash$ between the states rather than a function that defines the next states from the previous one.

The action of the parser is defined on β CAG as follows. In the definition, only synthesized attributes are manipulated, so attribute evaluation means calculation of synthesized attributes of the LSYM, using synthesized attributes of RSYMs on the stack. All of the actions (1) to (3) in the definition below are selected nondeterministically. ${}^k z$ denotes the first k symbols of z and $\lg(\beta)$ is the number of symbols of $\beta \in V^*$.

Definition 6: Action of the Parser.
In $\beta CAG = < G, At, Val, E, C, D >$ with $G = < V, \Sigma, P, S >$, when the parser is in a state that has $ID(\gamma T, z, \rho)$, where $\gamma T \in \{T_0\} \times (V \times L \times Q_G)^*, z \in \Sigma^*, \rho \in P^*$, the transition to the next ID is represented by a binary relation '$\vdash$' over the set of IDs, as follows:

(1) When *reduce* $p \in action(T, {}^k z)$, $\;p = A \rightarrow \beta$, let v be a set of results of attribute evaluation, in which synthesized attributes of A are obtained by synthesized attributes of β on the top $3 \times lg(\beta)$ symbols of stack γT according to the semantic rule in βCAG rule p.

(a) If the value of attribute *cond* is defined in v and it is false, then

$$(\gamma T, z, \rho) \vdash error.$$

(b) Or, if $\gamma' = \Lambda$, $T' = T_0$, $A = S$, and $z = \Lambda$,then

$$(\gamma T, z, \rho) \vdash (T_0 S v T_m, \Lambda, p\rho) \stackrel{def}{=} terminate.$$

(c) Or, if $goto(T', A) = error$, then

$$(\gamma T, z, \rho) \vdash error.$$

(d) Otherwise,

$$(\gamma T, z, \rho) \vdash (\gamma' T' A\, v\, goto(T', A), z, p\rho).$$

(2) When $shift \in action(T,^k z)$,

(a) if $z = \Lambda$, then

$$(\gamma T, z, \rho) \vdash error.$$

(b) Or, if $z \neq \Lambda$, let $z = bz', b \in \Sigma, z' \in \Sigma^*$,

(i) If $goto(T$, b)=$error$, then

$$(\gamma T, z, \rho) \vdash error.$$

(ii) Otherwise,

$$(\gamma T, z, \rho) \vdash (\gamma T\, b\, v\, goto(T, b), z', \rho),$$

where v=D(b) is a set of synthesized attribute values of terminal symbol b.

(3) When $action(T,^k z)$= ϕ , then

$$(\gamma T, z, \rho) \vdash error.$$

3.5 Generation of Attribute Evaluation Functions and Attribute Evaluation

In this section, we discuss an algorithm for generating attribute evaluation functions for synthesized attributes of the start symbol, and attribute evaluation in the CAG evaluator.

First, we define the structure of a parse tree, which is uniquely constructed from the parse obtained by the parser mentioned in the previous section.

Definition 7: Parse Tree.
In $CAG =< G, At, Val, E, C, D >$ with $G =< V, \Sigma, P, S >$,

(1) A terminal symbol $a \in \Sigma$ with a set D(a) of its synthesized attribute values is a partial parse tree (leaf of a tree).

(2) If there are partial parse trees $t_1, \ldots, t_n$ with respective roots $A_1, \ldots, A_n$ and there is a production rule $A \rightarrow A_1 \ldots A_n \in P$, then t=$A[t_1, \ldots, t_n]$ is a partial parse tree.

(3) The parse tree is a partial parse tree with the start symbol as its root node.

An attribute evaluation function defines one synthesized attribute value, using the parse tree and inherited attribute values as its input arguments.

Definition 8: Attribute Evaluation Function.

(1) For every synthesized attribute occurrence $a.A$, function $H_{a,A}$ is defined as follows: $H_{a,A}(t, x_1, \cdots, x_n)$

$$\stackrel{def}{=} \begin{array}{rlll} & \textbf{if} & prod(t) = p_1 & \textbf{then} \quad h_{a,A,p_1} \\ \textbf{else} & \textbf{if} & prod(t) = p_2 & \textbf{then} \quad h_{a,A,p_2} \\ & \cdots & & \\ \textbf{else} & \textbf{if} & prod(t) = p_l & \textbf{then} \quad h_{a,A,p_l} \end{array}$$

where predicate $prod(t) = p_i$ $(1 \le i \le l)$ indicates that p_i is the production rule applied to the root of subtree t and we assume that n is the number of synthesized attributes of LSYM A in all production rules.

(2) h_{a,A,p_i} in (1) is an expression obtained by application of the following rules to the attribute definition for synthesized attribute a of LSYM A in CAG rule p_i:

(a) Replace inherited attribute occurrences $i_k.A$ of LSYM A by x_k.

(b) When A_i is a nonterminal symbol, replace synthesized attribute occurrences of RSYM A_i by

$$H_{o,A_j}(t_j, i_1.A_j, \cdots, i_m.A_j)$$

(where $i_1, \ldots, i_m$ are inherited attributes of A_j and t_j is a partial parse tree of t),

or when A_i is a terminal symbol, replace them by

$$val(t_j, o)$$

(where $val(t_j, o)$ is the value of synthesized attribute o of partial parse tree (leaf) t_j).

(c) Replace inherited attribute $i_k.A_j$ of RSYM A_j by the attribute definition for $i_k.A_j$ in CAG rule p_i.

The attribute evaluation in CAG evaluator proceeds as follows. The action of the parser defined in Definition 6 is nondeterministic, and many parse trees are constructed from an ambiguous sentence. Let T be a set of the resulting parse trees.

(1) Construct a set of parse trees T.

(2) For all parse trees $t \in T$,

(a) evaluate the attribute evaluation function $H_{cond,S}(t)$ to obtain the synthesized attribute value *cond* of the start symbol S;

(b) if $cond.S = true$ is obtained in step (a), evaluate all synthesized attributes o_j of the symbol S by using the attribute evaluation function $H_{o_j,S}(t)$.

4 Application to Natural-Language Processing

In this chapter, we describe an application of the CAG system to natural-language processing and give some results.

4.1 A Grammar: CAG_{ENG}

The grammar used in the application is based on an English grammar given by [15], which consists of about 400 CAG rules (hereafter we call this grammar CAG_{ENG}). CAG_{ENG} aims to construct only valid parse trees of English sentences. Therefore, attributes and applicability conditions on CAG_{ENG} are used to exclude invalid parse trees of English sentences. CAG_{ENG} can also be expanded to handle some semantic analysis by adding semantic attributes, their definitions, and applicability conditions to the original CAG_{ENG}. It is, of course, possible to control parsing by using semantic information. In this application the following types of sentences can be analyzed:

(1) declarative sentences;

(2) imperative sentences;

(3) propositional interrogatives.

Attributes introduced in CAG_{ENG} are shown in Fig. 4. Figure 5 shows a part of the CAG rules. In this figure, <attribute name> _0, for instance, a_0, is an attribute occurrence of the LSYM, and <attribute name> $\_n$, such as form_3, is an attribute occurrence of the nth RSYM.

Inherited Attribute

nform_i	Used to denote the pattern of words that can follow this symbol.

Synthesized Attributes

a	Temporarily used according to the applied production rule
embed	Used to indicate whether this symbol denotes an embedded sentence
form	Used to indicate the original form, inflection, or tense of a word
nbr	Used to indicate the number of a word
nform_s	Used to denote the pattern of words that can follow this symbol
noadv	Used to restrict the modification of an adverb
psn	Used to denote the person of a noun phrase
pro	Used to restrict the modification of a reflexive pronoun
role	Used to indicate whether a noun phrase is subject or object
vpat	Used to indicate verb patterns.

Fig. 4 Primary attributes in CAG_{ENG}.

We explain each line of Fig. 5 as follows:

[**rule 470**] adjective phrase $\longrightarrow$ no/any, more, adjective phrase

1. The LSYM of this rule is *adjp* (adjective phrase), and it has

   inherited attribute *form* (which is not used in this rule),

   synthesized attribute *a* (which denotes the inflection and is a member of $\{more, most, er, est\}$),

   and synthesized attribute *nbr* (number).

2. The first RSYM is *a* (which denotes the indefinite determiner) with synthesized attribute *a* (which denotes the original form).

3. The second RSYM is *q* (which denotes on indefinite quantifier) with synthesized attributes *a* (original form) and *form* (not used in this rule).

4. The third RSYM is *adjp* (adjective phrase) with inherited attribute *form* and synthesized attributes *a* and *nbr*.

```
(470 (adjp (form) (a nbr))                              ···1
     =>
     ((a nil (a))                                       ···2
      (q nil (a form))                                  ···3
      (adjp (form) (a nbr)))                            ···4
     when
     (and (member a_0 '(no any) (eq 'more a_2))         ···5
     with
     ((a_0 = a_3)                                       ···6
      (nbr_0 = 's)                                      ···7
      (form_3 = 'more)))                                ···8

(3730 (vp (nform_i) (form vpat))                        ···9
     =>
     ((v nil (for vpat))                                ···10
      (obj1 nil (nform_s nbr psn))                      ···11
      (obj2 nil (nform_s nbr psn)))                     ···12
     when
     (and (vp_form nform_i_0 form_1)
           (intersect '(vp12a vp12b vp12c) vpat_1))     ···13
     with
     ((form_0 = from_1)                                 ···14
      (vpat_0 = vpat_1)))                               ···15
```

Fig. 5 Sample description of a CAG (in machine representation).

5. The applicability condition of this rule is a predicate to check whether this rule is applicable to an adjective phrase of the form 'no/any, more, adjective phrase.'
6. *a_0* is given *a_3*.
7. *nbr_0* is given 's' because the noun phrase modified by this adjective phrase is singular.
8. *form_3* is given 'more' to tell RSYM *adjp* that the RSYM *adjp* must be made comparative by adding 'more'.

   [rule 3730] verb phrase ⟶ verb, object1, object2

9. The LSYM of this rule is VP, and it has inherited attribute $nform\_i$ (which denotes on acceptable verb), and synthesized attributes $form$ (which denotes the inflection of the verb) and *vpat* (which denotes the verb pattern).
10. The first RSYM is v (which denotes a verb), and it has synthesized attributes $form$ (which denotes the inflection of the verb) and *vpat* (which denotes the verb pattern).
11. The second RSYM is *obj*1 (which denotes object1), and it has synthesized attributes $nform\_s$, *nbr* (which denotes the number) and *psn* (which denotes

the person).

12. The third RSYM is *obj*2 (which denotes object2), and it has synthesized attributes $nform\_s$, *nbr* (which denotes number) and *psn* (which denotes person).

13. The applicability condition of this rule is a predicate to check whether $form\_1$ contradicts $nform\_i\_0$ and whether a set $vpat\_1$ is a subset of {vp12a, vp12b, vp12c}.

14. The value of $form\_1$ is directly passed to $form\_0$.

15. The value of $vpat\_1$ is directly passed to $vpat\_0$.

4.2 Dictionary and Morphological Analysis

The input sentences are preprocessed as follows, and the results are used by the CAG evaluator:

(1) Divide an input sentence into words. This application aims at analyzing English sentences, so this process can be easily implemented by the function *read*.

(2) Morphologically analyze each word obtained in step (1). This analysis proceeds mechanically with no semantic analysis. When the tail of a word is *s, ed, ing, er, est*, or *ly*, remove this tail from the word, and after proper treatment the original form is found. In this step the original form is not determined uniquely; a list, whose elements are '(original form . termination),' is obtained.

(3) Input each original form obtained in step (2) into the dictionary function and transform each element into a sequence of terminal symbols and their attribute values. For words with inflection, the termination obtained in step (2) is inserted in the sequence as an attribute value. Incorrect analysis in step (2) is detected by failing to find an entry of the word in the dictionary.

Finally, a list whose elements are '(terminal symbol + its synthesized attribute values)' is obtained by the preceding analysis. Such a list structure results from homonyms of a word.

Each word in the dictionary is a list with the following elements:

(1) Word: word in the input sentence.

(2) Category: its category (terminal symbol).

(3) *Synthesized attribute value*$_1$: the first synthesized attribute value of this terminal symbol.

(4) *Synthesized attribute value*$_2$: the second synthesized attribute value of this terminal symbol.

...

(n+2) *Synthesized attribute value*$_n$: the nth synthesized attribute value of this terminal symbol, where n must correspond to the number of synthesized attributes of the terminal symbol. The dictionary items of verbs are shown in Fig. 6 as an example. The first element of the item is a verb in an input sentence, the second element is its category (the name of the terminal symbol), the third element is the termination of the verb, obtained by the morphological analysis mentioned above, and the last element is verb patterns that indicate possible sentence patterns [3].

```
(give v nil (vp2a vp2c vp3a vp6a vp12a vp12b vp13a vp15b vp16a))
(gave v ed (vp2a vp2c vp3a vp6a vp12a vp12b vp13a vp15b vp16a))
(given v en (vp2a vp2c vp3a vp6a vp12a vp12b vp13a vp15b vp16a))
(go v nil (vp2a vp2b vp2c vp2d vp2e vp3a vp4a))
(went v ed (vp2a vp2b vp2c vp2d vp2e vp3a vp4a))
(gone v en (vp2a vp2b vp2c vp2d vp2e vp3a vp4a))
(interpret v nil (vp2a vp6a vp16b))
```

Fig. 6 Part of the dictionary (the last element is the verb pattern [3]).

4.3 Generation of the Action/Goto Table and Attribute Evaluation Functions

We present in this section the results of generation of the action/goto table, translation from CAG_{ENG} to its inner representation, and generation of attribute evaluation functions for CAG_{ENG}. Our system is written in Franz Lisp and can be run on a VAX 11/780 processor, under the UNIX 4.2 BSD operating system. The following data was collected on the VAX 11/780.

(1) Computation time:

The results for computation time (and its overall ratio) are shown below:

Table generation	484 s (58%)
Translation to inner representation	198 s (24%)
Generation of attribute evaluation function	152 s (18%)

The generation of the action/goto table takes about 60% of the total preprocessing time. However, that does not seem critical: On the construction of some grammar in a CAG, there will be many more modifications to semantical descriptions of CAG rules, such as revision of attribute definitions, than to syntactical descriptions. Generation of the action/goto table, which takes a lot of CPU time and is restricted only to syntactical modifications, is not so frequently required. Since attribute evaluation functions can be compiled, the analysis can be done faster by using compiled functions when the construction of CAG rules has been completed. In CAG_{ENG} it takes 169 s of CPU time to compile attribute evaluation functions.

(2) Action/goto table:

The LALR(1) action/goto table of CAG_{ENG} has a feature shown in Fig. 7. In this figure, 17.2% of entries in the table have shift/reduce or reduce/reduce conflicts. Moreover, these conflicts amount to 30% of the entries other than error actions, that is, possibly correct actions. These conflicts suggest there may be multiple actions that lead to correct analyses, and the selection of these actions is not determined before actual analysis. Figure 7 suggests that a mechanism for controlling syntax analysis by means of semantic information is required.

Production rules	391	Error actions	8,611	(41.5%)
Nonterminal symbols	35	Reduce actions	5,836	(28.2%)
Terminal symbols	31	Shift actions	2,708	(13.1%)
States	668	Shift/reduce conflicts (one shift, one reduce)	1,713	(8.3%)
		Reduce/reduce conflicts (more than one reduce)	1,197	(5.8%)
		Others (one shift, more than one reduce)	643	(3.1%)

Fig. 7 Action table.

4.4 Experiment and the Results

Figure 8 gives the experimental results for analysis of the sentences in Fig. 9. In Fig. 8, the columns contain the following information:

Column 1: "(1) Trees not taking attributes into account" gives the number of trees and the CPU time of the experimental results without taking account of attribute evaluations.

Column 2: "(2) The number of trees returned in phase 1" gives the number of parse trees returned in phase 1 — that is, the number of parse trees satisfying the applicability conditions that are written only with synthesized attributes.

Column 3: "(3) Trees taking attributes into account" gives the number of parse trees and the CPU time, when full analysis of attributes and applicability conditions is done. Inherited attributes are also taken into account in these results.

Column 4: "$\frac{(1)-(2)}{(1)-(3)} \times 100$" gives the percentage of the total number of deleted trees that were deleted in phase 1 . From this it is found that more than 50% of invalid parse trees are deleted in phase 1 (during the syntax analysis phase). Thus, control by applicability conditions with attribute values works efficiently even though there are many conflicts in the LALR(1) action/goto table.

The CPU time in Fig. 8 is for compiled attribute evaluation functions, which are about 37% faster than interpreted functions.

We give an example of a parse tree in Fig. 10.

5 Conclusion

In this paper we have presented a conditioned attribute grammar (CAG) and a method for evaluating it, and we have confirmed its describability by an application to natural-language processing. In DCG [11], known as a formalism for describing

Sentence	(1) Trees not taking attributes into account		(2) The number of trees returned in phase 1	(3) Trees taking attributes into account		$\frac{(1)-(2)}{(1)-(3)}\times 100$
1	3	(1,088)	2	2	(765)	100
2	3	(1,241)	2	2	(850)	100
3	3	(1,003)	2	2	(765)	100
4	1	(493)	1	1	(493)	100
5	2	(1,972)	1	1	(1,139)	100
6	14	(5,015)	3	1	(1,683)	85
7	97	(52,955)	31	1	(8,296)	69
8	19	(9,180)	7	1	(1,853)	67
9	60	(48,246)	1	1	(4,947)	100
10	1	(1,377)	1	1	(918)	100
11	15	(11,764)	12	2	(6,681)	23
12	38	(27,982)	8	1	(9,656)	81
13	3	(3,723)	1	1	(2,312)	100
14	9	(6,222)	5	3	(3,009)	67
15	9	(3,213)	6	1	(1,377)	38
16	144	(168,725)	30	2	(72,216)	80
17	14	(2,822)	1	1	(714)	100
18	108	(100,657)	2	1	(8,415)	99
19	13	(8,500)	6	1	(2,159)	58
20	93	(84,711)	16	2	(25,857)	52
21	14	(2,958)	7	1	(1,020)	54
22	10	(4,879)	5	2	(1,649)	63
23	24	(13,702)	12	1	(3,434)	52
24	24	(34,085)	12	1	(11,407)	52
25	3	(1,207)	2	2	(986)	100

Fig. 8 Number of constructed parse trees (and CPU time in ms).

of grammars by means of Horn clauses, the description becomes hard to read and complicated when the numbers of arguments of predicates are large or when patterns embedded in the arguments are complicated. In CAG, on the other hand, attribute definitions are described separately in a special part of the semantic rules.

The action/goto table of CAG_{ENG} for English syntactical analysis has about 3,500 conflicts, as shown in Fig. 7. However, control by applicability conditions makes the evaluator efficient. Almost the same grammar as CAG_{ENG} was constructed on a DEC 2060 Prolog system [15], and its speed was almost equal to that of CAG_{ENG}. Therefore, taking into account the machine speed of the VAX 11/780 relative to that of the DEC 2060, the CAG evaluator is faster.

Roughly speaking, the syntactical ambiguity increases in proportion to the length of a sentence in natural language. Therefore, the computation time of the LR parser seems to increase exponentially; however, in CAG, the ambiguities are restricted by the applicability conditions. As can be seen from the experimental results (Fig. 8), our method is efficient for sentences of fewer than 10 words.

1. There are 3 on the table.
2. There are 3 on the table now.
3. There are some men from the city.
4. There are some men here from the city.
5. Those are the books she reads.
6. Were they given to her ?
7. Could she have been given many of them ?
8. I saw that they were there.
9. The books that were on the table are difficult to read.
10. My uncle gave the girl several books.
11. She was given some books by her uncle.
12. The books were given her by her uncle.
13. He gave up the books to her.
14. That hammer could break this vase easily.
15. We saw it coming.
16. Did not those people want him to try to do it ?
17. Are there any more left ?
18. Is this any harder for him to do than that was ?
19. The system for interpreting dialogues is developed.
20. She was given more difficult books by her uncle.
21. Do not do that !
22. Be very careful not to do it too quickly.
23. Read these books , if you have time.
24. If you have time , read these books.
25. There are some apples in the basket.

Fig. 9 Example sentences.

CAG_{ENG} is a general-use English grammar that is intended only to construct parse trees. Particular applications with semantic processing will be our next research subject. For semantic processing, the rules of CAG_{ENG} can be extended by adding semantic attributes and their definitions to the original CAG_{ENG}. Moreover, this semantic information can be used to control syntactical analysis by means of applicability conditions.

Our future tasks seem to be as follows: (1) to reuse the values of synthesized attributes that are evaluated in syntactical analysis for full attribute evaluations, (2) to reformulate attribute evaluation functions as equations in which simultaneously computable synthesized attributes are defined [7], and finally (3) to introduce LR attribute grammars [4].

Finally, we compare CAG with DCG [11]:

(1) An applicability condition of a CAG corresponds to the constraint exerted by Prolog predicates. The augmentations in DCG are used (a) to control the application of rules and (b) to compute information within the rule, whereas in a CAG the applicability conditions correspond to use (a) in DCG. Use (b) above corresponds to the use of Lisp functions for attribute definitions.

```
?? my uncle gave the girl several books.
no.1
s_sentence
nil
parse tree
|-sentence
  |-sdec
     |-subj
     |  |-np
     |     |-nomhd
     |        |-adjp
     |        |  |-adj---my
     |        |-nomhd
     |           |-n---uncle
     |-vp
        |-v---gave
        |-obj1
        |  |-np
        |     |-ddet
        |     |  |-det---the
        |     |-monhd
        |        |-n---girl
        |-obj2
           |-np
              |-a---several
              |-nomhd
                 |-n---books
t
Total time = 1989 ms
```

Fig. 10 Example of output.

Backtracking can occur for homonyms and syntactically ambiguous rules in a CAG. Moreover, backtracking may also occur for augmentations in DCG.

(2) Attributes are synthesized or inherited (not both) and have a direction of information flow (in the direction of the leaves for inherited attributes and in the opposite direction for synthesized attributes), whereas parameters in DCG clauses are bidirectional. In a CAG, every attribute definition is assumed to be computable (i.e., to include total functions), but there are uncomputable (ununifiable) cases in a DCG, in which case the DCG rule cannot be applied. The reason for this difference is that a CAG is functional (each symbol corresponds to a multiple-valued function with inherited attributes as inputs), whereas a DCG is logical (a DCG is based on the logic programming language Prolog).

(3) DCG is not allowed to use what are called left-recursive rules, because the grammar is usually loaded into a Prolog environment and analysis is top-down. In the BUP system [9], in which this problem is solved, ϵ-rules are not

allowed, for efficiency. In a CAG, however, left-recursive rules are allowed, and for some grammars ϵ-rules are also allowed.

Acknowledgments. The authors wish to thank Prof. Hozumi Tanaka of the Tokyo Institute of Technology for his insightful comments and encouragement.

References

[1] Bochmann, G. V. : Semantic Evaluation from Left to Right, *Comm. ACM*, Vol. 19, No. 2 (1976), pp. 55–62.

[2] Harrison, M. A. : *Introduction to Formal Language Theory*, pp. 501–558, Addison Wesley, 1978.

[3] Hornby, A. S. : *Guide to Patterns and Usage in English*, Oxford University Press, 1975.

[4] Jones, N. D. and Madsen, M. : *Attribute-Influenced LR Parsing*, Lecture Notes in Computer Science, Vol. 94 (1980), pp. 393–407, Springer.

[5] Kastens, U. : Ordered Attributed Grammars, *Acta Inf.*, Vol. 13 (1980), pp. 229–256.

[6] Katayama, T. : HFP: A Hierarchical and Functional Programming Based on Attribute Grammar, *Proc. 5th ICSE* (1980), pp. 343–352.

[7] Katayama, T. : Translation of Attribute Grammars into Procedures, *ACM Trans. Prog. Lang. Syst.*, Vol. 6, No. 3 (1984), pp. 345–369.

[8] Knuth, D. E. : Semantics of Context-Free Languages, *Mathematical Systems Theory*, Vol. 2, No. 2 (1968), pp. 127–145.

[9] Matsumoto, Y. and Tanaka, H. : BUP: A Bottom-up Parser Embedded in Prolog, *New Generation Computing*, Vol. 1, No. 2 (1983), pp. 145–158.

[10] Nagao, M. et al. : *Processing of Numbers, Expressions, and Sentences* (in Japanese), Jyohokagaku, Vol. 23 (1981), Iwanami-Shoten.

[11] Pereira, F. and Warren, D. : Definite Clause Grammar for Language Analysis – A Survey of the Formalism and a Comparison with Augmented Transition Networks, *Artif. Intell.*, Vol. 13 (1980), pp. 231–278.

[12] Pohlmann, W. : LR Parsing for Affix Grammars, *Acta Inf.*, Vol.20 (1983), pp.283–300.

[13] Pratt, V. R. : A Linguistic Oriented Programming Language, *IJCAI3* (1973), pp.272–381.

[14] Purdom, P. and Brown, C. A. : Semantic Routines and LR(k) Parsers, *Acta Inf.*, Vol. 14 (1980), pp. 299–315.

[15] Takakura, S. : A Parser of English in Prolog, B.S.thesis, Tokyo Institute of Technology (in Japanese), 1984.

[16] Takeda, M. and Katayama, T. : On Defining Denotational Semantics for Attribute Grammars, *J. Inf. Process.*, Vol. 5, No. 1 (1982), pp. 21–29.

[17] Tanaka, H., Sato, T. and Motoyoshi, H. : Extended LINGOL — A Programming System for Natural Language Processing (in Japanese), *IECE Japan*, J60-D, 1977.

[18] Watt, D. A. : The Parsing Problem for Affix Grammars, *Acta Inf.*, Vol. 8 (1977), pp. 1–20.

[19] Watt, D. A. : *Rule Splitting and Attribute-Directed Parsing*, Lecture Notes in Computer Science, Vol. 94 (1980), pp. 363–392, Springer.

Initially published in "Computer Software", Vol. 3, No. 3, in Japanese.

Naoyoshi Tamura
Department of Electrical and Computer Engineering
Yokohama National University
156 Tokiwadai, Hodogaya-ku,Yokohama
240 Japan

Shin Takakura
Advanced Software Development
IBM Japan, Ltd.
1623–14 Shimo Tsuruma, Yamato
242 Japan

Takuya Katayama
Department of Computer Science
Tokyo Institute of Technology
2–12–1 Oookayama, Meguro-ku, Tokyo
152 Japan

An Object-Oriented Implementation of TCP/IP Network Protocols

Ken-ichiro Murakami

Summary. This paper describes an object-oriented implementation of TCP/IP network protocols. The system is implemented based on a *connection-oriented implementation model.* Since the model regards each connection as an individual module, each connection can employ a different protocol at each layer in a system. The feature allows multiple protocols to coexist in a layer and provides the capability to localize the effect of protocol modification to a single connection during debugging.

This paper focuses on the connection-oriented implementation model, its mapping to object-oriented programming languages, and the internal structure of the TCP/IP implementation. In addition, approaches to some issues related to the model are discussed.

1 Introduction

In conventional network systems, network software is designed and implemented based on a layered reference model [1]. Every time a new protocol or a modified protocol is required, the corresponding software module and its interface with adjacent layer modules must be modified. Since a module processes all the incoming and outgoing packets, the modification affects all the packets. Therefore, it is difficult to localize the degradation of the software caused by the modification. This is an especially serious problem on network development systems where prototyping is required in a multiple protocol environment or where protocols are frequently modified.

To cope with these problems, a *connection-oriented implementation model* is proposed. Unlike conventional network implementations, this model regards each connection that offers a virtual circuit as a separate module. Thus, the effects caused by protocol modification can be localized to a single module, that is, one connection. In addition, it provides flexibility that enables multiple protocols to coexist in a single layer. Another advantage of this implementation model is that it can be easily implemented using an object-oriented programming language. In this paper, a TCP/IP protocol implemented using the TAO language is described in detail. The TCP/IP protocol suite [2] is a de facto standard protocol suite in the research and development community. TAO [3, 4] is a LISP dialect that harmoniously incorporates an object-oriented language, similar to Flavors, with a logic programming language. It also provides a multi-programming facility. This implementation shows the applicability of the model and addresses what is required of

ISBN 0–12–037103–0

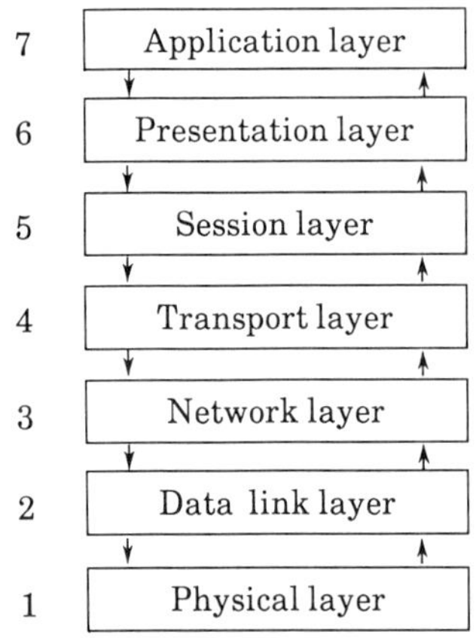

Fig. 1 Layered reference model (OSI reference model).

object-oriented programming languages when building multitask realtime systems, such as a network system.

This paper proposes the connection-oriented network implementation model and describes the TCP/IP network implementation in the TAO language. Section 2 presents issues related to the conventional network implementation model. The section then explains the connection-oriented network implementation model and its network structure. Section 3 describes a relationship between the connection-oriented implementation model and object-oriented programming. Section 4 focuses on the TCP/IP network protocol implementation and the internal structure. It compares two class structures and explains processes and objects. Finally, section 5 discusses the applicability of the model and approaches to some issues.

2 Implementation Model

First, this section describes the conventional implementation model and its issues. Then, it explains structure of the connection-oriented implementation model and an approach to issues related to the conventional implementations.

2.1 Conventional Implementation Model and Its Issues

To reduce complexity, network systems are designed to have highly structured modules that perform the functions required by protocol suite based on a layered network model, in Fig. 1. In this model, a protocol is implemented at each layer as an independent software module. In that module, a process handles all the incoming and outgoing packets, and passes them to adjacent layer modules with some control information. This software structure focuses on the functions in each layer, and the movement of packets through the modules.

Figure 2 shows the software structure and the packet flow. In this implementation, each layer module, L, processes packets according to the protocol specification.

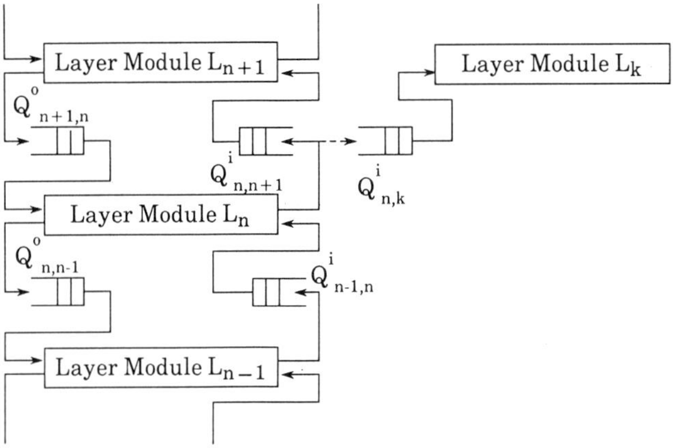

Fig. 2 Software structure.

In this model, each layer module consists of two submodules, one for outgoing packets and the other for incoming packets. Through a queue, Q, a layer module passes processed packets to an adjacent layer module. For example, layer module L_n dequeues a packet from queue $Q^i_{n-1,n}$. The packet has already been processed by the lower layer module L_{n-1}. After it processes the packet, it enqueues the packet on queue $Q^i_{n,n+1}$ to pass the packet to the upper layer module L_{n+1}. A process on each layer module continually repeats this cycle.

An issue in this implementation is the modification of existing modules. When a protocol in a layer is changed, the corresponding software module must be modified. When a new layer L_k is required on top of layer L_n, the interface to the upper layer in the module must be also modified. This then requires that a part of the layer module that switches the next queue $Q^i_{n,n+1}$ and $Q^i_{n,k}$ be modified so that a packet for the new protocol can be properly delivered to layer module L_k. Since each layer module serves all the packets, a module modification failure affects all the packets. Therefore, it's difficult to localize a problem caused by that kind of failure. In addition, network services stop while the module is being modified.

2.2 A Connection-Oriented Implementation Model

To cope with the problems present in the conventional implementation, each connection that offers a virtual circuit is regarded as a module in the connection-oriented implementation.

One of the main functions in network systems is multiplexing user data on a real medium and providing a user with a virtual circuit. An entity that offers the virtual circuit service is called a *connection*. Figure 3 shows the virtual circuit. Many virtual circuits coexist in a system, and each of them has its own unique identifier. A connection consists of a data structure and the related virtual circuit service operations. The data structure has fields to store data such as the connec-

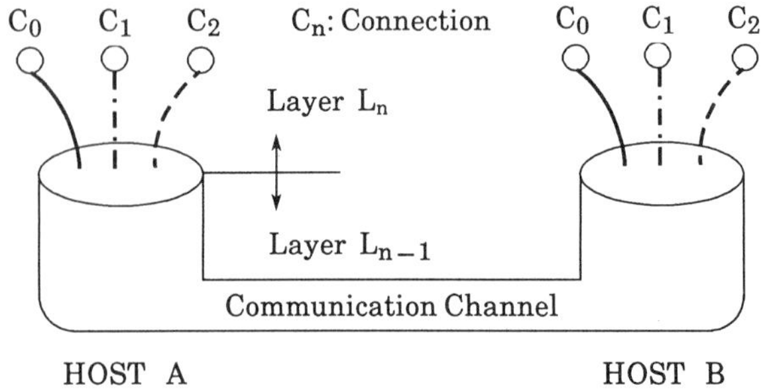

Fig. 3 Virtual circuit.

tion state, identifier. Since the layer module is uniquely determined at each layer in the conventional implementation, the structure has no field for pointers to layer modules through which packets on each virtual circuit are processed. However, in the connection-oriented implementation, a data structure for a connection has pointers to layer modules. Therefore, each connection can employ a different protocol at each layer in a system. In this respect, this model regards not only each layer but also each connection as a module. A set comprising a data structure for the connection and a collection of related packet operations is called a *connection module*. In this model, each layer module is a passive entity. Unlike the conventional implementation, no resident process runs in a layer module. Instead, functions in the layer module are invoked through the connection module by system processes.

When a new protocol is implemented or a protocol is modified, this implementation model allows debugging using a connection that does not affect other existing connections. In the connection module being debugged, only a pointer to the layer module corresponding to the old protocol is exchanged with a pointer to the new layer module. Even if the modification fails, only the connection is affected. Thus, this implementation localizes problems caused by a modification failure and enables existing network services to continue during debugging. These features are especially important in a development environment where protocol modules are frequently modified and software is developed in an incremental manner.

2.3 Structure of a Connection Module

Figure 4 shows the structure of the connection-oriented implementation model. Each connection module, C, consists of a buffer for storing the packet, pointers to layer modules, working registers, registers to save each connection state, and connection identifiers. Unlike the conventional implementation, there is no process in each layer module. Instead, a daemon process is prepared for each layer. Each daemon has an event queue. When an event occurs in a layer, it is enqueued in the queue of the corresponding daemon. After the daemon process dequeues the event, it finds a connection module where the event occurred by analyzing the event. Then, it invokes a protocol function corresponding to the event by referring to the pointer in the connection module. The daemon process only invokes these functions

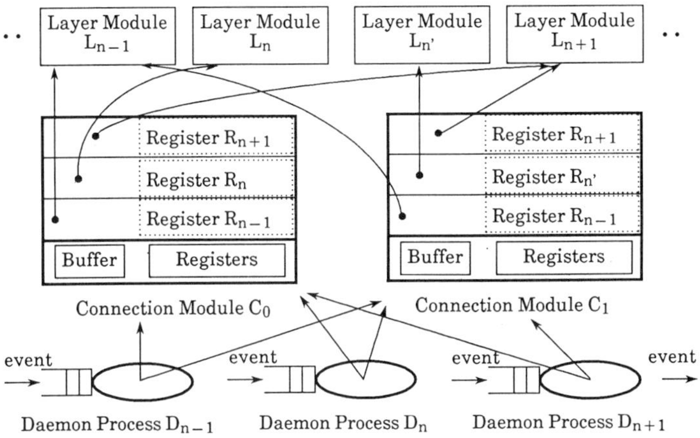

Fig. 4 Connection-oriented implementation model.

and never applies specific functions to the connection. Thus, the daemon process works like a process dispatcher that assigns the processor to each connection on a timesliced basis. Since events occur on a connection independently, a number of processes run on a connection module simultaneously. These concurrent processes operate a buffer in the same connection module using working registers.

Prior to establishing a connection and setting up a virtual circuit, a connection module is created and initialized. The connection module has variables to hold pointers to protocol functions in each required layer modules. Ordinarily, they hold pointers to standard protocol functions. Since the pointer is used instead of the function itself, the program code is shared by connection modules and memory space is saved. When a new protocol or modified protocol is required for the connection, a new layer module for the protocol is prepared. The module includes data structures and a collection of protocol functions. An entry point for the new layer module is assigned to the corresponding variable in the connection module. This implies that different protocols can coexist in a single layer.

The above discussion assumes connection-oriented service. Since it has overhead in establishing and closing connections, a connectionless service is adopted for low overhead transaction processing. The service requires neither the establishment nor the closing of connections. To apply the same model also to connectionless services, the connection-oriented implementation model regards the connectionless service as a connection-oriented service. That is, connectionless communication is assumed to establish a connection virtually prior to the first datagram transfer.

3 Implementation Model and Object-Oriented Programming

In this section, mapping between the implementation model and mechanisms in object-oriented programming languages is explained. Also, the changing of protocol

Table 1. Mapping between the implementation model and an object-oriented programming language

Implementation Model	Object-oriented Programming Language
layer	abstract class (layer class)
working register in a layer	instance variable in layer class
statistics on a layer	class variable in layer class
connection	class that inherits multiple layer classes (connection class)
event	message passing

combinations is described.

3.1 Mapping to Mechanisms in Object-Oriented Programming Languages

A network system based on the connection-oriented implementation model can be implemented using conventional languages that can handle multiple processes. However, mechanisms embedded in object-oriented programming languages enable easy implementation of the model. Table 1 shows the mapping between the connection-oriented implementation model and the mechanisms of object-oriented programming languages.

Each layer is mapped to an abstract class on a one-to-one basis. The class is called a *layer class*. Since the layer class is an abstract class, it is not instantiated. Operations and data structures required in a layer are mapped to methods and instance variables in the class, respectively. A template for connection modules is mapped to another kind of class, a *connection class*. Using the multiple inheritance facility, a connection class inherits the layer classes required for the connection as its *superclasses*. Prior to establishing a connection, a network user instantiates the required connection class and get a connection module. In Fig. 4, a pair compring layer L and register R is implemented as a layer class. Connection C is implemented as an instance of a connection class. A method, which is defined in a layer class, handles packets according to the protocol specified for the layer. Instance variables are utilized in saving data such as the connection state, variables, and the buffer to be processed. They are local to each connection. Shared variables such as statistics, which are accessed by instances of a class, are defined as class variables.

A daemon process exists for each layer class and serves all the connections that inherit the same layer class. When the daemon process detects an event on a connection, it sends a message to the appropriate instance. Therefore, all the instances of the layer class must be registered in advance. To perform that function, a class variable is utilized. In the class definition, registration of the instance for the class variable is defined as an option. This option enables each instance to be registered automatically when it is instantiated.

3.2 Protocol Combination

Ordinarily, network users utilize only some standard services. This means that only a few specific protocol combinations are required in a system. Consequently, only a limited number of standard connection classes are prepared to satisfy the service requirements. However, special protocol combinations are required when a new protocol or a new service is developed. The connection-oriented implementation model provides the development system with a flexible workbench that allows the creation of any protocol combination.

When the combination of protocol layers is changed, a new connection class is defined. It inherits all the required layer classes. Of course, this modification has no effect on instances that have already been created. Even if a specific protocol in a layer is changed, direct modification of the existing layer class is not required. The protocol modification is performed as follows:

(1) Define a new layer class that inherits the existing layer class for the layer.

(2) Define new methods in the new layer class. It is possible to combine a new method with the existing method using the method combination facility.

(3) Define a new connection class that inherits the newly defined layer class instead of the existing one.

This procedure makes the new protocol or the modified protocol available. Thus, application of the mechanism embedded in the object-oriented programming language makes it easy to implement a flexible network system based on the connection-oriented implementation model.

4 Implementation in Object-Oriented Programming

To prove the applicability of the connection-oriented implementation model, a network system has been developed using object-oriented programming. First, this section describes the TCP/IP protocol suite and the implementation language TAO. Next, the structure of the software is explained in detail.

4.1 Protocol Suite and Implementation Language

This subsection describes the TCP/IP protocol suite and the TAO language.

4.1.1 TCP/IP Protocol Suite

The TCP/IP Protocol suite [2] was developed in ARPANET (Advanced Research Project Agency NETwork) [5] and now is a de facto standard in the research and development community. It was developed for internetworking, which enables multiple networks to be connected and operated like a single large network. It utilizes communication media such as leased lines, public data networks, and satellite communications. This protocol is employed in large worldwide internetworks such as CSNET (Computer Science Network), NSFNET (National Science Foundation NETwork) and ARPANET [5]. Figure 5 shows the network protocol layers.

Various media such as Ethernet and serial line are supported at the lowest layer. The IP protocol insulates upper-layer protocols from these medium dependencies. To map IP addresses to these media addresses, the ARP (Address Resolution Protocol) is employed. The IP protocol also provides host-to-host unreliable datagram delivery through long-haul packet-switched networks and local networks. TCP is

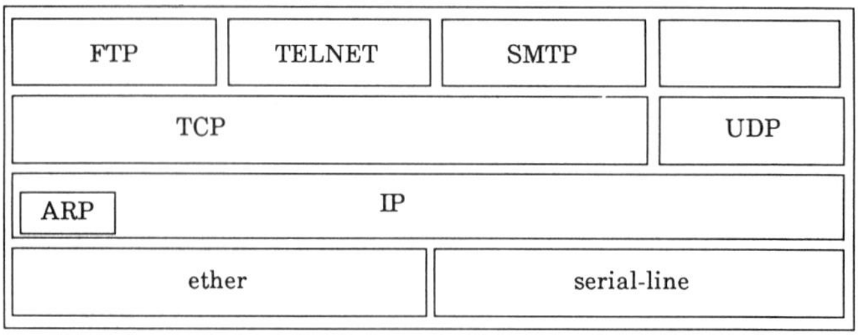

Fig. 5 TCP/IP protocol layers.

a connection-oriented, reliable, and byte-stream protocol on top of IP. TCP detects transmission errors and recovers them by retransmission. The flow control in TCP allows a receiving TCP to regulate the rate at which data arrives from a sending TCP. TCP allows multiple application programs on a given machine to communicate simultaneously, and it demultiplexes incoming TCP traffic among application programs. Hence, each application program can regard the connection as a dedicated hardware circuit for that program. UDP (User Datagram Protocol) is another protocol on top of IP. Connection multiplexing is also provided by UDP. However, UDP is an unreliable and transaction-oriented protocol.

TELNET, FTP (File Transfer Protocol), and SMTP (Simple Mail Transfer Protocol) are application programs that run on top of TCP. TELNET, FTP, and SMTP provides virtual terminal services, file transfer services, and mail transfer services, respectively.

4.1.2 ELIS and Kernel Language TAO

To implement the TCP/IP protocol, the TAO language on the LISP machine ELIS is employed. ELIS [3] is an interpreter-oriented LISP machine developed at the NTT Electrical Communications Laboratories. In the ELIS machine, a fully microcoded interpreter is implemented. The kernel language is called TAO [4]. TAO is a LISP dialect and harmoniously incorporates an object-oriented language and a logic programming language. It provides a multi-user and a multi-process environment. The features of TAO are summarized as follows:

(1) It is basically a LISP language. It is similar to Zetalisp in many aspects, and mostly upwardly compatible with Common LISP. It emulates Common LISP in the area where the two languages differ fundamentally. About half of the TAO functions are microcoded.

(2) It incorporates an object-oriented programming paradigm, similar to Flavors. It accommodates a syntactical variant of Smalltalk-like message passing and handles all primitive data types as objects.

(3) It incorporates a logic programming paradigm, based on the Horn clause, unification and backtracking. Unifications and ordinary function calls can be nested within each other.

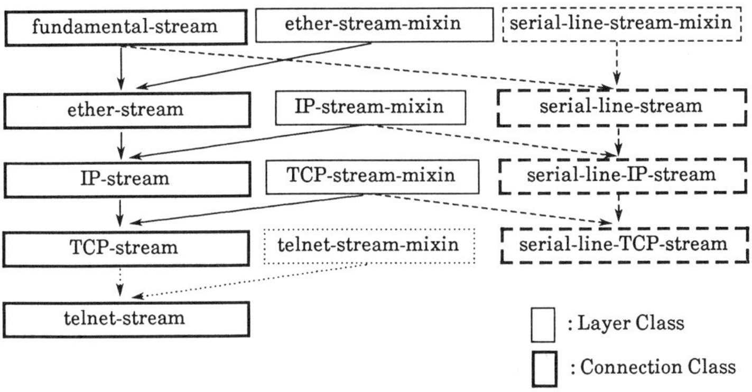

Fig. 6 A class hierarchy (1).

(4) It supports concurrent programming and a multi-user environment. There are primitives for process synchronization, mutual exclusion and process-interrupts. It can run up to 128 processes, and support up to eight users concurrently.

All the system software is written in TAO, but is microcoded where high-speed execution is required. For example, almost all programs for the I/O system, process management, and memory management are microcoded. A LAP (List Assembled Program) interpreter also written in microcode executes compiled code. These features meet the requirements for implementing network systems. The network software is characterized by modularity derived from the layered structure of protocols, multitask realtime systems, and finite automatons.

4.2 Architecture of the Network Implementation

This subsection explains the relationship between the protocol layers and classes. Two kinds of class hierarchy are discussed. Then, the subsection describes some features derived from the object-oriented implementation.

4.2.1 Protocol Layers and Class Hierarchy

The TCP/IP program on ELIS is written in S-expression and is about 13K steps long. Some of the special microcode, such as the checksum operation, was developed for performance improvement. Figure 6 shows a part of the class hierarchy.

As described in Subsection 3.1, there are two kinds of classes: the *connection class* and the *layer class*. The layer class is an abstract class that has no instance. Each layer class corresponds to a protocol at a layer, as shown in Figs. 6 and 7. It defines a collection of specific operations and services for the corresponding protocol. For example, `IP-stream-mixin` and `TCP-stream-mixin` are layer classes and define operations and services for the IP protocol and TCP protocol, respectively. The connection class inherits the required layer classes and provides network users with a standard network interface, that is, stream. In TAO, streams

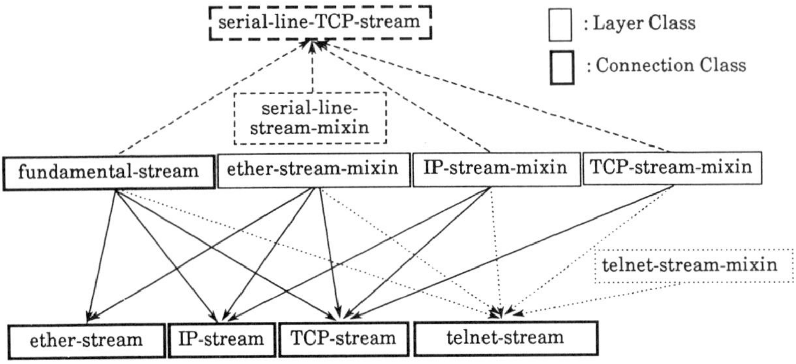

Fig. 7 A class hierarchy (2).

provide generic input/output access methods and are implemented as an object. To establish a connection and create a virtual circuit, the network user instantiates a connection class such as `TCP-stream`.

There are two ways to inherit layer classes and define a connection class. In Fig. 6, every connection class inherits the adjacent class corresponding to a lower layer as one of its superclasses, considering the upper layer inherits the characteristics of all the lower layers. In contrast, Fig. 7 shows another kind of class hierarchy. It regards all the layer classes as parts of connection classes, and each connection class inherits all the required layer classes directly. A comparison of these class hierarchies shows the following characteristics:

(1) Flexibility in the lower layer modification or extension.
For example, suppose that a serial line is supported as a new medium. It is obvious that a new layer class for the serial line must be prepared. Another new connection class, which inherits the layer class, is also prepared to offer users network services using the serial line. Assume that the new layer class name is `serial-line-stream-mixin` and the new connection class name is `serial-line-TCP-stream`. In Fig. 6, all the intermediate connection classes that inherit `ether-stream-mixin` as their superclasses are affected. For example, `serial-line-IP-stream` must be also defined to define the subclass `serial-line-TCP-stream`. On the other hand, the class hierarchy shown in Fig. 7 never affects other classes when supporting the serial line. That is because the class hierarchy of `serial-line-TCP-stream` is quite similar to that of `TCP-stream`, except that the former inherits `serial-line-stream-mixin` directly instead of `ether-stream-mixin`.

(2) Flexibility in the upper-layer modification or extension.
For example, suppose that a new protocol is supported on top of `TCP-stream`. In this case, two new classes are prepared. One is a layer class that corresponds to the new protocol and the other is a connection class that offers users with the new service. In the class hierarchy shown in Fig. 6, the new connection class only has

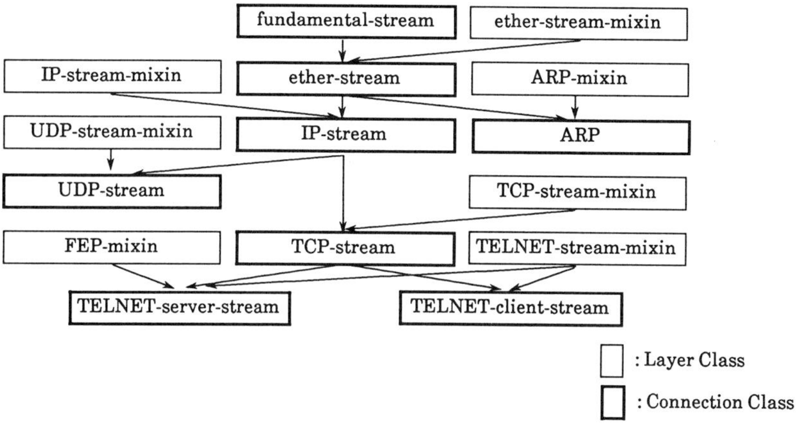

Fig. 8 Class hierarchy in the TAO/ELIS implementation.

to inherit the new layer class and `TCP-stream`. However, in the class hierarchy shown in Fig. 7, the new connection class is required to inherit all the required layer classes. This implies that knowledge about all the layer classes is necessary to extend or modify a subclass.

This comparison shows that the class inheritance shown in Fig. 6 is suitable for modifying or extending higher protocol layers. In contrast, the class inheritance shown in Fig. 7 is suitable for modifying or extending of the lower protocol layers. In the TAO/ELIS implementation, the former is adopted, since the network is developed from the lower layer (superclass) to the higher layer (subclass) and almost all the modification and extension always takes place in the upper layer. Figure 8 shows the complete class hierarchy. Although `UDP-stream` supports a connectionless protocol, each datagram is regarded as a short-term connection and is implemented as a connection class.

4.2.2 Features of the Object-Oriented Implementation Approach

This object-oriented implementation approach has the following features:

(1) Compatibility and high-speed access to buffer memory.
To be compatible with conventional input and output, connection class is implemented as a stream in TAO/ELIS. This results in a high-speed buffer access facility.

The class `fundamental-stream` in TAO defines the basic input and output data structure and its operation. Since all the conventional file and terminal stream classes inherit the class `fundamental-stream`, these streams can be treated in the same manner. The accessing methods, such as `read-char` and `write-char`, are fully implemented in microcode and provide a high speed buffer access facility. All the network streams also inherit `fundamental-stream` and network stream objects are implemented as a stream. Therefore, microcoded `read-char` and `write-char` can be applied to the streams, and these methods allow the network users to access

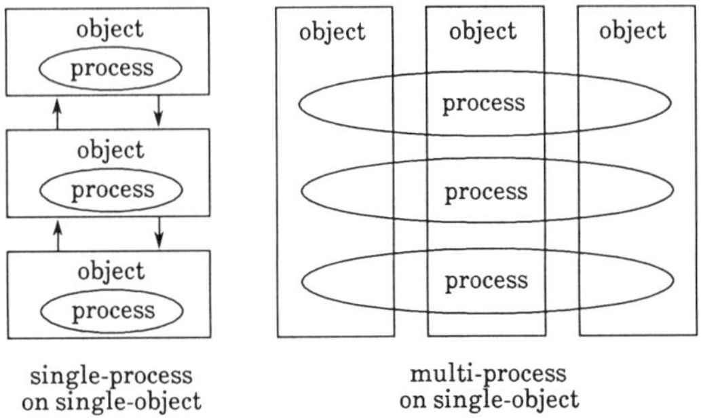

Fig. 9 Processes and objects.

the buffer memory directly. This results in fast access to communication buffers as conventional file streams and terminal streams in TAO.

(2) Simple structure
The class hierarchy is simple and clear because of the one-to-one correspondence between each protocol layer and each layer class. The exception is `FEP-mixin`, which is one of the superclasses of `TELNET-server-stream`. The TELNET server provides the capability to login from a remote host through a network as well as a terminal that is directly attached to the local host. In the case of the terminal, the FEP (Front End Processor) supports flow control and interrupts character processing and code conversion. The abstract class `FEP-mixin` emulates the FEP for network users.

4.3 Processes and Objects

4.3.1 Multiple Processes on an Object

In conventional network implementations, a protocol is implemented at each layer as an independent software module based on the layer model. On each layer module, a process operates all the incoming and outgoing packets and passes them to adjacent layer modules with some control information (`Single-Process on Single-Object`). In contrast, the object-oriented implementation considers each connection as a module and a number of processes handle the incoming and outgoing packets on that module, as shown in Fig. 9 (`Multi-Process on Single-Object`).

Each connection is implemented as a *stream object* that is an instance of a connection class. Since the connection class inherits all the required layer classes, each object is considered to have all the methods required to operate packets in each layer. Several daemon processes, each corresponding to a layer, invoke these methods in a stream object asynchronously through message passing. That is, multiple processes run simultaneously on a single object, unlike the situation in conventional network implementations.

For example, there are three processes that run independently on a `TCP-stream` object, as shown in Fig. 10. They are (1) a daemon process, `TCP-in-daemon`, that

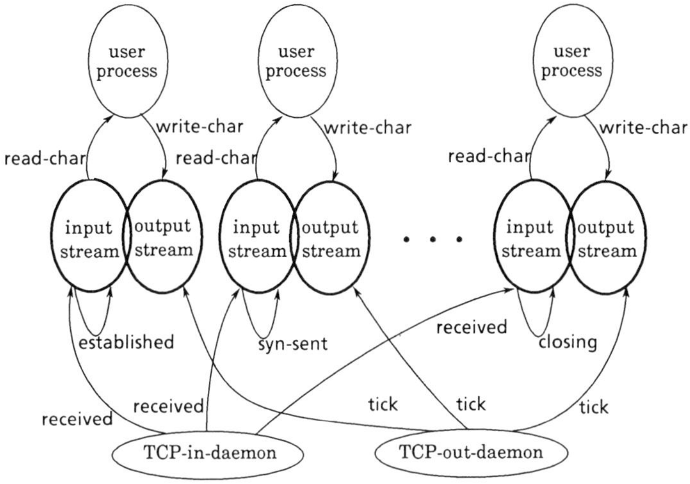

Fig. 10 Three processes on a TCP-stream object.

manages events on incoming TCP packets; (2) a daemon process, `TCP-out-daemon`, that manages the primitive retransmission timer; and (3) a user process that reads or writes data. Whenever `TCP-in-daemon` detects an event such as packet reception, it send a message to the appropriate stream object that should process the incoming packet. The message invokes a method that processes the packet based on the TCP protocol. In this respect, the daemon works like a process dispatcher in the conventional operating systems. Not the daemon but each stream object knows how to process the packet. The process `TCP-out-daemon` manages the primitive retransmission timer and send a message, `tick`, to all the stream objects periodically. The message invokes a method, `tick`, that increments the retransmission timer in each stream object. Timeout is detected by the method in each stream object, since each connection has a different timeout value, as determined by the state of the connection or the state of the communication channel. When timeout is detected, each stream object retransmits its packets. This means `TCP-out-daemon` only sends a message and does not have any knowledge about retransmission. The third process, the user process, runs on a stream object when the user reads or writes data from or to the stream buffer. Since these three processes run asynchronously and send messages to a stream object independently, multiple processes run on a single object simultaneously.

To send a message, each daemon process must manage all the stream objects that inherit a given corresponding layer class. A class variable is utilized to hold them, since it can be accessed by all the instances of the class. If a daemon has to send a message to objects directly, the class variable holds an associative list. An element in the list is a pair of user stream identifier and user stream object. If a daemon process communicates with other processes through a mailbox, an element in the associative list is the user stream identifier and mailbox pair. Registration in the association list is executed automatically every time a stream object is instantiated. For this purpose, execution is specified by the `:eval-when-instantiation` option of the defclass function in TAO.

4.3.2 State Transition and Message Passing

The action of a protocol is decided by the connection state and the event that causes a state transition. In the TAO/ELIS implementation, the state is represented by a state name in an instance variable. The event is provided to a stream object through message passing, as described in Subsection 4.3.1.

For example, a method in a stream object is invoked by `TCP-in-daemon`, which detected an event. In this case, the appropriate method must be invoked according to the connection state. The TAO/ELIS implementation approaches it by adopting the state name as the method name, or in other words, as the message selector. There are 11 states in TCP. They are `listen`, `syn-sent`, `syn-received`, `established`, `fin-wait1`, `fin-wait2`, `close-wait`, `last-ack`, `closing`, `time-wait` and `closed`. Therefore, the layer class, `TCP-mixin`, has at least 11 methods that have the same name as the state name. Each stream object stores its state name in one of its instance variables. Every time `TCP-in-daemon` detects an event such as packet reception, it send a `received` message to a stream object. The `received` method in the stream object is invoked by the message. First, it accesses the instance variables in which the connection state is stored. Then, it sends the state name as a message to itself. After the method processes a received packet, it changes its state by assigning the next state name to the instance variable. This state transition allows the next message from the daemon to invoke an appropriate method according to the connection state.

5 Evaluation

In this section, an evaluation of and the issues associated with the connection-oriented implementation model are discussed.

5.1 Applicability of the Implementation Model

The implementation based on this model only requires primitive mechanisms such as multiple inheritance and method combination. They are embedded in every object-oriented programming language. In this respect, the model is considered to be easily implemented.

As for performance, effective implementation requires a facility to run multiple processes on a single object in the implementation language, as described in Section 4.3. In this implementation, message passing by a daemon process is equivalent to a process dispatch from the dispatcher in a conventional operating system. The message passing allocates the processor to a stream object and switches to active process. The method must be invoked immediately after message passing, since the process switching speed determines the system performance in a multitask realtime system. Some concurrent object-oriented programming languages serialize methods to an object and allow only one process to run on an object. In this case, a dispatch delay causes performance degradation and make it difficult to implement a multitask realtime system. Thus, effective implementation requires a facility to run multiple processes on an object. These multiple processes may access the same resources, such as buffer and class variables, simultaneously. This indicates that conventional process synchronization and exclusion facilities, such as semaphores or interrupt inhibition, are also required.

Performance measurements of a file transfer program on top of the TAO/ELIS network indicated a transfer rate of about 30Kbyte/s. The order of the speed is equal to the file copy speed on a local host. Thus, the speed is limited not by the network software, but by the file system on FEP and ELIS or by the channel speed between the FEP and ELIS. This indicates that the network implementation model does not degrade the performance of the network system.

5.2 Issues in Designing Methods in Stream Object and Daemon Processes

There are some design issues related to designing methods and daemon processes. The TAO/ELIS network approaches them as follows:

(1) Critical section.
User processes and methods that are invoked by daemon processes access the same resources simultaneously, since they run on an object asynchronously. These resources include buffer memory, class variables, and so on. Therefore, access to these resources is mutually excluded by semaphores. Since the long-term lock by an interrupt inhibition stops process switch and degrades the system performance, a semaphore is adopted to allow the process switch. When a short-term lock is required, an interrupt inhibition is adopted.

(2) Suspension avoidance.
Each daemon process serves all the stream objects that inherit a given corresponding layer class. Therefore, daemon process suspension in a stream object leads to performance degradation or deadlock. To cope with this problem, methods invoked by daemon processes must be designed not to hang. There is also another issue in the design of daemon processes. An unexpected error in a method can stop a daemon process. This also stops the network service. Therefore, daemon processes are designed to catch error events and restart the service in other streams.

6 Summary

This paper proposed a connection-oriented implementation model and described its TCP/IP implementation in an object-oriented programming language. In the model, neither protocol modification nor protocol extension requires direct modification of the existing software module. Therefore, it is possible to localize or prevent adverse effects caused by modification or extension. The feature also allows multiple protocols to coexist in a layer.

The TCP/IP implementation in the TAO language proves that the model is easily implemented by employing object-oriented programming. The features are as follows:

(1) The protocol hierarchy is reflected in the structure of the class hierarchy. Each layer class corresponds to each protocol layer on a one-to-one basis, and the classes for upper layer inherit those for the lower layers. This leads to a clear and simple software structure.

(2) Since network streams inherit `fundamental-stream`, the implementation provides compatibility with conventional streams and a high-speed buffer access facility.

(3) Since daemon processes and a user process send a message to a stream object asynchronously and independently, multiple processes run on a stream object.

The precise performance evaluation of the network is also a topic for the further investigation.

Acknowledgments. The author wishes to acknowledge the contributions and thoughtful suggestions made in this study by I. Takeuchi, Leader of Takeuchi Research Group, Basic Research Laboratories, and N. Ohsato, Strategic Technology and Business Planning Department.

References

[1] Ahuja, V. : Design and Analysis of Computer Communication Networks, McGraw-Hill (1982).

[2] Postel, J. B. : Internetworking Protocol Approaches, *IEEE Trans. Comm.*, Vol. COM-28, No. 4, pp. 604–611 (1980).

[3] Hibino, Y., Watanabe, K. and Ohsato, N. : The Architecture of Lisp Machine ELIS (in Japanese), *IPSJ SIG-SYM Notes 24-3*, pp. 70–79 (1983).

[4] Takeuchi, I., Okuno, H. and Ohsato, N. : A List Processing Language TAO with Multiple Programming Paradigms, *New Generation Computing*, Vol. 4, No. 4, pp. 401–444 (1986).

[5] Quarterman, J. S. and Hoskins, J. C. : Notable Computer Networks, *Comm. ACM*, Vol. 29, No. 10, pp. 932–971 (1988).

[6] Murakami, K. and Okuno, H. : An Object-oriented Implementation Model for Network Protocols (in Japanese), *Proc. of 32nd IPSJ Conference*, 6F-6, (1986).

[7] Murakami, K. : An Object-oriented Implementation of LAN Protocols (in Japanese), *Proc. of 34th IPSJ Conference*, 1F-7, (1987).

Initially published in "Computer Software", Vol. 6, No. 1, in Japanese.

Ken-ichiro Murakami
NTT Software Laboratories
3-9-11, Midori-cho, Musashino-shi, Tokyo
180 Japan

RACCO : A Modal-Logic Programming Language for Writing Models of Real-Time Process-Control Systems

— Toward Computer-Aided Generation of Real-Time System Software —

Takashi Hattori Reiji Nakajima Naoyuki Niide
Takashi Sakuragawa Kazuki Takenaka

Summary. RACCO is a programming language for modeling and describing real-time process-control systems in order to develop and maintain software rapidly and correctly. Its design is intended to facilitate concise and natural description of highly complex and dynamic systems where each component within the system behaves autonomously, but with mutual interaction. A model described in RACCO can be simulated, then equivalently converted or compiled to lower level code. This paper will show the grammar and semantics of RACCO and will also cxplain its formal semantics and implementation. In addition, the design concept of RACCO will be discussed.

1 Introduction

This paper introduces RACCO, a programming language that is designed to model and describe process-control software of real-time systems naturally.

RACCO is the name of the language and is also the name of an environment for developing and maintaining process-control software. These are called the RACCO language and the RACCO environment, respectively. The RACCO environment is intended to carry out a chain of developing real-time process-control software rapidly, including specifications, writing documents, and efficient maintenance.

Since computers have developed an increasing importance within factories, many methods and languages for developing process-control software have been discussed. For example, in the Jackson method [3], the structure of a system software is determined under relations between components of the target system. Then, a detailed specification and code are drawn up. There is the contrasting approach of "executable-specification" in which the specification is directly written in a higher-level, yet executable programming language. [7] is a functional executable-specification language. RACCO belongs to this type of language.

RACCO is a logic programming language in which such concepts as modules, pipes, and interface of interaction between processes are uniformly treated as modalities. As with temporal logics, time is also treated as a modality. Since the model-theoretic semantics of RACCO can be strictly defined, theoretical and

ISBN 0–12–037103–0

precise discussions about program transformation, compilation, or optimization are possible.

[6] is another approach similar to RACCO, though it is not declared to be an executable-specification language. [6] uses the production system to control systems. Descriptions are accomplished by if-then rules that are similar to the logic-programming style of RACCO. The main difference between [6] and RACCO is that it does not consider the notion of time separately. In addition, RACCO has structures to build module hierarchies and model-theoretic formal semantics.

In this paper, we introduce the RACCO language informally and explain its main features in Section 2, its semantics and implementation in Section 3, and its design concept in Section 4.

2 A Primer of RACCO

In this section, we informally present RACCO's syntax, semantics, and use by a simple example.

RACCO is a modular programming language based on modal and temporal logic, and whose design is intended to facilitate concise and natural description of highly dynamic and complex real-time process-control systems, where each of various components within the system behaves autonomously, but with mutual interaction. We call such a component a "process," and it is syntactically represented by a "module" in RACCO. (Note that these notions are conceptually different from the conventional relationships of an abstract data type vs. instances and of a class vs. objects.)

2.1 The Conceptual Features of RACCO

2.1.1 Temporal Logic

The description of process actions in RACCO is based on Temporal Prolog [5], a logic programming language with tense. In Temporal Prolog, a state of the world is assigned to each point of time. The truth values of predicates vary depending on the points of time. A change of truth values in time can be written using temporal operators.

2.1.2 Process Interactions

- Message-Passing

  Process interaction is accomplished by message-passing. Message passing to a process is realized by setting to true a particular predicate defined by the module representing the process.

- Sockets and Pipes

  Although process interactions can generally be undertaken by message-passing, a process will often exchange a variety of information at the same time with a single opponent process. Hence, it is important both for efficiency and simplicity to deal with such cases effectively. For this purpose, RACCO provides special devices, "sockets" and "pipes."

Sockets are defined on both sides of the communicating processes. All predicates to be exchanged are encapsulated in the socket. Then, a pipe is defined to connect the sockets together in order to transfer information between the processes. This will enable the user to treat processes as components and will allow the user to define a larger module by combining several smaller modules. Hence, modular programming becomes easier. In addition, a relation of interaction between processes can be defined clearly by describing the connection of a pipe in an upper-level module which includes the modules connected by the pipe.

- Modality

  RACCO is defined in a uniform formal basis of modal logic. Such concepts as modules and sockets, as well as the notion of time, are treated as modalities. Pipes are simply axiom schemes that express equivalence between (possibly nested) modal operators.

2.2 An Example—Elevator Control

In the following example, we sketch the main features of RACCO. (RACCO has already been exposed to real-life problems— beyond those of toy examples [2].)

In this section, we adopt a bottom-up and more-or-less intuitive approach to introduce the reader to the main features of the RACCO language. (RACCO has been designed in a bottom-up fashion.) Motivations and discussions are given in Section 3.

We will be describing an elevator control system using RACCO. Some simplifications have been made on the system: The door-open button and door-close button are omitted and the door opens and closes automatically.

The elevator moves from the basement (the 0th floor) to the 4th floor. There is a single *box* to carry people up and down. It is equipped with a group of *destination-buttons*. When one of the *buttons* is pushed, the *box* moves to the corresponding floor. Also, a couple of (upward and downward) *call-buttons* are installed on each floor. The *box* moves to the floor on which a *call-button* is pushed. Once pushed, each *button* maintains the state of "being pushed" until it is reset. When the *box* reaches its destination, the *destination-button* is reset, and the *call-button* in the corresponding direction is reset to the floor.

2.3 Processes and Modules

Each component within the *elevator-system*, such as the *box* or a *button*, is represented by a process that is syntactically represented by a module. This includes not only the items that exist in the actual elevator system, but any item that may conceptually appear or be needed throughout the design and refinement steps. An approximately one-to-one correspondence between processes and modules exists. As usual, a module consists of two parts, the **interface** for the declaration and the **realization** for describing actions and structures.

First, the *elevator-system* [a,b] is defined to represent the whole system. In [a], no declaration is given in the **interface** part, since this module is at the top of the hierarchy and is not needed to interact with other external processes. In

```
interface elevator-system                                              [a]
end interface

realization elevator-system with                                       [b]
            the-box               is box;
            the-calling-board     is calling-board;
      end with

      {the-box}{up-button} ⇔ {the-calling-board}{up-button};          [c]
      {the-box}{down-button} ⇔ {the-calling-board}{down-button};
end realization

interface box
      door-open;                                                       [d]
      door-closed;
      current-floor : int;
      direction : int ;             /* 1=up, 0=down */
      {up-button}pushed(int);                                          [e]
      {up-button}reset(int);
      {down-button}pushed(int);
      {down-button}reset(int);
      {destination-button}pushed(int);
      {destination-button}reset(int);                                  [f]
end interface

realization box with
            operation-board is elevator-button;                        [g]
      end with

      local                                                            [h]
            must-move(int);
            must-move-up(int);
            must-move-down(int);
            moving;
            arrived;
            go;
      end local

      {destination-button} ⇔ {operation-board}{control};               [i]

      {up-button}pushed(X) |                /* '|' reads 'or' */
      {down-button}pushed(X) |
      {destination-button}pushed(X) ⇒ must-move(int);
```

Note: [a], [b], ..., etc., are not part of the program; they are only reference points.

Fig. 1 The elevator program.

```
must-move(X) & (current-floor < X) ⇒
        must-move-up(X);
must-move(X) & (current-floor > X) ⇒
        must-move-down(X);

●door-closed & (current-floor = X) & ●must-move(X) ⇒
        arrived;                                                    [j]
●door-closed & (current-floor = X) &
●{up-button}pushed(X) ⇒
        direction = 1;
●door-closed & (current-floor = X) &
~●{up-button}pushed(X) & ●{down-button}pushed(X) ⇒
        direction = 0;

●moving & (current-floor = X) &
●{destination-button}pushed(X) ⇒
        arrived;
●moving & (current-floor = X) & ●(direction = 1) &
●{up-button}pushed(X) ⇒
        arrived;
●moving & (current-floor = X) & ●(direction = 0) &
●{down-button}pushed(X) ⇒
        arrived;
●moving & (current-floor = X) & ●(direction = 1) &
●{down-button}pushed(X) & ~●{up-button}pushed(X) &
~●must-move-up(Y) ⇒
        arrived & (direction = 0);
●moving & (current-floor = X) & ●(direction = 0) &
●{up-button}pushed(X) & ~●{down-button}pushed(X) &
~●must-move-down(Y) ⇒
        arrived & (direction = 1);

●door-closed & (current-floor = X) & ~●must-move(X) &
●must-move-up(Y) ⇒
        go & (direction = 1);
●door-closed & (current-floor = X) & ~●must-move(X) &
~●must-move-up(Y) & ●must-move-down(Z) ⇒
        go & (direction = 0);

arrived ⇒ door-open until door-closed;                              [k]
arrived & (current-floor = X) ⇒
        {destination-button}reset(X);                               [l]

arrived & (current-floor = X) & (direction = 1) ⇒
        {up-button}reset(X);
```

Fig. 1 The elevator program (cont'd).

```
    arrived & (current-floor = X) & (direction = 0) ⇒
            {down-button}reset(X);

    arrived ⇒ {operation-board}ring;                                    [m]

    door-closed & ~must-go(X) ⇒ ○door-closed;                           [n]

    go ⇒ moving until arrived;

    initial
            direction = 1;                                              [o]
            current-floor = 0;
            door-open;
end realization

interface calling-board
end interface

realization calling-board with
            up-calling is group-of-buttons(3,0);
            down-calling is group-of-buttons(4,1);
    end with

    {up-button} ⇔ {up-calling}{control};
    {down-button} ⇔ {down-calling}{control};
end realization

interface elevator-button is group-of-buttons(4,0)                      [p]
            ring;
end interface

realization elevator-button
    ring ⇒ {bell}ring;              /* bell is defined externally */
end realization

interface group-of-buttons(int,int)                                     [q]
            push(int);
            {control}reset(int);                                        [r]
    state {control}pushed(int);                                         [s]
end interface

realization group-of-buttons(upper-limit,lower-limit)
    push(X) & (lower-limit ≤ X) & (X ≤ upper-limit) ⇒
            {control}pushed(X) until {control}reset(X);                 [t]
end realization
```

Fig. 1 The elevator program (cont'd).

the **realization** part [b], the **with** ... **end with** contains two internal processes, *the-box* and *the-calling-board.* (The use of **is** is explained in Section 2.6.)

2.4 Interface of Module

The **interface** part of the module *box* declares two predicates and two functions:

door-open; [d]
door-closed;
current-floor : *int*;
direction : *int*;

Their (truth) values are visible to and manipulatable by a process that is defined outside this module. *door-open* and *door-closed* are 0-ary predicates, whereas the others are 0-ary integer-valued functions. Here, functions are mainly used to keep particular values for a period of time, whereas in procedural language, this would be undertaken by variables. Note that a predicate is automatically reset to false unless otherwise indicated.

The predicates that are used only internally are declared in **local** ... **end local** in the **realization** part. The six lines

must-move(*int*); [h]
...
go;

are internal, and the first two lines have integer-valued functions with an integer argument.

2.5 Realization

Actions are specified as they are in Temporal Prolog. For instance,

arrived ⇒ *door-open* **until** *door-closed*; [k]

reads "when *arrived* holds, then *door-open* continues to hold until the predicate *door-closed* becomes true." Consider other examples:

●*door-closed* & (*current-floor* = X) & ●*must-move*(X) ⇒
arrived; [j]

reads "if *door-closed* holds at the previous point of time (specified by the temporal operator ●) and *current-floor* is equal to some X at the present time, and *must-move*(X) holds at the previous time, then *arrived* holds."

door-closed & ∼*must-go*(X) ⇒ ○*door-closed*; [n]

reads "if *door-closed* holds and *must-go*(X) does not hold for any X, then door-closed holds at the next time (specified by the temporal operator ○)."

Some other temporal operators are:

□*f*	*f* holds forever from the present point of time
◆*f*	*f* was true at some point of time in the past including now
■*f*	*f* has been always true until now
f **atnext** *g*	*f* holds at the next time when *g* holds
f **since** *g*	*f* has been true since *g* held last time

2.6 Is

Within

interface *elevator-button* **is** *group-of-buttons*(4,0) [p]

elevator-button becomes a specialization of the module *group-of-buttons*(4,0), i.e., all definitions of the latter (both **interface**, **realization**) are automatically included in the former (cf. sype-type relations in IOTA [4] and inheritance of object-oriented languages).

is has another usage in the definition of the **realization** part of the module *box* [g]. *box* has a submodule *operation-board* where its definition is not explicitly declared. Instead, **is** indicates that the defintion of *elevator-button* is used as the definition of *operation-board.*

A formal definition of **is** is given in Section 3.

2.7 Socket

The declaration

$\{up\text{-}button\}pushed(int);$ [e]

in the **interface** part indicates that a socket *up-button* in the process *box* exists, and within the socket a 1-ary predicate *pushed* is defined in which the predicate *pushed* is accessed and manipulated only through the socket *up-button.* In RACCO, modules and sockets are all regarded as modalities.

For example, assume that a predicate *reset* is defined in a socket *up-button* of a module *box.* If one writes:

$\{box\}\{up\text{-}button\}reset(X)$

somewhere outside of *box*, the execution of this formula forces the predicate *reset* to set to true for the argument X.

2.8 Pipe

Two modules that are included in the same module can be connected by their sockets. For instance, in the *elevator-system,*

$\{the\text{-}box\}\{up\text{-}button\} \Leftrightarrow \{the\text{-}calling\text{-}board\}\{up\text{-}button\};$ [c]

connects the socket *up-button* in *the-box* with the socket *up-button* in *the-calling-board.* (Note that both *the-box* and *the-calling-board* are component modules of *elevator-system.*)

In RACCO, such a statement has a special name, "pipe." In logic, a pipe is simply an equivalence between modal operators. In other words, if two sockets are piped, the predicates of the same name in both sockets will have the same truth value (for the same argument, if any). A predicate *reset* is defined in both the sockets $\{the\text{-}box\}\{up\text{-}button\}$ and $\{the\text{-}calling\text{-}board\}\{up\text{-}button\}$. Therefore, by the pipe above, if *reset*(3) becomes true in the former socket, then *reset*(3) becomes true in the latter, and vice versa. In this way, pipes are useful when many messages are sent together to a single opponent process at the same time.

Piping can also be done between a socket of a module and a socket of its submodule. Therefore, the socket *destination-button* in *the-box* and the socket *control* in *operation-board* can be connected.

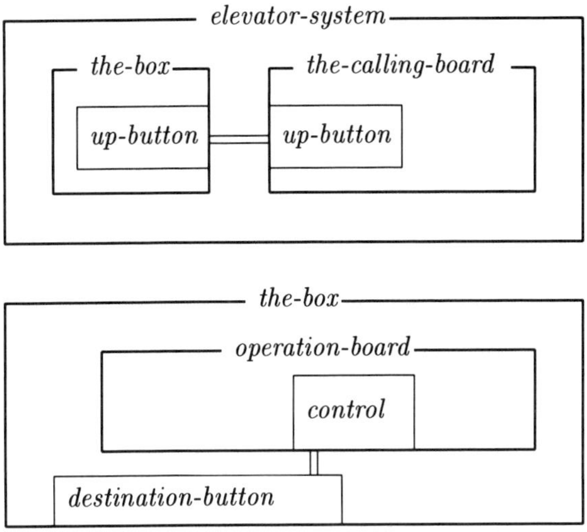

Fig. 2 Examples of piping.

{*destination-button*} ⇔ {*operation-board*}{*control*}; [i]

In this case, the lower-level interface {*the-box*}{*operation-board*}{*control*} is exposed to the higher-level interface {*the-box*}{*destination-button*}.

The Figure 2 shows two possible cases in which pipes can be defined.

By using sockets and pipes, we can make modules independent from each other. All interactions are concentrated in sockets so that explicit specification of opponent modules can be eliminated. Instead, pipes combine modules in the higher-level module. Thus, commonly used components may be implemented as reusable modules from which a module hierarchy can be constructed.

2.9 Initialization

Initialization of a process is done by the **initial** construct in the **realization** of the corresponding module. Here, at the time of system initialization, three conditions within *box* are true:

direction = 1; [o]
current-floor = 0;
door-open;

2.10 Parameterization

The module *group-of-buttons* is parameterized by two integers:

interface *group-of-buttons*(*int*,*int*) [q]

Formally, this indicates that *group-of-buttons* is defined for all possible integer pairs (*i*,*j*).

2.11 State

In the **interface** of the module *group-of-buttons*, **state** is used to declare the predicates that are visible but not manipulatable by other processes.

state $\{control\}pushed(int)$; [s]

2.12 Execution

Let us simulate and illustrate how a RACCO program operates the elevator. In the **realization** of the module *box*, refer to the following two formulas:

arrived ⇒ *door-open* **until** *door-closed*; [k]
arrived & (*current-floor* = X) ⇒
{*destination-button*}*reset*(X); [l]

When the *box* arrives at the jth floor, a message "current floor is the jth" is sent to *the-box*. Namely, the value of the function *current-floor* is set to j. Then, the system checks whether *arrived* is true by using the other formula in the module. If it is true, the predicate *door-open* becomes true by [k] and holds until *door-closed* becomes true. In addition, by [l], the predicate *reset*(j) in the socket *destination-button* becomes true.

A real elevator system contains a control system that stops and starts the box, opens and closes the door, etc.; information is interchanged between the system and the program. We will not consider such ideas at this stage.

The socket *destination-button* and the socket *control* in the module *operation-board* are piped by the formula

{*destination-button*} ⇔ {*operation-board*}{*control*}; [i]

When the *reset*(j) in the {*destination-button*} becomes true, the *reset*(j) also becomes true in {*operation-board*}{*control*}. Namely, a message is sent to the process *operation-board* that forces the *destination-button* for the jth floor, which is in a state of "pushed," to be "reset." Since *operation-board* is a specialization of *group-of-buttons*, its **realization** should contain the formula

push(X) & (*lower-limit* $\leq X$) & ($X \leq$ *upper-limit*) ⇒
{*control*}*pushed*(X) **until** {*control*}*reset*(X); [t]

which resets the *button* to indicate that the *box* is moving to the jth and so forth.

Because of the semantics of RACCO as given by the minimal model, when {*control*}*reset*(X) becomes true, {*control*}*pushed*(j) becomes false, because {*control*}*pushed*(j) need not be true to keep [t] true when {*control*}*reset*(X) is true.

Finally, Fig. 3 illustrates the hierarchical relationships between modules and sockets and the piping system between them.

3 Semantics and Implementation

3.1 Semantics

As mentioned previously, modules and sockets are all regarded as modality in modal logic. Therefore, a program in RACCO simply defines a theory in modal logic in which sentences in **realizations** act as axioms. For instance, the **is** relationship between two modules,

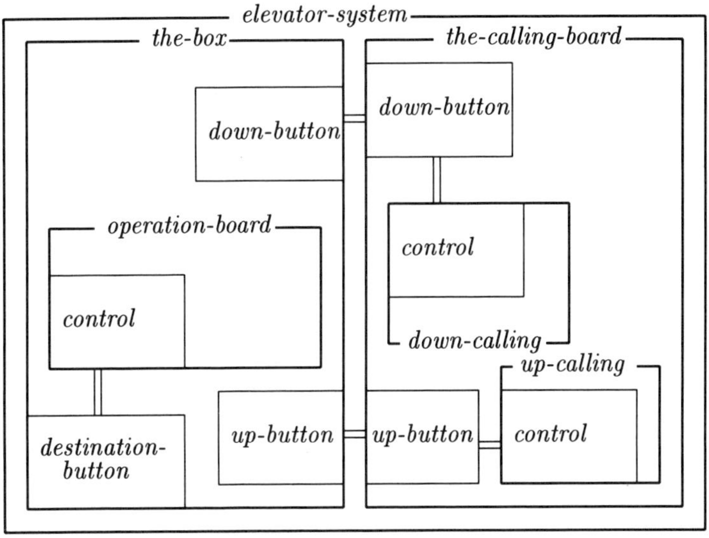

Fig. 3 Relations between modules and sockets.

A **is** *B*,

formally defines a rule of inference in the form of

$$\frac{\{B\}\ (\Box\&\blacksquare)f}{\{A\}\ (\Box\&\blacksquare)f}$$

for all formulas f where $(\Box\&\blacksquare)f$ stands for $\Box f\&\blacksquare f$.

In RACCO, pipes are simply axiom schemes with limited use. For example, when sockets G and H are connected by the statement

$$\{E\}\{G\} \Leftrightarrow \{F\}\{H\}\ ,$$

it denotes an axiom scheme

$$\{E\}\{G\}\mathit{atomic\text{-}formula} \Leftrightarrow \{F\}\{H\}\mathit{atomic\text{-}formula}\ .$$

A model theoretic semantics for Temporal Prolog is given in [5]. By discarding all modalities derived from the modules and sockets, a model for RACCO can be easily derived from that of Temporal Prolog. As explained in the next section, the current version of RACCO is executable after being transformed into Temporal Prolog. Hence, the formal semantics of RACCO can be defined by the transformation and the formal semantics of Temporal Prolog. Since modules and sockets have their proper meanings, it should be considered when semantics is defined. This is especially important when dealing with program transformations in RACCO. Inside a particular module, transformation based on Temporal Logic can be utilized. When spanning two or more modules, however, it is expected that semantics based on modality-specific models can produce a more sophisticated transformation. It is a subject of further work to construct modality-specific models.

3.2 Implementation

An efficient implementation scheme for a temporal and modal logic programming language is surely a challenging research problem. Although the implementation issue is not the main topic of this paper, we will briefly mention how the initial version of RACCO interpreter works according to a straightforward strategy:

The basic idea is to assemble all sentences in all modules and transform them into standard formulas or pseudo-PROLOG sentences. Then, by backward reasoning, the model at each point of time is determined.

1. Type checking

   In the first step, static type checking is applied to all predicates (including those derived from functions).

2. Transformation to Temporal Prolog

   All predicates are renamed uniquely, regardless of the modal operators for modules and sockets, and all modal operators for modules and sockets are removed. Here, for any two sockets that are piped to each other, the predicates in those sockets with the same name are renamed to the same name, i.e., are identified.

3. Transformation to normal form

   By a mechanical method, all temporal modal operators except $\bullet$, $\Rightarrow, \&, \sim$ are removed from sentences by equivalence preserving transformations into a normal form. (Refer to [5] for a concrete presentation of the transformation procedure.)

   $$a_1 \ \& \ a_2 \ \& \ \cdots \ \& \ a_n \Rightarrow b$$

   where $a_1, \cdots, a_n$ are atomic formulas or their negations, possibly preceded by $\bullet$, and b is an atomic formula.

   For instance,

   $$\bullet\bullet p \Rightarrow q \ \ \textbf{atnext} \ \ r$$

   is transformed into

   $$\begin{array}{l} \bullet p \Rightarrow s \\ \bullet s \Rightarrow t \\ \bullet t \ \ \& \ \ \bullet \sim r \Rightarrow t \\ t \ \ \& \ \ r \Rightarrow q \end{array}$$

4. Execution

   The resulting sentences in normal form are executed. Namely, the truth value of each predicate in the sentences is determined by cycling through the following loop:

(a) Assert the external predicates that are true at the current point in time.

(b) Assert those predicates that are true at the current point in time. This can be accomplished, for example, in the same manner as the Prolog interpreter.

(c) Let N be the maximal length of sequences of ● appearing in the program, and delete the history of truth values older than the point of time that is N units before the current time.

(d) Increase time by one unit. Those predicates that were true at the current time are now assumed to be true in the previous time, and so on.

Repeat (4a) through (4d) infinitely. Since any history older than a certain interval is deleted at (4c), the possibility that history will overflow never occurs.

Table 1 Results of benchmark test

The elevator example	$6step/sec$†
● $at(X)$ & $Y := X + 1 \Rightarrow at(Y)$	$850step/sec$‡
naive reverse(30)	1.3KLIPS‡, 500LIPS†

† includes garbage collection
‡ does not include garbage collection

The current implementation from (1) through (4) is written in Common LISP. Efficiency is the main concern in (4) since it is the interpreter. Table 1 shows statistics when executing on Data General MV10000 and Kyoto Common LISP with 400KB for the cell region. The elevator example described in Section 2.2 executes in about 0.16 seconds to proceed time by one unit. For reference, Table 1 also includes statistics for a program which changes $at(n)$ true at the nth point of time and the program of naive reverse. Since Prolog compilers faster than 10KLIPS on microprocessors are available, a possible RACCO compiler could execute the elevator example in 8 ms/step if the ratio was preserved.

To increase efficiency, we can decrease the number of predicates asserted in (4b). For example, it is not necessary to assert predicates that do not vary over time. We only examine and assert predicates that depend on time, and the former predicates may be used in resolution steps for the latter predicates.

2 Discussion

We have seen many arguments against the so-called waterfall styles of software development and for the merits and infeasibility of the so-called transformational approach. In the latter approach, the first stage of development is writing executable specification in formal language that can be checked and processed by mechanical methods. When the specification is well debugged, an efficient program could result from a mechanized (but not necessarily automatic) procedure.

The following assertions are our observations on this issue:

1. Algebraic or equational specification is the most popular approach to executable specification. It has good mathematical foundation and can be well treated formally. However, its expressive power is not strong enough for real and concrete applications.

2. The idea of transformation seems promising but has been used to mean many different ideas. As far as the authors of this paper are aware, regrettably, no solid and generally acceptable method or algorithm has been developed as was the case in compiler technology decades ago.

3. The study of programming has largely tended to search for generality. Model-oriented or domain-specific features should receive more attention in research into languages, methodologies, and environments specifically geared toward specification issues.

In this paper we have limited our attention to the domain of real-time process control systems. As is well known, rapid developments of computer-controlled equipment and its manufacture, such as factory automation and various large-scale plants, have made increasingly important and urgent the introduction of innovative improvements in the technology for production and maintenance of software for real-time process-control systems. The following difficulties apply to general software production, but especially so to real-time system software:

1. The cost of real-time control software has been increasing — occasionally to more than half of the total system cost. It is generally believed that this ratio will continue to increase.

2. Reliability is the key issue in real-time systems. While malfunctions have disastrous consequences, real-time control software is often too dangerous to test in actual system settings. No solution to this issue, however, has been found that satisfies project managers and system analysts.

3. Real-time systems tend to be large, complex, and inevitably inflexible due to concurrency issues. Hence, adapting software to change or enhancement of the whole system requires challenging work that, in some cases, is impossible to perform.

These points should justify our intention to limit the domain to the real-time system software. The next step is to verify that it is, indeed, profitable to limit the domain. The following points should be examined.

If we limit our goal to some particular domain of computer application and to try utilizing the domain-specific features:

1. Is it possible to facilitate natural and simple expression that is easy to debug, and

2. is it possible to work out effective schemes of transformation, optimization, and compilation (if they should be treated differently) to provide powerful environments that are better than existing technology ?

If work under such a guideline is to be successful, it must be started bottom-up from real and concrete problems — quite the opposite to the usual attitude in programming languages and methodologies.

For instance, when one of the authors of this paper designed IOTA [4] years ago, he started with a theory and a formalism in a top-down approach, and then tried to find toy examples in which the ideas could be neatly applied.

Therefore, in this research work, we started purely from concrete problems with collaboration between computer scientists and system engineers of process control. So far, the design of the language RACCO has been based on attacking a number of real problems. Attention has been devoted to pragmatism rather than elegance or novelties.

We assert that the present specifications of RACCO are enough to cover various (though, of course, not all) problems of process control without excessively redundant features.

The following will be the procedure of system development for RACCO. As widely pointed out, language design should go hand in hand with the design consideration of the support environment.

First, the model of the system is constructed from the designer's view of the required specification of the intended system. It begins similarly to the method suggested in [3], where the designer lists all items to appear in the system, including those that may appear in the design and refinement steps. Then, the designer points out all relationships that will be later expressed by specialization (**is**) and 'consist-of' (**with** ··· **end with**) relations between modules in RACCO.

Next, the designer determines under what plan the system will work and elaborates the behavior of each item and interactions among them so that the items will evolve into "processes" in RACCO. Although all actions within the system are initiated and controlled by computers, the items at this stage of model description have autonomy, and each plays its role according to a script. (The RACCO language is designed for this type of script.) Thus, the designer can construct a model that is natural to his or her point of view without being overwhelmed by the actual details of the computer setting. To convert such a script to meet the demands of an actual situation is one of the objectives of the transformation.

Although model construction is trivial in the elevator example of Section 2, it generally requires challenging work to deal with real life-size problems (see [2]). Hence, a systematic environment support is indispensable.

Once the model of the system is constructed and described, its behavior will be visually simulated in a graphic environment furnished by a high-resolution bit-map display. This process will be highly interactive by using the various support tools. As previously discussed, simulation during the early stage will be useful for rapid prototyping. Note also that it is important for the system designer to understand visually the outcome of the simulation.

When a model is convincingly well validated, it will enter into an interactive and semi-automatic process of compilation (and transformation) to yield code executable on actual computers. Although RACCO is a purely formal language with straightforward semantics, it does not lose practical feasibility, unlike many requirement specification languages with similar objectives in the field of software engineering. For instance, in promoting reuse of modules, which is a key issue in this field of work, RACCO's sockets and pipes are useful devices and do not require complicated operational semantics.

We have further optimism and expectations for the "RACCO environment," but that will be the topic of another paper.

Acknowledgments. The authors express their deep gratitude to Mr. Tamao Yokoi of Sumitomo Metal Industries for his constant encouragement to the RACCO project.

References

[1] Hattori, T. : Time Extraction for Temporal Logic, *J. Comput. Syst. Sci.* (appear).

[2] Hattori, T., Nakajima, R., Niide, N., Sakuragawa, T. and Takenaka, K. : *A Work out Example of Tube Mill in RACCO*, Technical Report in RIMS 561(J), Kyoto University, 1986 (in Japanese).

[3] Jackson, M. A. : *System Development*, Prentice-Hall, 1983.

[4] Ed. Nakajima, R. and Yuasa, T. : *The IOTA Programming System*, LNCS 160, Springer-Verlag, 1982.

[5] Sakuragawa, T. : Temporal Prolog, *Comput. Softw.*, Vol. 4, No. 3 (1987), pp. 15–27 (in Japanese).

[6] Tashiro, T., Komoda, N. and Tsushima, I. : A System Description Method Based on Rule Description, *Journal of the Society of Instrument and Control Engineers*, Vol. 22, No. 9 (1983), pp. 42–46 (in Japanese).

[7] Zave, P. : An Operational Approach to Requirements Specification for Embedded Systems, *IEEE Trans. Softw. Eng.*, SE-8 (1982), pp. 250–269.

[8] Zave, P. : The Operational versus the Conventional Approach to Software Development, *Comm. ACM*, Vol. 27, No. 2 (1984), pp. 104–118.

Appendix. SYNTAX

1. Characters

   alphanumeric, hiragana, katakana, chinese character, special symbol

2. Reserved Words

   after, atnext, end, for, initial, int, interface, is, list, socket, realization, since, state, until, with

3. Syntax Rules

program ::= *interface* ··· *realization* ··· *initiation*

interface ::=
        interface *module-name* [(*list-of-types*)] [**is** *list-of-module-descript*
                [*declaration* ···]
                [**state** *declaration* ···]
        end interface

realization ::=
        realization *module-name* [(*list-of-variable-names*)]
                [**with** (*module-name* **is** *list-of-module-descriptors*;)
                  ··· **end with**]

```
                [ local declaration ··· end local ]
                [ ( formula; ) ··· ]
                [ initial ( formula; ) ··· ]
        end realization

initiation ::=
        initial
                ( formula; ) ···
        end initial

declaration ::=
        [ {socket-name} ] predicate-name [ (list-of-types) ] ; |
        [ {socket-name} ] function-name [ (list-of-types) ] :type;

list-of-types ::= type | list-of-types,type
type ::= int | socket | module-descriptor | list (type)

list-of-module-descriptors ::=
        module-descriptor | list-of-module-descriptors,module-descriptor
module-descriptor ::= module-name [ (list-of-terms) ]

conditional ::=
        atomic-formula | ~conditional |
        conditional&conditional | conditional'|'conditional |
        ●conditional | ◆conditional | ■conditional |
        conditional since conditional | conditional after conditional |
        conditional for integer |
        {module }conditional | {socket }conditional

formula ::=
        atomic-formula | formula &formula | conditional ⇒formula |
        □formula | ○formula |
        formula until conditional | formula atnext conditional |
        {module }formula | {socket }formula |
        [ {module} ] {socket} ⇔ [ {module} ] {socket}

atomic-formula ::= predicate-name [ (list-of-terms) ]

list-of-terms ::= term | list-of-terms ,term

term ::=
        module-name | socket-name | variable-name | [term|term] |
        function-name [ (list-of-terms) ] |
        {module}term | {socket}term

module ::= module-name | variable-name
```

socket ::= *socket-name* | *variable-name*

list-of-variable-names ::= *variable-name* | *list-of-variable-names*,*variable-name*

predicate-name ::= *name*

function-name ::= *name*

variable-name ::= *name*

name ::= *character* ···

character ::= *alphanumeric* | *hiragana* | *katakana* | *chinese-character*

Initially published in "Computer Software", Vol. 5, No. 3, in Japanese.

Takashi Hattori
Research Institute for Mathematical Sciences
Kyoto University
Kita-Shirakawa Oiwake-cho, Sakyo-ku, Kyoto
606 Japan

Reiji Nakajima
Research Institute for Mathematical Sciences
Kyoto University
Kita-Shirakawa Oiwake-cho, Sakyo-ku, Kyoto
606 Japan

Naoyuki Niide
Research Institute for Mathematical Sciences
Kyoto University
Kita-Shirakawa Oiwake-cho, Sakyo-ku, Kyoto
606 Japan

Takashi Sakuragawa
Research Institute for Mathematical Sciences
Kyoto University
Kita-Shirakawa Oiwake-cho, Sakyo-ku, Kyoto
606 Japan

Kazuki Takenaka
Control & OR Department
Sumitomo Metal Industries
1–3 Nishi-Nagasu-Hondori, Amagasaki
660 Japan

Formalizing Computer Program Traces

Shigeki Goto

Summary. This paper proposes a new language, Formal LISP, for expressing and reasoning about traces of computer programs. Each statement in the language looks like a logical formula, and a program takes the form of a logical proof. We can apply the normalization theorem of logical proofs to the new expressions to verify the equivalence between two computer programs. The normalization theorem states that a trace is divided into three parts: decomposition, basic operation and composition. This indicates that we have a specific programming style in this language. This paper also suggests that a single trace can represent a set of traces of a program if the program satisfies some conditions of uniformity. The class of uniform programs covers several interesting examples by Boyer and Moore, who have shown how their explicit induction schemes are useful.

1 Introduction

It is well known that a computer program looks like a logical proof (Manna [8], McCarthy [11]). This paper shows a new straightforward correspondence between traces of computer programs and logical proofs based on constructive logic (Constable *et al.* [3], Hayashi and Nakano [5], Martin-Löf [9]).

Martin-Löf explains in his proposal of constructive logic that the form of a proof can be classified according to the form of the formula to be proved (Table 1) [9]. $\bot$ in Table 1 stands for a propositional constant that is always $false$. &, $\vee$, $\supset$, $\forall$ and $\exists$ are logical connectives. (a, b) represents a pair of a and b. $i(\cdot)$ is a canonical injection from A to the direct sum A+B, and $j(\cdot)$ is a canonical injection from B to A+B. $\lambda x.b(x)$ is a lambda expression.

Table 1 Logical formulas and proofs

Formula	Proof
$\bot$	none
$A \& B$	(a, b)
$A \vee B$	$i(a)$ or $j(b)$
$A \supset B$	$\lambda x.b(x)$
$\forall x.B(x)$	$\lambda x.b(x)$
$\exists x.B(x)$	(a, b)

ISBN 0-12-037103-0

This paper concerns the second row of Table 1. It reads, "If a is a proof for a logical formula A and b is a proof for B, the term (a, b) is a proof for the formula $A\&B$". The following is a rule in [9] that justifies the second row of Table 1.

$$\frac{\mathrm{a} \in \mathrm{A} \qquad\qquad \mathrm{b} \in \mathrm{B}}{(\mathrm{a,b}) \in \mathrm{A\&B}}$$

In this paper, we are interested in the left hand side of "∈," i.e., proofs, and we often omit the expressions like "∈A," "∈B," and "∈A&B."

The programming language LISP (McCarthy [12], McCarthy *et al.* [13], Steel [17]) has "pair" as a basic constituent. Our Formal LISP adopts the same notation as traditional LISP to represent pairs. A pair (a, b) is written as `(a.b)` in LISP, where "`.`" is called a *dot*. We sometimes use a *list* `(a b)` to represent a pair (a, b) because it is customary to use lists rather than dot notation in daily LISP programming. Precisely speaking, the list `(a b)` is an abbreviation for the dotted term `(a.(b.nil))`.

Since a dotted pair, or a list, can be interpreted as a proof term for an AND (&) formula, we can formalize LISP operations in accordance with the logical inference rules. Figure 1 shows logical inference rules for AND (&) in Natural Deduction formalism (Prawitz [14]), where &I and &E mean "AND Introduction" and "AND Elimination" respectively. The introduction rule puts a logical symbol AND (&) in the conclusion **A&B**, whereas the elimination rule removes it from the premise of the inference rule.

$$\frac{\mathtt{A} \quad \mathtt{B}}{\mathtt{A\&B}}\ \mathtt{\&I} \qquad\qquad \frac{\mathtt{A\&B}}{\mathtt{A}}\ \mathtt{\&E} \qquad\qquad \frac{\mathtt{A\&B}}{\mathtt{B}}\ \mathtt{\&E}$$

Fig. 1 Logical inference rules for AND (&).

The inference rules for the dot (`.`) take exactly the same form as logical inference rules for AND (Fig. 2). We can extend the rules to cover lists. The names of the rules `cons`, `car`, and `cdr` correspond to the names of the functions in LISP that perform the same operations as the inference rules.

$$\frac{\mathtt{a} \quad \mathtt{b}}{\mathtt{(a.b)}}\ \mathtt{cons} \qquad\qquad \frac{\mathtt{(a.b)}}{\mathtt{a}}\ \mathtt{car} \qquad\qquad \frac{\mathtt{(a.b)}}{\mathtt{b}}\ \mathtt{cdr}$$

$$\frac{\mathtt{a} \quad \mathtt{(b)}}{\mathtt{(a\ b)}}\ \mathtt{cons} \qquad\qquad \frac{\mathtt{(a\ b)}}{\mathtt{a}}\ \mathtt{car} \qquad\qquad \frac{\mathtt{(a\ b)}}{\mathtt{(b)}}\ \mathtt{cdr}$$

Fig. 2 Inference rules for dots and lists.

Inference rules `car` and `cdr` are frequently combined to improve the readability of proof figures, as shown in the following.

$$\frac{\mathtt{(a\ b\ c)}}{\mathtt{a}}\ \mathtt{car} \qquad \frac{\mathtt{(a\ b\ c)}}{\mathtt{(b\ c)}}\ \mathtt{cdr} \qquad \frac{\mathtt{(a\ b\ c)}}{\mathtt{a} \quad \mathtt{(b\ c)}}\ \mathtt{car{-}cdr}$$

```
A    B              A    B
------- &I          ------- &I
  A&B                 A&B
------- &E          ------- &E
   A                   B
```

Fig. 3 Redundant proofs.

```
  A&B
------- car-cdr
A    B
------- &I
  A&B
```

Fig. 4 Redundant proofs (continued).

The resemblance between logical inference rules and LISP operations suggests that there is a similar relationship between logical proofs and LISP programs. In fact, they have many properties in common. We will later apply the normalization theorem of logical proofs to Formal LISP programs.

Normalization is a process of repeatedly applying reduction rules to a proof, thereby removing the redundant parts.

Definition 1. *If no reduction rules can be applied to a proof, then it is called* **normal**.

In this paper, we have only one logical connective, & (AND), and two inference rules, &I and &E. The redundant (sub-)proofs are shown in Figs. 3 and 4.

Both of the proofs in Fig. 3 introduce &s (ANDs) in the second line by the rule &I and immediately eliminate them by the rule &E in the next line. They are apparently redundant because the left proof can be reduced to `A` without changing the conclusion and the right one to `B`. In general, the reduction procedure cancels both of the applications of &I and &E, if the rule &I is immediately followed by the rule &E. The reduction rules in Fig. 3 are represented in LISP notation as `(CAR (CONS A B))` ▷ `A` and `(CDR (CONS A B))` ▷ `B`, where ▷ means "is reduced to." The two reduction rules are useful in LISP programming.

The proof in Fig. 4 is also redundant and can be reduced to `A&B`. The reduction rule in Fig. 4 rarely appears in the proof normalization literature. An exception is Prawitz [15], who utilizes the rule in the reverse direction. He uses it to expand a proof, minimizing the complexity of the minimal formula in the proof. Furthermore, the reduction rule in Fig. 4 is treated together with the rules in Fig. 3 in the literature of typed lambda calculus. It is well known that all the proofs are strongly normalizable with respect to the reduction rules in Figs. 3 and 4. (In [6], strongly normalizable terms are called *bounded* terms.) We will make use of these reduction rules.

In LISP, the reduction in Fig. 4 is represented as `(CONS (CAR (CONS A B))(CDR (CONS A B)))` ▷ `(CONS A B)`. The property is well known among LISP programmers.

A program in Formal LISP is treated as a logical proof. Thus, a normal program can be obtained by successively applying reduction rules to a program. A normal

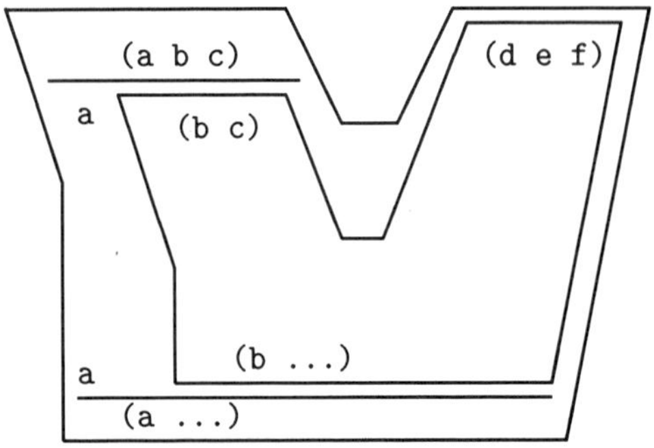

Fig. 5 Making a trace of (APPEND A B).

program can be thought of as a standard or canonical form of the program. In Section 2, we will apply the normalization theorem to Formal LISP programs to verify the equivalence between two programs. The list programs in Section 2 only handle fixed length lists. Section 3 will generalize the method in Section 2 by the use of an implicit mathematical induction scheme. Section 4 applies the same technique to other data structures, such as natural numbers and S-expressions. The summary is given in Section 5, as well as the plan for the future.

2 T-equivalence between Programs

Since Formal LISP has three inference rules (car, cdr, and cons), it can express simple operations. The following LISP program, described by Boyer and Moore [1], asserts that the function APPEND is associative.

```
(EQUAL (APPEND (APPEND A B) C)
       (APPEND A (APPEND B C)) )
```

We will prove this assertion using Formal LISP. First, the definition of the function APPEND is

```
(APPEND X Y)
= (IF (LISTP X)
      (CONS (CAR X) (APPEND (CDR X) Y))
      Y)
```

where (LISTP X) is a predicate defined in [1], which tells if the argument X is a list or not.

Since we only have car, cdr, and cons, the function APPEND cannot be directly translated into Formal LISP. However, traces of the APPEND program are represented in Formal LISP. If we substitute the list (a b c) for A and (d e f) for B, then the trace of the program (APPEND A B) is shown in Fig. 5. The input data (a b c) is decomposed into a and (b c). The function APPEND is recursively applied to (b c). Finally, the output is constructed from a and the result of the recursive application of APPEND.

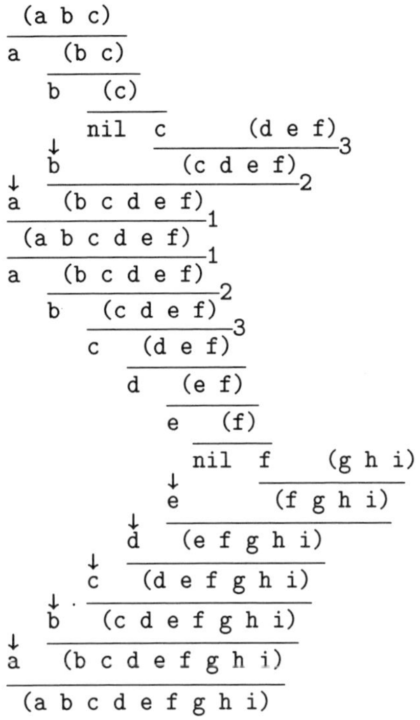

Fig. 6 (APPEND (APPEND A B) C).

After filling the blanks in Fig. 5 and substituting `(g h i)` for `C`, the final trace of `(APPEND (APPEND A B) C)` is shown in Fig. 6. Hereafter, a trace is also called a "proof" because it takes the form of a proof in Formal LISP.

Some additional notations are used in Fig. 6. The arrows (↓) over `a` and `b` indicate that they are identical to the terms `a` and `b` above. Formally, the upper term `a` is the real term, and the lower `a` with an arrow is an echo of the upper term. The echo term makes the proof figure readable. The numbers attached to the inference rules (`1, 2, 3`) are used for reference in the text.

The proof in Fig. 6 can be normalized. First, both of the inference rules marked `1` are canceled, because the upper rule is `cons` and the lower one is the combination of `car` and `cdr`. The two rules `1` form an "&I-&E" sequence, which is a redundant part in the proof. By removing the rules `1`, we can get the proof in Fig. 7.

The reduction steps for `2` and `3` are similar to the reduction procedure for `1`. The final normal proof is shown in Fig. 8. The proof in Fig. 8 has no "&I-&E" sequences because it is normal.

On the other hand, if we append `B` and `C` first, the proof figure for `(APPEND B C)` is shown in Fig. 9. The final proof figure for `(APPEND A (APPEND B C))` is shown in Fig. 10. It is identical to Fig. 8 and therefore normal.

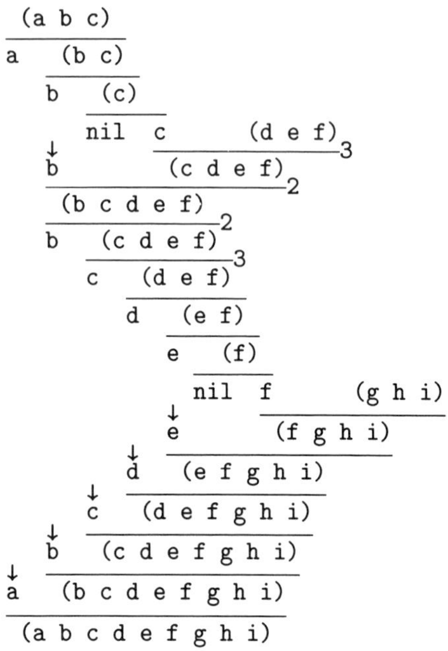

Fig. 7 After canceling the rules 1.

We have shown that `(APPEND (APPEND A B) C)` and `(APPEND A (APPEND B C))` are **t-equivalent** as defined by the following.

Definition 2.

1. *If two programs $P_1(x)$ and $P_2(x)$ have traces $P_1(a)$ and $P_2(a)$ that are equivalent when normalized, the programs are called* **t-equivalent at "a."**
2. *If two programs $P_1(x)$ and $P_2(x)$ are t-equivalent at all x, they are simply called* **t-equivalent**.

Since each reduction rule does not change the conclusion (the lower formula) of inference rules, t-equivalent traces have the same conclusion. The conclusion of the proof corresponds to the final value of the program. Thus, t-equivalent programs are equivalent in the usual sense, i.e., they have the same value.

The above proof of equivalence is much shorter than the proof in Boyer and Moore [1], which covers three pages. However, some alert readers may notice that we have only proved the t-equivalence at `(a b c)`, `(d e f)`, and `(g h i)`. On the other hand, the proof in [1] showed the equivalence for all input data `A`, `B`, and `C`. The proof in [1] cannot be replaced by our new method unless the t-equivalence at all data can be shown.

It is worth while to differentiate our proof method from the Boyer-Moore method. While the Formal LISP approach shows the equivalence only for some

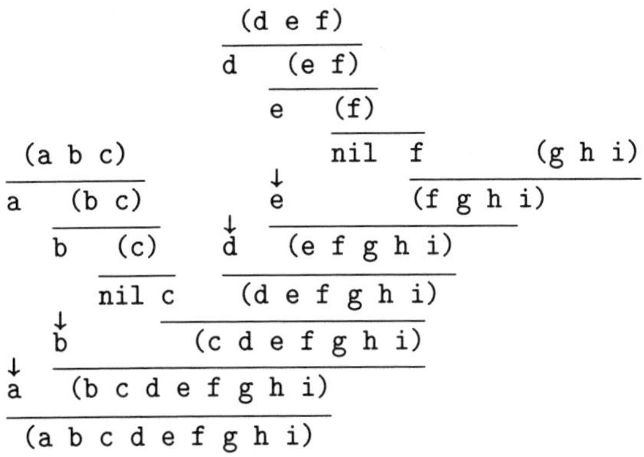

Fig. 8 Normalized proof.

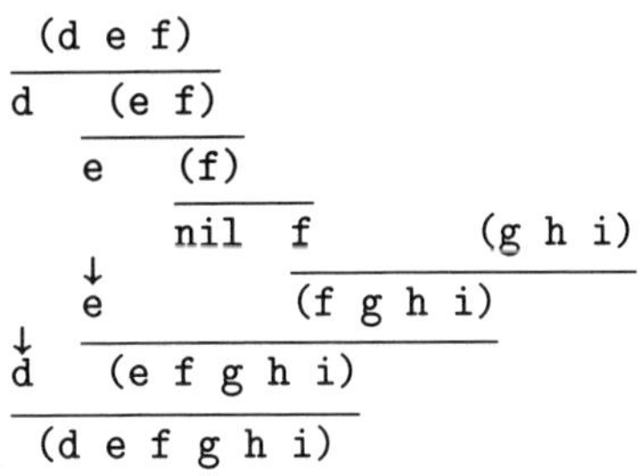

Fig. 9 `(APPEND B C)`.

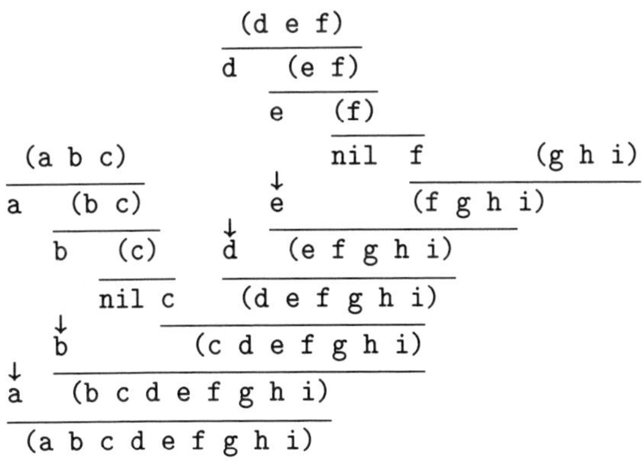

Fig. 10 `(APPEND A (APPEND B C))`.

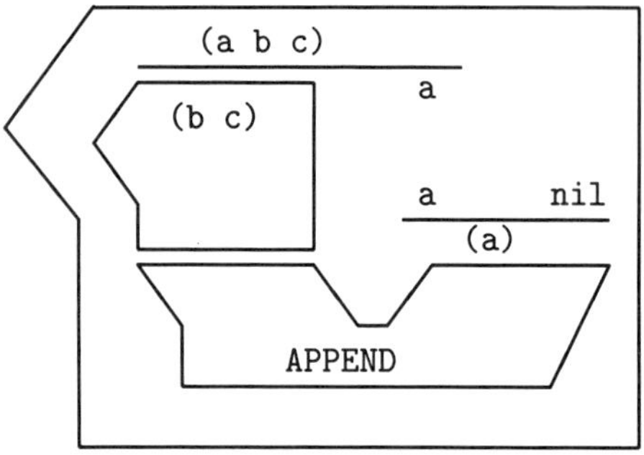

Fig. 11 Trace of `(REVERSE X)`.

specific data, the proof figure demonstrates the trace of the computation as well as the result of the computation. Human intelligence can utilize the trace information to generalize the result. Section 3 will try to extend our result and show how to generalize the normalization method to deal with general data. Before investigating the generalization technique, one more LISP program is introduced to illustrate our Formal LISP method.

```
(EQUAL (REVERSE (REVERSE X)) X)
```

The above problem, also discussed in Boyer and Moore [1], asserts that `(REVERSE (REVERSE X))` is equal to `X`. Actually, Boyer and Moore state an additional condition, "`X` is a list". We omit this condition because only lists are considered in this section. A proof figure is made by substituting `(a b c)` for `X`. First, the trace of `(REVERSE X)` is illustrated in Figs. 11 and 12, based on the definition of "naive `REVERSE`" given below.

```
(REVERSE X)
= (IF (LISTP X)
      (APPEND (REVERSE (CDR X))
              (CONS (CAR X) NIL) )
      NIL)
```

The trace in Fig. 12 is not normal. The reduction rules are applied, and the normal proof is shown in Fig. 13.

Next, two `REVERSE` proofs are linked in Fig. 14 to solve the problem. The proof in Fig. 14 is not normal. The reduction steps for Fig. 14 are similar to the proof of `APPEND`. The intermediate stage is shown in Fig. 15 with all &I-&E sequences eliminated.

Further reduction rules are applied to the inference rules marked 4, 5, and 6. The final proof is Fig. 16, which consists of a single formula, `(a b c)`.

It is possible to apply the reduction rules in a different order than that used in this paper. The final normal proof is guaranteed to be unique regardless of the order employed because the proofs are strongly normalizable.

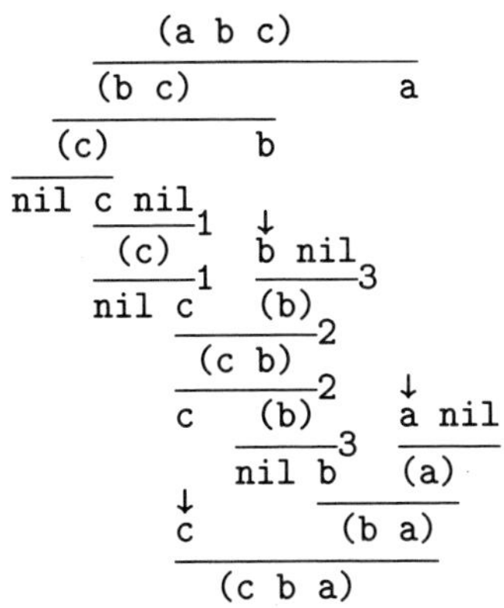

Fig. 12 Naive REVERSE.

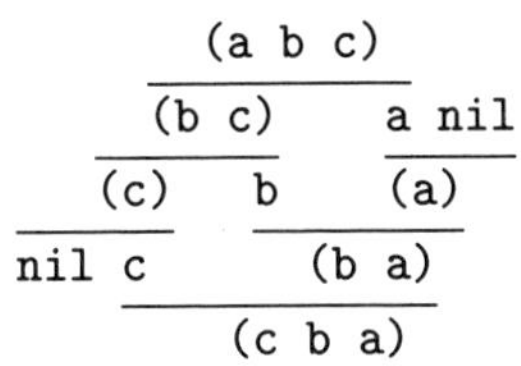

Fig. 13 Normalized (REVERSE X).

The normalized proof demonstrates that reversing X twice is t-equivalent to the identity function at (a b c). Thus, the problem has been solved. However, the usefulness of our method depends on how to handle general terms because we are not satisfied with the simple result for (a b c). This will be discussed in Section 3.

The celebrated normalization theorem is described elsewhere [14] [18].

Theorem 1. *A proof takes the form of a tree. A* **spine** *is a series of logical formulas beginning at a leaf of a tree and ending at the root of the tree. Any spine of a* **normal** *proof can be divided into three parts: The uppermost part is the* **elimination** *part, where only elimination rules appear; the middle part is the* **basic operation** *part; and the lowermost part is the* **introduction** *part, where only introduction rules are used.*

The normalization theorem can be applied to Formal LISP traces. This means there exists the standard or canonical form of a trace.

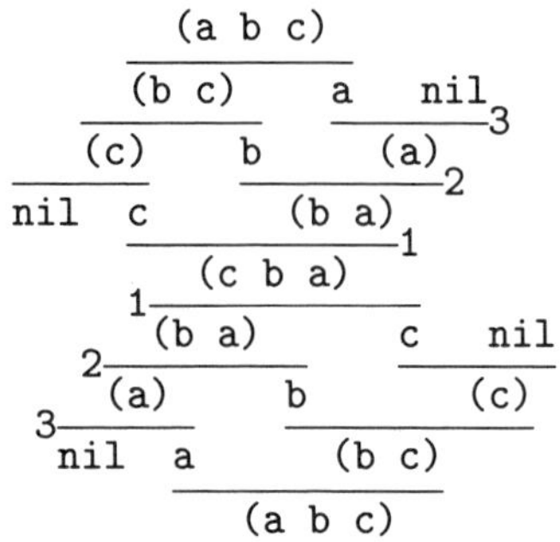

Fig. 14 (REVERSE (REVERSE X)).

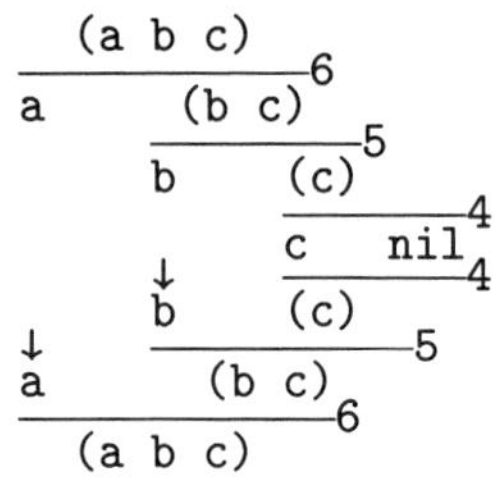

Fig. 15 After eliminating &I-&E sequences.

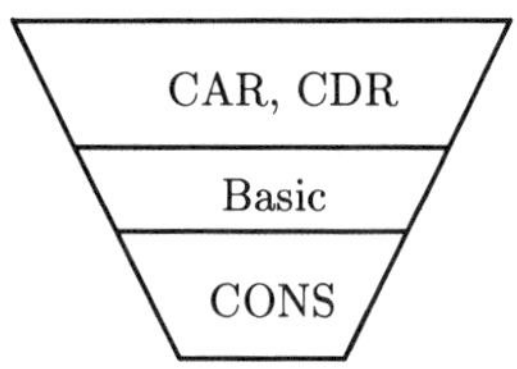

In fact, the traces shown in Figs. 8 and 13 have only cars and cdrs, which are the elimination rules, in the upper part of the proof. And they have only cons rules, which are just the introduction rules in LISP, in the lower part. This illustrates that the normalization theorem is valid for Formal LISP traces. Figure 16 is also a normal proof. However, all parts are degenerated.

This section has no *basic operations* concerning equality rules and properties of primitive recursive functions in logic.[1]

3 Stereoscopic Program Extension

In the previous section, the normalization theorem was successfully applied to Formal LISP programs to verify the equivalence between two LISP programs. The

[1] Since this paper discusses only the inference rule for AND (&), the definition of *spine* is extremely simplified. For more detailed definition, please refer to p. 299 in Troelstra [18].

```
(a b c)
```

Fig. 16 Final proof.

method is theoretically well justified, but the usefulness is limited because we could only show the result for some specific lists, such as `(a b c)` and `(d e f)`. We had to verify the result for `(a b c d)` separately, to prove the equivalence for it. We will show how to extend the method to cover general terms in Formal LISP.

A common technique to solve this kind of problem is to apply the mathematical induction scheme. In principle, our method is based on the mathematical induction. However, this paper proposes to use the induction scheme implicitly.

Our method constructs a longer term `(a b c d)` from `(a b c)`. First, each entry `a`, `b`, or `c` in the term `(a b c)` is thought of as a variable. Thus, `(a b c)` can represent any list of length three. If two programs are t-equivalent at `(a b c)`, they are t-equivalent at all the lists of length three.

`(a b c)` ↔ `(x y z)`

However, a list `(x y z w)` has a length of four, and there is no simple substitution for `(a b c)` that makes `(x y z w)` and `(a b c)` equivalent.

There are two possible ways to adjust for the difference in the length of lists `(a b c)` and `(x y z w)`. Our method uses both of the adjustments.

(1) `(x y z w)` is decomposed into subterms `x` and `(y z w)`. The term `(y z w)` is of length three and can be regarded as `(a b c)`.

(2) Using the dot notation, `(a b c)` is written as `a.b.c.nil`. Similarly, `(x y z w)` is `x.y.z.w.nil`. A set of associated pairs are taken beginning on the left: `a` ↔ `x`, `b` ↔ `y`, `c` ↔ `z`, `nil` ↔ `w.nil`. They can be made equal: `a=x`, `b=y`, `c=z`, `nil=w.nil`, where special care should be taken to avoid inconsistency due to `nil=w.nil` (to be discussed later).

The decomposition (1) is the top-down approach to list manipulation that is popular in LISP programming.

On the other hand, method (2) adjusts the length of the list at the rightmost entry. It seems peculiar at first sight.

The equation `nil=w.nil` is justified as follows. In Formal LISP, the dot "." appears in the proof for an AND (&) formula. If `w` is a proof for `W` and `nil` is a proof for the formula `NIL`, then a term `w.nil` is a proof for the formula `W&NIL`. If `w` is `T`, where `T` is a propositional constant and always true, then `T&NIL` and `NIL` are logically equivalent. `T` is thought of as an axiom, and the proof of `T` is `T` itself. The logical equivalence can be extended to the proofs by applying the equivalence relation to all the formulas in the proof. The proofs `T&nil` and `nil` are logically equivalent. Thus, a list `(a b c)` of length three is equivalent to a list `(x y z T)` of length four.

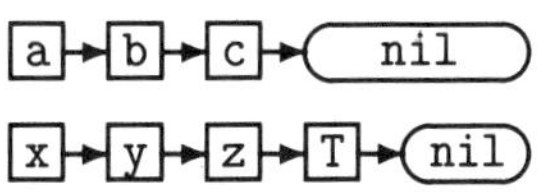

The constant `T` is also useful in method (1). If we substitute `T` for `x` in `(x y z w)`, the resultant list `(T y z w)` is logically equivalent to `(y z w)`. This gives another explanation for decomposition (1).

In summary, a list `(a b c)` is made from `(x y z w)` either by substituting `T` for `x` or by substituting `T` for `w`. The special constant `T` is a unit element for the dot "`.`" operation. That is, `T.y = y` and `x.T = x` hold.

It is extremely important to have two different schemes of making `(a b c)` out of `(x y z w)` because we can simultaneously use them in a *stereoscopic* way. Stereoscope means using both the right eye and the left eye together to identify an object. In the right eye, `(a b c)` is identified with `(T y z w)`, and in the left eye, `(a b c)` is `(x y z T)`. The real picture `(x y z w)` is composed from the two pictures. The composition is formally explained by the concept of anti-unification (Lassez *et al.* [7]).

In Fig. 17, `x`, `y`, `z`, and `w` are variables, and `T` is a constant. The two expressions `T.y.z.w.nil` and `x.y.z.T.nil` are unifiable, and the most general instance is `T.y.z.T.nil`, where most general unifier is a substitution {x←T, w←T}. On the other hand, the most specific generalization is `x.y.z.w.nil`. The most specific anti-substitution is a *generalization* {x→T, w→T}. A generalization is an "anti" operation to the substitution, which replaced a variable with a constant.

A list `(a b c)` of length three can be stereoscopically extended to a list `(x y z w)` of length four. The extension method is repeatedly applied to a list to obtain a list of arbitrary length.

The stereoscopic technique can be applied to proof figures as well as list terms. For example, a `REVERSE` proof for `(x y z w)` is obtained from the `REVERSE` proof for `(a b c)`.

(1) The list `(x y z w)` is decomposed into `x` and `(y z w)`. The `REVERSE` proof for `(y z w)` is *isomorphic* to the proof for `(a b c)`. The variable `x` is treated as `T`, and the term `T.nil` is equal to `nil` in the proof for `(y z w)`.

(2) The list `(x y z w)`, i.e., `x.y.z.w.nil`, is equal to `x.y.z.nil` if `T` is substituted for `w`. The proof for `x.y.z.nil`, or `(x y z)`, is *isomorphic* to the proof

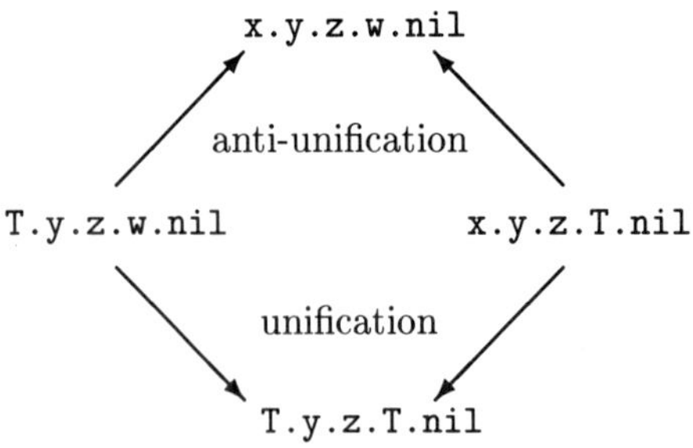

Fig. 17 Anti-unification and unification.

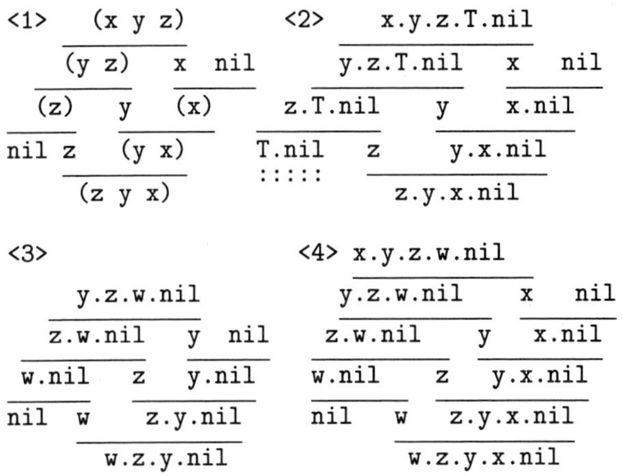

Fig. 18 Stereoscopic extension of **REVERSE**.

for `(a b c)`. The term `w.nil` is equivalent to `nil` and cannot be decomposed into `w` and `nil`.

The two proofs are *isomorphic* if they are identical through variable renaming and neglecting `T`s.

The trace **REVERSE** for `(x y z)` is easily obtained by renaming the variables `(a b c)` in Fig. 13 (<1> in Fig. 18). The first extension is <2> in Fig. 18, where `nil` in `x.y.z.nil`, or `(x y z)`, is replaced by `T.nil`. The term `T.nil` is not decomposed further (indicated by `:::::` in <2>, Fig. 18).

Secondly, another extended **REVERSE** trace for `(y z w) = y.z.w.nil` is written according to the trace for `(x y z)` (<3> in Fig. 18).

The final trace for `x.y.z.w.nil` <4> is stereoscopically composed from <2> and <3>, where the term `y.z.T.nil` in <2> is associated with `y.z.w.nil` in <3>. At the same time, the term `x.nil` in <2> is associated with `nil` in <3>.

Using graph notation, the stereoscopic composition is explained again. A graph represents a proof figure or a trace. The nodes of the graph, such as `(y z w)`, `y`, and `nil`, represent the terms in the proof. It is easy to see that the graphs <2> and <3> can be associated with each other if `T` in <2> is thought of as `w`, and `T` in <3> is thought of as `x`. The composed graph results in program <4> in Fig. 18.

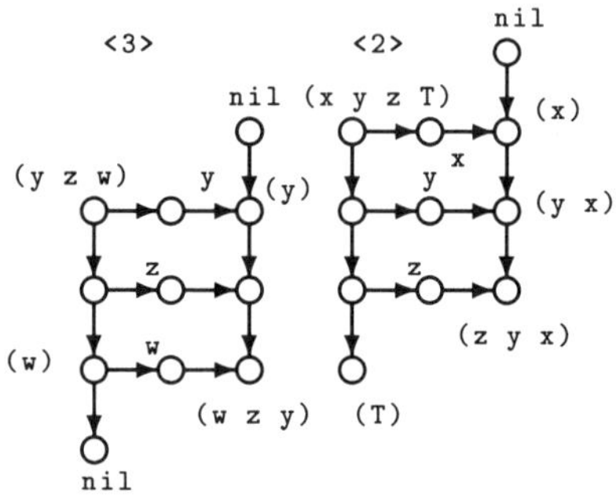

The stereoscopic composition is described in detail, and the associated nodes (matching pairs) in the graphs <2> and <3> are classified into three groups.

(1) The terms of two associated nodes are identical, for example, `y` and `z`.

(2) One term (list) is *more general* than the other. For example, `(y z w)` in <3> is more general than `(y z T)` in <2>. Similarly, `(y x)` in <2> is more general than `(y)` in <3>.

(3) There is no associate node in the other graph. For example, `nil`, `(x y z T)` and `x` in <2>, and `w` and `(w z y)` in <3> have no counterparts.

A list X is **more general** than a list Y if there is a substitution $\sigma = \{v_1 \leftarrow \mathtt{T},\ v_2 \leftarrow \mathtt{T}, \ldots\}$ such that $X\sigma = Y$, where v_1, v_2,... are variables in X. Conversely, Y is called **more specific** than X. The new graph is composed according to the classification of the nodes.

(1) If the two associated nodes have an identical term, then the term is not changed in the composed graph.

(2) If one term is more general than the other term, the more general term is selected to be a new term in the composed graph.

(3) If the associated term is missing, then the existing term is selected in the composed graph, where the existing term may be generalized in the process of (2).

It is clear that the new composed graph represents a proof or a trace. The terms in (1) present no problem. The more general terms in (2) do not violate the proof if the generalization is uniform throughout the graph. In the present example of `REVERSE`, the generalizations for graph <2> are all $\{\mathtt{w} \rightarrow \mathtt{T}\}$. Moreover, the generalizations for <3> are all $\{\mathtt{x} \rightarrow \mathtt{T}\}$. Thus, they are uniform throughout each graph and keep the graph a proof. The augmented terms in (3) are meaningful either in proof <2> or <3>. Then, the composed graph represents a proof.

The selection of the more general term in (2) is formally well justified because the selection is to pick up the *most specific generalization*, according to the terminology in anti-unification [7]. In our examples of `REVERSE` and `APPEND`, one of the associated terms happens to be the most specific generalization of the pair. This makes the story simple. (A more sophisticated example will appear in Section 4.)

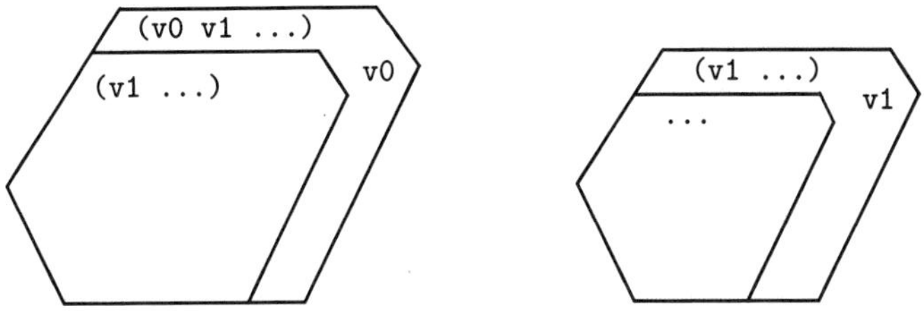

Fig. 19 (REVERSE X) is uniform w.r.t X.

The extension method is applicable when the proof is *uniform*.

Definition 3.

1. *Two proofs are* **isomorphic** *if they are identical by variable renaming and neglecting the logical constant* T.
2. *P is* **uniform with respect to** L, *if a proof* $P(\ldots,\mathtt{L},\ldots)$ *has a list* L=(v_0 ... v_n) *at the topmost position, and all the proofs* $P(\ldots,\mathtt{L}\{v_i \leftarrow \mathtt{T}\},\ldots)$ *are isomorphic, where* $\{v_i \leftarrow \mathtt{T}\}$, $0 \le i \le n$, *are substitutions.*

The uppermost formula is an assumption of the proof. In general, a proof has several uppermost formulas, which are the leaves of the proof tree.

The uniform proofs have isomorphic subproofs that are produced by substitutions. Our stereoscopic extension applies the anti-unification to the subproofs. Namely, a proof for a list of length four is obtained by anti-unifying two proofs of length three.

Property 1. *The proof* (REVERSE X) *is uniform with respect to* X.

Proof. Using mathematical induction, we will prove that (REVERSE X) is uniform with respect to a list X=(v_0 ... v_n) which is of length $n+1$ under the condition that (REVERSE X) is uniform with respect to a list of length n or shorter (Fig. 19). Substitutions are classified into two groups.

(1) $\{v_i \leftarrow \mathtt{T}\}$, $i \neq 0$: The resultant proofs are all isomorphic because (REVERSE X) is uniform with respect to lists of length n or shorter.

(2) $\{v_0 \leftarrow \mathtt{T}\}$: The resultant proof is decomposed as is shown in Fig. 19 (right) into the subproofs for the leftmost element v_1 and the rest of the list (v_2 v_3 ... v_n). The proof figure is isomorphic to one of the resultant proofs in 1 (above). (Renaming the variable v_0 to the variable v_1 in the proof for $\{v_1 \leftarrow \mathtt{T}\}$.) **[QED]**

Property 2. *The proof of* (APPEND A B) *is uniform with respect to* A *as well as to* B.

The proof for A is treated similarly (Fig. 20). It is clear that the proof is uniform with respect to B.

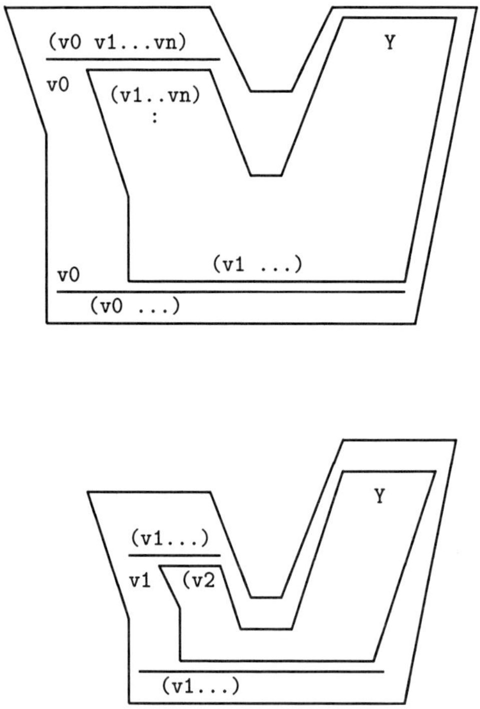

Fig. 20 (APPEND A B) is uniform w.r.t A B.

Property 3. *If a proof* $P(\ldots, \mathtt{L}, \ldots)$ *is uniform with respect to* L *and a proof* $Q(\ldots, \mathtt{M}, \ldots)$ *is uniform with respect to* M, *and the conclusion of* P *(the root of the tree) is identical to the list* M, *then the composition of two proofs* $Q(\ldots, P(\ldots, \mathtt{L}, \ldots), \ldots)$ *is uniform with respect to a list* L.

Proof. Let $\mathtt{L=(v_1\ \ldots\ v_n)}$. The subproofs $P(\ldots, \mathtt{L}\{\mathtt{v}_i \leftarrow \mathtt{T}\}, \ldots)$ of the composed proof $Q(\ldots, P(\ldots, \mathtt{L}\{\mathtt{v}_i \leftarrow \mathtt{T}\}, \ldots), \ldots)$ are isomorphic by the hypothesis on P. Moreover, all the conclusions of the subproofs are isomorphic. Thus, the new composed proof is uniform with respect to L by the hypothesis on Q. **[QED]**

We can compose a large uniform proof based on the small uniform proofs. The examples in this paper are composed proofs of APPEND and REVERSE. It should be noted here that mathematical induction is used in the proof of uniformity of each small proof. Our stereoscopic extension does not eliminate mathematical induction

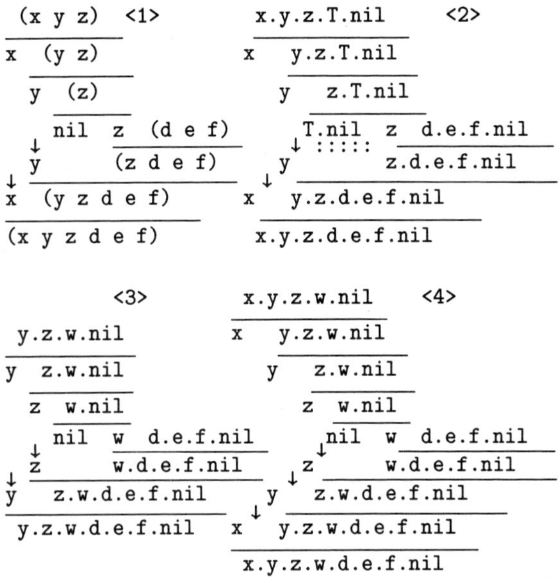

Fig. 21 `APPEND` for `(x y z w)`.

at all, but it realizes a simple equivalence proof through normalization and anti-unification based on the small uniform proofs. The simple or small proofs are shown to be uniform by mathematical induction.

A uniform proof (program) is written by `MAPCAR` in traditional LISP. The function `MAPCAR` does not cover all the classes of recursive programs, but it gives a straightforward source code. `MAPCAR` greatly reduces the chances of program "bugs," because a uniform program takes a simple and readable form.

It is easy to see that the program `APPEND` is also uniform, and we can extend it to cover general terms as shown in Fig. 21.

The graph notation illustrates the extension method for `APPEND`, which is similar to `REVERSE`.

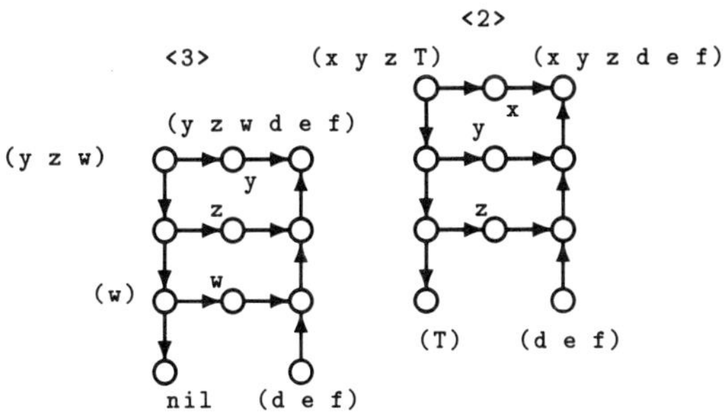

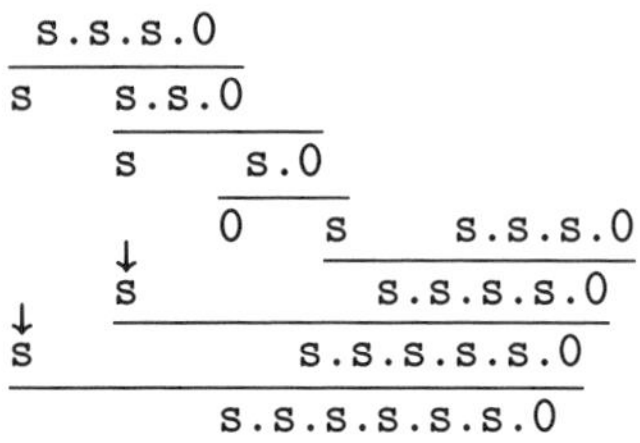

Fig. 22 Addition program.

The same technique is applied to a program to make a larger program. Conversely, it is fairly easy to make a program smaller. We only have to apply a substitution $\{\mathtt{v}_i \leftarrow \mathtt{T}\}$ to a proof for `L` to get a smaller proof. The following two substitutions make typical smaller programs:

(1) Substituting `T` for $\mathtt{v}_1$ in $\mathtt{L=(v_1} \ \ldots \ \mathtt{v}_n\mathtt{)}$ throughout the program.

(2) Substituting `T` for $\mathtt{v}_n$ in $\mathtt{L=(v_1} \ \ldots \ \mathtt{v}_n\mathtt{)}$.

The two small programs made by (1) and (2) coincide if the original proof is uniform.

4 Natural Numbers and S-Expressions

Our method is applicable to data structures other than lists. It is easy to see that natural numbers can be represented in symbolic terms as is shown in the following table.

0	0
1	s.0
2	s.s.0
:	:
n	s.s. . .s.0
:	:

It is common to interpret the number "5" as $s(s(s(s(s(0)))))$ in the programming language Prolog. Our encoding scheme is slightly different from Prolog. If the natural numbers are coded in lists, the trace of the addition program takes the form of **APPEND** on lists (Fig. 22). This means the addition program is associative. It is also concluded that we can extend the addition program to cover general numbers because the same extension method is applicable to the addition program.

Next, the method is applied to LISP S-expressions. S-expressions are much more complex than lists. The third problem from Boyer and Moore [1] claims that **FLATTEN** is equivalent to **MC.FLATTEN**, which is more efficient. The program **FLATTEN** gathers all the tip nodes (leaves) of an S-expression.

```
(FLATTEN X)
= (IF (LISTP X)
```

```
        (APPEND (FLATTEN (CAR X))
                (FLATTEN (CDR X)) )
        (CONS X "NIL") )

(MC.FLATTEN X ANS)
= (IF (LISTP X)
      (MC.FLATTEN (CAR X)
                  (MC.FLATTEN (CDR X) ANS) )
      (CONS X ANS) )
```

The program in Fig. 23 deals with a simple S-expression that has only four tip nodes.

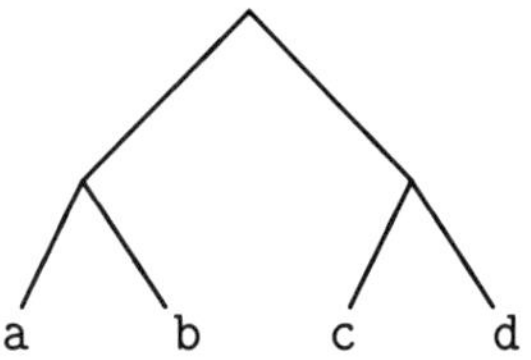

The first trace is written in Fig. 23 <1>. It follows the definition of the function **FLATTEN**, which divides the S-expression into two subexpressions and appends the subresults of the two subexpressions.

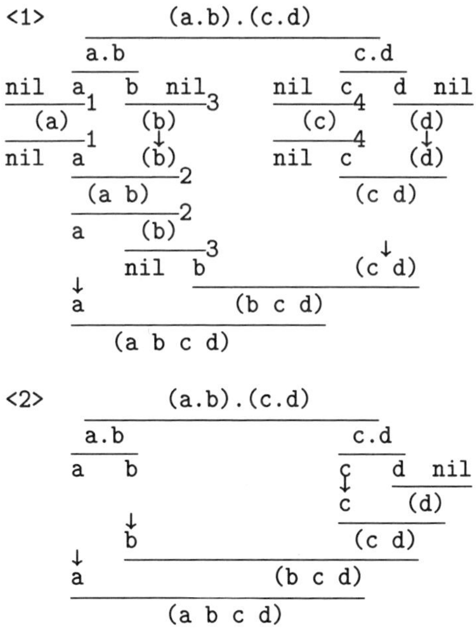

Fig. 23 Program for **FLATTEN**.

The reduction procedure for <1> cancels inference rules 1, 2, 3, and 4. The normal program is shown in <2>, which exactly represents the trace of the `MC.FLATTEN` program.

This example shows how the normalization method works for S-expressions. The final question to answer is if our stereoscopic extension method is also applicable to S-expressions. The answer is yes. However, the anti-unification procedure is much more sophisticated. For example, we will compose a `MC.FLATTEN` proof for `(a.b).(c.d)` out of the proof for `a.c`. The procedure is illustrated in Fig. 24.

First, the graph is written for `a.c`. Next, `a.T` is substituted for `a`, and `c.T` is substituted for `c`. The new graph for `(a.T).(c.T)` is only partially meaningful. It is necessary to augment it using the fine structures for `a.b` and `c.d`.

Our extension method compares two graphs node by node. If the two graphs `(a.T).(c.T)` and `c.d` are compared, some identical terms are found by neglecting `T`s. Then, we search for the pairs of nodes that have *more general* relations among them.

(1) There are only two nodes, `nil` and `c.T=c`, that are identical in the two graphs.

(2) The upper `c.T` is compared with the lower `c.d`. If `T` is substituted for `d` in `c.d`, the entire small graph for `c.d` becomes a graph for `c`. It represents a proof from `c` and `nil` to get the conclusion `(c)`. Thus, the small graph for `c.d` seems to be more general than an upper subgraph for `c.T`.

It is necessary to extend the definition of *more general*, because two graphs should be compared instead of two terms or nodes. If X and Y are two graphs and there is a substitution $\sigma = \{v_1 \leftarrow \mathtt{T},\ v_2 \leftarrow \mathtt{T}, \ldots\}$, such that $X\sigma = Y$, then X is **more general** than Y, where the equation $X\sigma = Y$ means that $X\sigma$ and Y are isomorphic.

The new definition of *more general* implies the more general relation between terms in Section 3.

Finally, the more general graph for `c.d` is selected as a subgraph. This extends the bigger graph for `(a.T).(c.T)` to the graph for `(a.T).(c.d)`. This intermediate proof has the conclusion `(a.b c d)`. The final step is to compose the subproof beginning at `a.b`. It is performed similarly. The term `(c.d)` is identified with `nil` when the term `a.b` is treated. The composed figure coincides with the program `MC.FLATTEN` in Fig. 23.

5 Concluding Remarks

In the literature, programs have often been represented in the tree form, especially when type information is essential. This paper further extended the use of treelike representation of computer programs so as to enjoy the normalization property. This paper also proposed a new method to extend a trace to cover general input data. It is applicable to a program if the program is uniform.

We plan to enlarge the application area to incorporate the basic operations discussed in Section 2 into the program.

Acknowledgments. The author wishes to thank Professor Martin-Löf at Stockholm University and Professor Masahiko Sato at Tohoku University for their valuable

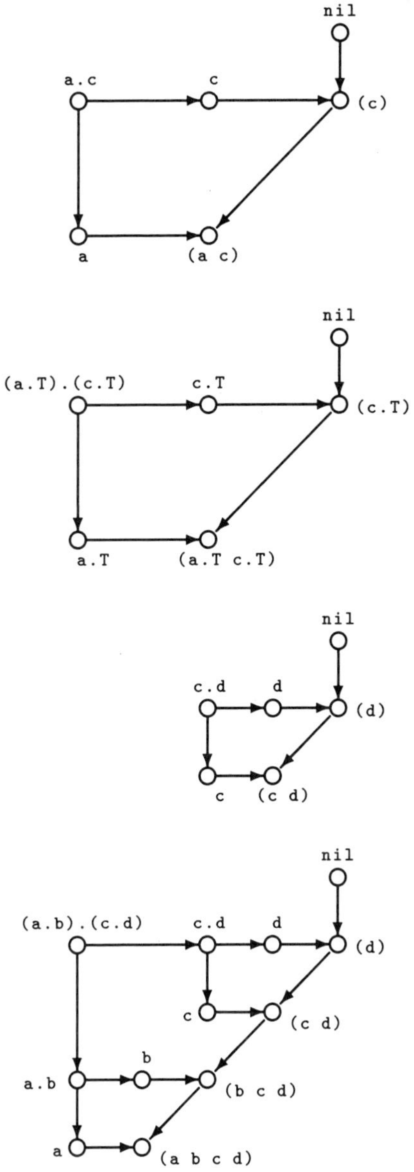

Fig. 24 Extension of MC.FLATTEN.

discussions.

References

[1] Boyer, R.S. and Moore, J.S., *A Computational Logic*, Academic Press, 1979.

[2] Clark, K.L. and Tärnlund, S-Å, A First Order Theory of Data and Programs, *Information Processing 77 (IFIP 77)*, 939–944, North-Holland, 1977.

[3] Constable, R.L., Allen, S.F., Bromley, H.M., Cleaveland, W.R., Cremer, J.F., Harper, R.W., Howe, D.J., Koblock, T.B., Mendler, N.P., Panangaden, P., Sasaki, J.T. and Smith, S.F., *Implementing Mathematics with the Nuprl Proof Development System*, Prentice-Hall, 1986.

[4] Goto, S., Normal Programs and Proofs in Formal LISP, *Proceedings of the Japanese – Czechoslovak Seminar on Theoretical Foundations of Knowledge Information Processing*, 13–21, Prague, 12–14 June, 1989.

[5] Hayashi, S. and Nakano, H., *PX: A Computational Logic*, The MIT Press, 1988.

[6] Lambek, J.L. and Scott, P.J., *Introduction to Higher Order Categorical Logic*, Cambridge University Press, 1986.

[7] Lassez, J-L., Maher, M.J. and Marriott, K.G., *Unification Revisited*, RC 12394 (#55630) IBM, T. J. Watson Research Center, 1986.

[8] Manna, Z., *Mathematical Theory of Computation*, McGraw-Hill, 1974.

[9] Martin-Löf, P., *Intuitionistic Type Theory*, Bibliopolis, Napoli, 1984.

[10] Martin-Löf, P., Nonstandard Type Theory, *Logic Colloquium '88*, p.14, Padova, 1988.

[11] McCarthy, J., Towards a Mathematical Theory of Computation, *Information Processing 62 (IFIP 62)*, 21–28, North-Holland, 1963.

[12] McCarthy, J., Recursive Functions of Symbolic Expression and Their Computation by Machine, Part I, *Comm. ACM*, Vol. 3, No. 4, 184–195, April, 1960.

[13] McCarthy, J., Abrahams, P.W., Edwards, D.J., Hart, T.P. and Levin, M.I., *LISP 1.5 Programmer's Manual*, The MIT Press, 1962.

[14] Prawitz, D., *Natural Deduction: A Proof-Theoretical Study*, Almqvist and Wiksell, Stockholm, 1965.

[15] Prawitz, D., Ideas and Results in Proof Theory, *Proc. 2nd Scandinavian Logic Symposium*, 235–307, North-Holland, 1971.

[16] Sato, M., Theory of Symbolic Expressions I, *Theor. Comput. Sci.* 22, 19–55, North-Holland, 1983.

[17] Steel, G.L., Jr., *Common LISP: The Language*, Digital Press, 1984.

[18] Troelstra, A.S. (ed.), *Metamathematical Investigation of Intuitionistic Arithmetic and Analysis*, Springer Lecture Notes in Mathematics, 344, Springer-Verlag, 1973.

Initially published in "Computer Software", Vol. 7, No. 2, in Japanese.

Shigeki Goto
NTT Basic Research Laboratories
3–9–11 Midori-cho, Musashino-shi, Tokyo
180 Japan

Regular Expressions with Semantic Rules and Their Application to Data Structure Directed Programs

Ikuo Nakata Masataka Sassa

Summary. Most input data have structures that can be defined by regular expressions, and it is often necessary to develop programs that process these input data not only syntactically but also semantically. One formal method of developing such programs is to use attribute grammars, that is, context-free grammars augmented with semantic rules. Context-free grammars, however, are often inferior to regular expressions as tools for representing data structures intuitively, and systems based on attribute grammars are rather complex. This paper proposes *regular expressions with semantic rules*, which can be used as tools for expressing the syntax and semantics of input data, and a method of generating programs for processing these input data. First, regular expressions with semantic rules will be defined as regular expressions intermixed with semantic statements. Then, an algorithm will be given for translating a regular expression with semantic rules to a nondeterministic finite automaton with semantic actions (NFAS), and another algorithm for translating an NFAS to a deterministic finite automaton with semantic actions (DFAS). Finally, our semantic rules and translation algorithms will be expanded so that the proposed method can be applied to programs that process data defined in terms of regular expressions with semantic rules, that is, to data-structure-directed programs.

1 Introduction

The methods of translating a regular expression to the corresponding finite automaton are well known [1, 5]. The resultant automaton recognizes the input that belongs to the language defined by the original regular expression. Usually, the semantic actions are performed after the syntactic recognition of the input. In the case of language processors, a lexical analyzer and a parser can be generated from the descriptions of a lexical grammar and a syntactic grammar defined in terms of regular expressions and by a context-free grammar, respectively. Recently, it has become possible to generate even a compiler from an attribute grammar, which is a combination of a context-free grammar and semantic rules [1, 2, 3, 4, 5].

However, when the structure of input data is rather simple, the structure and its semantics can be expressed in terms of regular expressions and semantic rules embedded in them. In this paper we propose such expressions, as well as a method for translating them into a finite automaton.

ISBN 0-12-037103-0

Our method can be compared with the usual method based on attribute grammars as follows. (The comparisons are meaningful only in the range where regular expressions can be applied. We do not claim that attribute grammars are totally inferior, as they can cover a wider range.)

(1) More intuitively understandable.
Regular expressions are known to be an excellent tool for describing the structure of various kinds of data, such as commands, in a simple and intuitively understandable form. For example, Jackson's method, which is a famous programming methodology, uses regular expressions practically as a fundamental tool. If we used grammars instead of regular expressions, we would have to write several productions to express a single regular expression. The same argument applies when we have additional semantic rules.

(2) Simpler program produced by simpler generator.
A regular expression with semantic rules can be transformed into a program that acts as a finite state automaton, by means of a simple algorithm described in this paper. On the other hand, the processing program that corresponds to an attribute grammar consists of a syntax analyzer and a semantic analyzer. The algorithm for generating these routines is not so simple. If the underlying context-free grammar of an attribute grammar is an LL(1) or an LR(1), the semantic analyzer can be embedded in the one-pass parser. But in other cases, we have to modify the underlying grammar if we want to apply the above one-pass technique, and we often lose the clear structure of the original grammar. (We will give an example of this later.)

We will now explain what we mean by the insertion of semantic rules into a regular expression. For example, for a regular expression

$$(\alpha|\beta)\gamma$$

we can insert semantic rules by writing

$$(\alpha[f(\alpha)]|\beta[g(\beta)])\gamma[h(\gamma)]$$

or

$$\begin{array}{ll} (\alpha & [f(\alpha)] \\ |\beta & [g(\beta)] \\ ) & \\ \gamma & [h(\gamma)] \end{array}$$

if the evaluation of $f(\alpha)$, $g(\beta)$, and $h(\gamma)$ is required for α, β, and γ, respectively. We call these expressions *regular expressions with semantic rules*. A processing program for this kind of expression can be expressed as a finite automaton for the underlying regular expression with semantic actions attached to the proper transitions. We call it a *finite automaton with semantic actions*.

Our process for generating the finite automaton with semantic actions from a regular expression with semantic rules is to follow the well-known process for generating a finite automaton from a regular expression and then attach semantic actions to proper transitions. In the above case, for example, $f(\alpha)$ is attached to the transition path corresponding to α. The problem here is that "the transition path corresponding to α" cannot always be simply determined. For example, if the given regular expression is

$$(a|ab)bc$$

that is, $\alpha = a$, $\beta = ab$, and $\gamma = bc$, then we cannot recognize α when we first read a, but only after we have read the last c. On the other hand, we can recognize β when we read two consecutive bs. When the given regular expression contains repetitions (we use the notation $\{\alpha\}$ for a repetition of α 0 or more times) the problem is even more complex.

One of the main objects of this paper is to propose an algorithm for generating a finite automaton with semantic actions from a regular expression with semantic rules.

The above regular expression $(a|ab)bc$ is transformed naturally to the following context-free grammar:

$$S \rightarrow Abc$$
$$A \rightarrow a$$
$$A \rightarrow ab$$

This grammar is neither LL(1) nor LR(1). Thus, it is an example of the previously mentioned non-LL(1) and non-LR(1) grammar.

A regular expression can be used not only to define a language by itself, but also in the right-hand side of production rules in an extended context-free grammar, or a *regular right part grammar*. Regular right part grammars are useful tools for expressing the syntax concisely in fewer rules, and their parsers are expected to be efficient. We said earlier that we do not need attribute grammars in simple cases. In more complex cases, however, if combined with regular right part grammars, attribute grammars may be useful for concise expressions of semantics. The method described in this paper can be applied to such cases.

2 Explanation by Simple Examples

First, we will explain our method by means of two simple examples.

2.1 Examples of Regular Expressions with Semantic Rules

Example 1. Suppose that there is a text editor with the following forms of commands:

(1) line-designation [, line-designation] command-name
(2) number-of-lines command-name

The intended meanings of these commands are as follows. (Here, $[\alpha]$ means optional α. But since we use [ ] with a different meaning in this paper, we rewrite optional α by using ε.)

```
(1) line-designation       -- integer (line-number) that indicates the first line
    (, line-designation    -- the last line. If it is absent then
    | ε )                  -- the last line = the first line
    command-name           -- if the command-name is d, delete all lines
                           -- from the first line to the last line
(2) number-of-lines        -- integer n
```

```
command-name        -- if the name is p, print n lines
                    -- starting from the current line
```

These meanings are rewritten a little more formally as follows:

(n	[L1←line(n)]
(, n	[L2←line(n)]
| ε	[L2←L1]
) d	[del(L1,L2)]
| n p	[prt(n)]
)	

(While the syntax of integer n can also be expressed by a regular expression, we treat it as an alphabet of regular expressions, because it is one of the fundamental elements of the commands in this example. This follows the usual way of defining a grammar of a programming language in two levels: the regular expression, which defines lexical elements, and the context-free grammar, which defines the syntax of the language. Of course we can replace n with the regular expression that defines the form of an integer.)

Example 2. As a slightly more complex example, we give the specification of a program that prints the total sum of a sequence of integers:

n	[init(n)]	-- The initial value of the total is n.
{, n	[add(n)]	-- Add n to the total.
| , n −	[sub(n)]	-- Subtract n from the total.
}		
(+		-- no action
| −	[negate]	-- Negate the total.
) Cr	[print]	-- Print the total.

This is not a good specification, but we use it to make the example a little complex.

2.2 Examples of a finite automaton with semantic actions

A well-known method of translating a regular expression into a finite automaton is to translate it first into a nondeterministic finite automaton, then into a deterministic one. Here, we adopt this method and augment it by adding semantic actions. The nondeterministic finite automaton and the deterministic automaton obtained from Ex. 1 are shown in Fig. 1 and Fig. 2, respectively. In Fig. 1, for example,

$$①\xrightarrow{n[\mathrm{L1}\leftarrow\mathrm{line}(n)]}②$$

shows that the transition from state 1 to state 2 occurs when n is read, and that on that occasion, [L1←line(n)] is evaluated.

In Fig. 2, state (2,4,5) is the union of states 2, 4, and 5 in Fig. 1. [N1←n] on the incoming arrow to this state is a semantic action. The union of states 2, 4, and 5 means that it is one of the states 2, 4, and 5, but that it is not yet determined which of these is the current state. If it is state 2 or 4, [L1←line(n)] should be executed, but not if it is state 5. Therefore, we assign the value n to a temporary variable N1 (it is shown as [N1←n] in Fig. 2) and execute [L1←line(N1)] instead

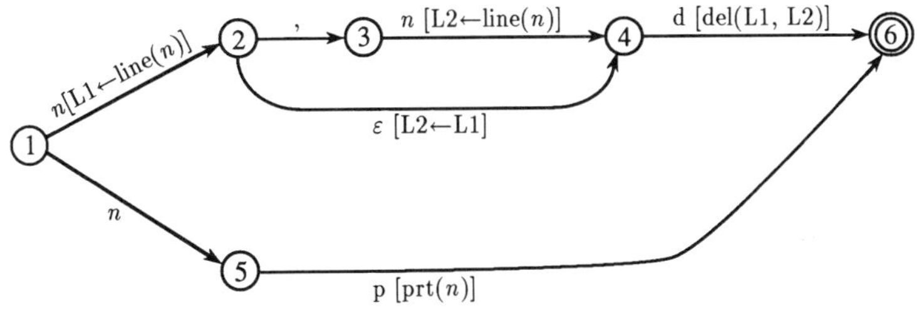

Fig. 1 Nondeterministic finite automaton with semantic actions for Example 1.

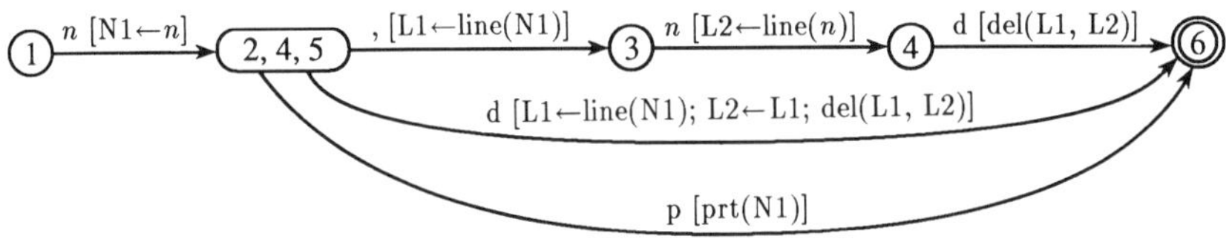

Fig. 2 Deterministic finite automaton with semantic actions for Example 1.

of [L1←line(n)] or [prt(N1)] instead of [prt(n)] later, when it becomes certain that the current state is 2 or 4, or 5, respectively.

The automata obtained from Example 2 are shown in Figs. 5 and 7; we will explain these figures after describing the general method of translation to automata. On that occasion, we will explain the automata for Example 1 once again, following the general method. Although they look a little different from the ones shown here, they are essentially the same.

3 Regular Expressions with Semantic Rules and Their Automata

3.1 Definition of Regular Expressions with Semantic Rules

Definition 1. A regular expression with semantic rules over an alphabet Σ (written as RES(Σ)) is defined as follows:

(1) $\varepsilon \in$RES(Σ).
(2) If $a \in \Sigma$ then $a \in$RES(Σ).
(3) If $\alpha,\beta \in$RES(Σ) then
$\alpha\beta$, $\alpha \mid \beta$, $\{\alpha\}\in$RES(Σ).
(4) If $\alpha \in$RES(Σ) and f is a semantic rule then
$\alpha[f]\in$RES(Σ).

Here, a semantic rule f is in general a function such that

$f : S \rightarrow S$,
S :Var→Val,

where S is a state of computation and Var is a set of variables and Val is a set of values. The set of semantic rules is written Ω.

Definition 2. The meaning of $\alpha \in$RES(Σ), a regular expression with semantic rules, is defined as follows: Let $\underline{\alpha}\in$RE(Σ) be the regular expression made from α by removing all $f \in \Omega$ in α, where RE(Σ) is the set of regular expressions over Σ. The set represented by $\underline{\alpha}$, that is, the language of $\underline{\alpha}$, is written L($\underline{\alpha}$).

Let $x \in$L($\underline{\alpha}$). When x is evaluated by α, the semantic rules that correspond to x are obtained from α. We denote them by $[x,\alpha]$. $[x,\alpha]$ is a function of the signature $S \rightarrow S$ and is defined as follows according to the definition of RES(Σ):

(1) If $\alpha = \varepsilon$ then $x = \varepsilon$ and $[\varepsilon, \varepsilon]$ is the identity function.
(2) If $\alpha = a \in \Sigma$ then $x = a$ and $[a, a]$ is the identity function.
(3) Let α,$\beta \in$RES(Σ), $x \in$L($\underline{\alpha}$), $y \in$L($\underline{\beta}$). Then

$$[x, (\alpha \mid \beta)] = [x, \alpha],$$
$$[y, (\alpha \mid \beta)] = [y, \beta],$$
$$[xy, \alpha\beta] = [y, \beta] \circ [x, \alpha],$$
$$[\varepsilon, \{\alpha\}] = [\varepsilon, \varepsilon],$$
$$[xx', \{\alpha\}] = [x', \{\alpha\}] \circ [x, \alpha],$$

where $x' \in$L($\{\underline{\alpha}\}$).
(4) If $\alpha \in$RES(Σ), $f \in \Omega$, $x \in$L($\underline{\alpha}$) then

$$[x, \alpha[f]] = f \circ [x, \alpha],$$

where $\circ$ is the operator for the composition of functions.

The meaning of α is defined as follows, using $[x, \alpha]$:

$$\{[x, \alpha] \mid x \in \mathrm{L}(\underline{\alpha})\}$$

The above step (3) is a nondeterministic definition. For example, if $x \in$L($\underline{\alpha}$) and $x \in$L($\underline{\beta}$) then $[x, (\alpha \mid \beta)]$ has two definitions. In this case, however, they may be equal, in which case $[x, \alpha] = [x, \beta] = [x, (\alpha \mid \beta)]$. We therefore give the following definition:

Definition 3. A regular expression with semantic rules α is called *deterministic* when $[x, \alpha]$ is uniquely defined for any $x \in$L($\underline{\alpha}$).

3.2 Translation from Regular Expressions with Semantic Rules to Nondeterministic Finite Automata with Semantic Actions

The method of translation is basically the same as that of translating regular expressions into finite automata [1, 5]. The nondeterministic finite automaton with semantic actions for $\alpha \in$RES(Σ) is called the *NFAS*, and is obtained as follows:

Algorithm 1. Algorithm for translation from regular expressions with semantic rules to NFASs

(1) If $\alpha = \varepsilon$ then 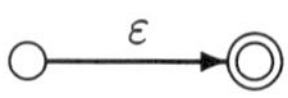

(2) If $\alpha = a \in \Sigma$ then 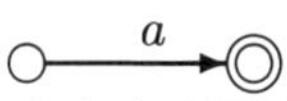

(3) Let α,$\beta \in$RES(Σ) and their NFASs be

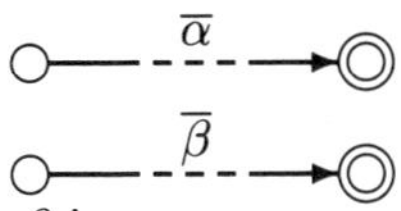

Then the NFAS for $\alpha\beta$ is

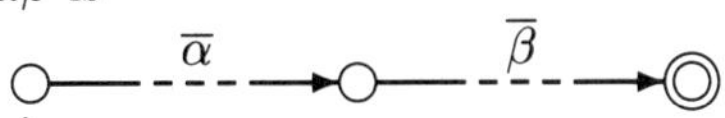

the NFAS for $(\alpha \mid \beta)$ is

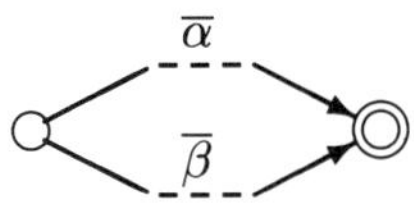

and the NFAS for $\{\alpha\}$ is

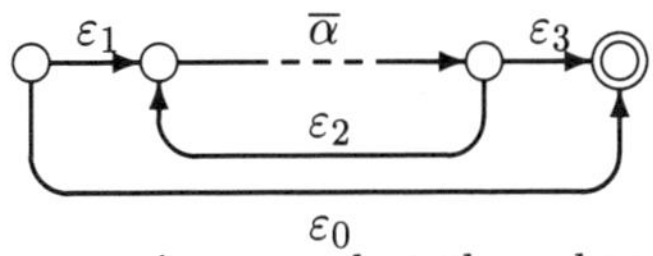

Here, ε_i has the same meaning as ε, but the subscripts are added for later reference in this paper.

(4) If $\alpha \in$RES(Σ), $f \in \Omega$ then the NFAS for $\alpha[f]$ is

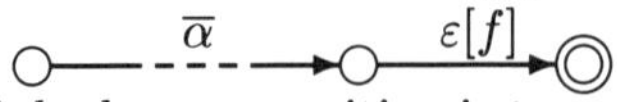

Here, the purpose of the last ε-transition is to evaluate f.

3.3 Translation from NFASs to Deterministic Finite Automata with Semantic Actions (DFASs)

A deterministic finite automaton with semantic actions is called a *DFAS*. The method of translation to DFASs is also basically the same as that of translating nondeterministic finite automata into deterministic ones. Let Q be the set of states of an NFA, and let $\tilde{Q}$ be the set of the corresponding DFA. The NFA has one initial state q_e and one final state q_f. Usually, the deterministic automata can be obtained as follows (we ignore semantic actions for the time being):

Algorithm 2. Algorithm for translation from an NFA to a DFA (without semantic actions)

(1) $\tilde{q}_e = \text{closure}(\{q_e\})$
$\tilde{Q} := \{\tilde{q}_e\}$ -- $\tilde{q}_e$ is the initial state of $\tilde{Q}$

(2) For any $\tilde{p} \in \tilde{Q}$ and $a \in \Sigma$
add $\tilde{q} = \text{closure}(\text{next}(\tilde{p}, a))$ to $\tilde{Q}$.
Repeat this until nothing remains to be added to $\tilde{Q}$.

(3) $\tilde{F} = \{\tilde{q} \mid q_f \in \tilde{q} \in \tilde{Q}\}$ -- $\tilde{F}$ is the final state of $\tilde{Q}$

Here, "closure" and "next" are defined for $R \subset Q$ as follows:

$$\text{closure}(R) = \{q \mid \exists p \in R : p \downarrow^* q\}$$
$$\text{next}(R, a) = \{q \mid \exists p \in R : p \xrightarrow{a} q\}$$

where $p \downarrow q$ means there is a transition $p \xrightarrow{\varepsilon} q$, and $\downarrow^*$ is the reflective transitive closure of $\downarrow$.

To extend the above method to cases with semantic actions, let us take some simple examples. If $\tilde{p} = \{p\}$ and $p \xrightarrow{a} q \xrightarrow{\varepsilon[f]} r (a \in \Sigma, f \in \Omega)$, then $\tilde{p} \rightarrow \tilde{r}$ should become $\tilde{p} \xrightarrow{a[f]} \tilde{r}$, where $\tilde{r} = \{q, r\}$. In the following more complex case,

$$\tilde{p} = \{p_1, p_2\}, \quad p_1 \xrightarrow{a} q_1 \xrightarrow{\varepsilon[f_1]} r_1, \quad p_2 \xrightarrow{a} q_2 \xrightarrow{\varepsilon[f_2]} r_2,$$

it can be considered that $\tilde{p} \xrightarrow{a} \tilde{r}$ and $\tilde{r} = \{q_1, r_1, q_2, r_2\}$, but it cannot be determined at the time of transition to $\tilde{r}$ which function should be executed, f_1 or f_2. Therefore, we modify $\tilde{r}$ as $\tilde{r} = \{q_1, r_1(f_1), q_2, r_2(f_2)\}$ to record the fact that process f_1 or f_2 has not yet been executed. Now, if the transitions from q_1 and q_2 are only ε-transitions, then the transitions from $\tilde{r}$ are determined only from r_1 or r_2, and q_1 and q_2 have nothing to do with this. Therefore, we eliminate q_1 and q_2 from $\tilde{r}$ to make the later translation simpler, that is, $\tilde{r} = \{r_1(f_1), r_2(f_2)\}$ (we also eliminate q from $\tilde{r} = \{q, r\}$ in the previous example, that is $\tilde{r} = \{r\}$), and write the above transition as

$$\tilde{p}(p_1, p_2) \xrightarrow{a} \tilde{r}(r_1(f_1), r_2(f_2)).$$

The memorized functions, or "carried over" functions, f_1 and f_2 are then propagated to the following states. For example, if there is a transition $r_1 \xrightarrow{b} s_1$, then the transition from $\tilde{r}$ becomes

$$\tilde{r}(r_1(f_1), r_2(f_2)) \xrightarrow{b} \tilde{s}(s_1(f_1), \cdots).$$

In this case, if there is no b-transition from r_2, then $\tilde{s} = \{s_1(f_1)\}$, and f_1 can be executed at $\tilde{s}$, because all $s_1 \in Q$ in $\tilde{s}$ have the same function f_1. Therefore, the above transition becomes

$$\tilde{r}(r_1(f_1), r_2(f_2)) \xrightarrow{b[f_1]} \tilde{s}(s_1).$$

This means that the carried-over function f_1 is executed at this b-transition.

A state $\tilde{r} \in \tilde{Q}$ is identified by the set of states $r_i \in Q$ and the memorized functions in $\tilde{r}$. For example,

$$\{q(f)\} \neq \{q(g)\}$$

if $f \neq g$, though they have the same set of states, $\{q\}$. Several carried-over functions may be accumulated in one state. These functions should be executed in the order in which they appeared in the original NFAS. Therefore, they should be memorized in states, such as $\tilde{r}(r(f;g), \cdots)$, and then placed in transitions, such as $\tilde{r}(r(f;g), \cdots) \xrightarrow{b[f]} \tilde{s}(s(g))$, in first-in first-out order.

From these considerations, we derived the following algorithm for cases with semantic actions:

(a) Algorithm for closure$_0(R) = C$

(i) $C := R$

(ii) For every $p(s) \in C$ (s is a sequence of $f_i \in \Omega$), repeat the following:

1) Add $q(s; f)$ to C for all q such that $p \xrightarrow{\varepsilon[f]} q, f \in \Omega$.
(If $p \xrightarrow{\varepsilon} q$, add $q(s)$ to C.)

2) Remove $p(s)$ from C if p has only an ε-transition.

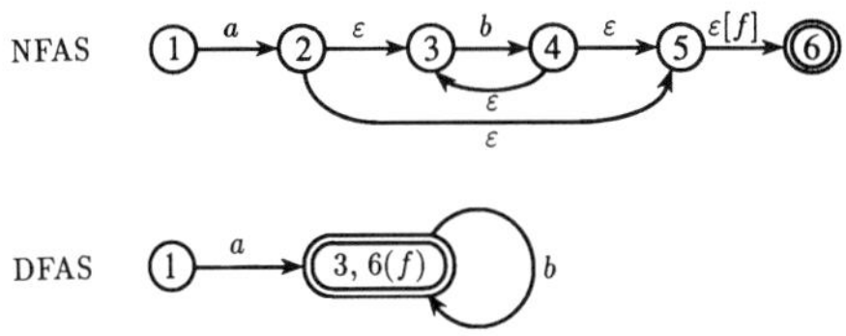

Fig. 3 NFAS and DFAS for $a\{b\}[f]$.

Here, "$s; f$" in 1) means the sequence, s followed by f, and loop (ii) is applied to every $q(s; f)$ added to C.

(b) Definition of next$_0(R, a)$

$\text{next}_0(R, a) = \{q(s) \mid \exists p(s) \in R : p \xrightarrow{a} q\}$
for any a such that $a \in \Sigma(a \neq \varepsilon)$

By using the above "closure$_0$" and "next$_0$", the DFAS can be obtained by the following algorithm.

Algorithm 3. Algorithm for translation from an NFAS to a DFAS

(1)$\tilde{q}_e = \text{closure}_0(\{q_e()\}), \tilde{Q} := \{\tilde{q}_e\}$
(2) For every $\tilde{p} \in \tilde{Q}$ and $a \in \Sigma$
$C = \text{closure}_0(\text{next}_0(\tilde{p}, a))$
If all s in the $q(s)$ of C have the common prefix s_h,
then remove it from every s in q, namely,
$s_h =$ the longest s_i such that $(\forall q(s) \in C, \exists s' : s = s_i; s')$
$\tilde{q} = \{q(s') \mid \exists q(s) \in C : s = s_h; s'\}$.
Add $\tilde{q}$ to $\tilde{Q}$, and make the transition from $\tilde{p}$ to $\tilde{q}$

$$\tilde{p} \xrightarrow{a[s_h]} \tilde{q} \qquad (*)$$

Repeat this process until nothing remains to be added to $\tilde{Q}$.
(3) $\tilde{F} = \{\tilde{q} \mid q_f(s) \in \tilde{q} \in \tilde{Q}\}$ is the set of final states of $\tilde{Q}$.

$q_f(s) \in \tilde{q} \in \tilde{F}$ in (3) means that s, if $s \neq \varepsilon$, cannot be executed in this automaton, and should be executed at the exit from this automaton. For example, let us take $a\{b\}[f] \in \text{RES}(\Sigma)$, where $a, b \in \Sigma, f \in \Omega$. The corresponding NFAS and DFAS are shown in Fig. 3, and f cannot be executed in that DFAS. The actual DFAS should be as follows:

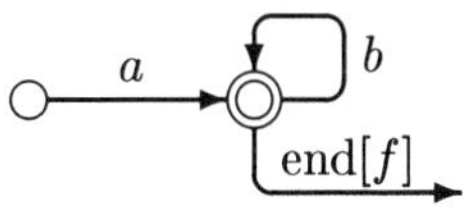

where the transition "end" is taken at the end of the input or when one of the symbols following this regular expression is read.

In the computation of $C = \text{closure}_0(\text{next}_0(\tilde{p}, a))$ in step (2) of the preceding algorithm, if there are two sequences s and s' for the same q, that is, if $q(s), q(s') \in C$, and $s \neq s'$, it means that there are two possible interpretations for a certain input. In this case the given regular expression with semantic rules is nondeterministic.

For example, the (simplified) NFAS for

$$(a[f] \mid a[g]b)\{b\}$$

is

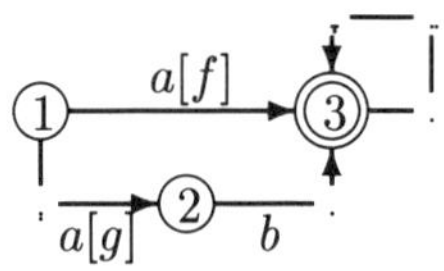

and the DFAS will be

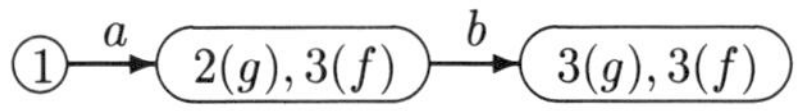

This is nondeterministic, because $3(g)$ and $3(f)$ are conflicting.

Consequently we can show that the following theorem holds.

Theorem. For any regular expression with semantic rules α, if the DFAS obtained by the previous two translation algorithms, (1) from regular expressions with semantic rules to the NFAS, and (2) from the NFAS to the DFAS, is deterministic, then it gives $[x, \alpha]$ for any $x \in \mathrm{L}(\underline{\alpha})$.

Outline of the proof. Let $[x, \alpha] = f_n \circ \cdots \circ f_2 \circ f_1$. $f_1, f_2, \cdots$ be on the path for x in the NFAS in this order. The path for x in DFAS is unique because DFAS is made essentially by the general translation algorithm for deterministic finite automata. On that path in the DFAS, $f_1, f_2, \cdots$ are placed in this order and each f_i is placed on the transition where it is specified that it should be executed. This specification for each f_i is always possible, because α is deterministic. Therefore, it suffices to prove that the last f_n is specified on the path for x. The algorithm (1) gives only one final state q_f for NFA, and the last state of the path for x is q_f. Similarly, let the last state of the path for x in DFA be $\tilde{q}_x \in \tilde{F}$. Then $\tilde{q}_x \ni q_f(s)$, and this $q_f(s)$ is the only one element of $\tilde{q}_x$ that corresponds to the path for x. Because α is deterministic, s is uniquely determined, as explained just before this theorem. If $s = \varepsilon$, f_n has already been specified before reaching the state $\tilde{q}_x$. If $s \neq \varepsilon$, s is specified at the exit of this automaton. The last element of s is f_n.

4 Application to Data-Structure-Directed Programs

Regular expressions with semantic rules and the algorithms for translation to automata can be applied to programs that process data whose structure is defined by a regular expression. For that purpose it is necessary to have a concrete syntax for these expressions and to modify the algorithms accordingly.

4.1 Descriptions of Semantic Rules

In the previous chapter, a semantic rule f is defined as

$$f : S \to S$$

Therefore, users can write any semantic rules by defining appropriate functions. In spite of this, we have selected three semantic rules as system-defined for the convenience of the user and to allow optimization by the system. We do not discuss their concrete syntax in this paper.

(1) As we saw in Exs. 1 and 2, we need to write semantic rules that have the value of $a \in \Sigma$, or some kind of attribute of a, as a parameter. Here, we assume that in a given semantic rule $\alpha[f] \in \mathrm{RES}(\Sigma)$, the system can judge whether f has $a \in \Sigma$ as a parameter or not, and can identify the occurrence of a in α if it is a parameter.

(2) As a semantic rule specific to regular expressions, we can write, for example,

$$(\alpha_1 \mid \alpha_2)\beta[f] \in \mathrm{RES}(\Sigma)$$

where f is of the form

$$\begin{aligned} f = \textbf{case } & \alpha_1 : f_1 \\ & \alpha_2 : f_2 \end{aligned}$$

This semantic rule behaves differently according to what was read previously.

(3) For $\{\alpha\}$, we can write a semantic rule that depends on the count of the repetition such as

$$\begin{aligned} f = \textbf{case } & \text{number-of } \alpha \textbf{ of} \\ & 0 : f_0 \\ & 1 : f_1 \\ & \geq 2 : f_2 \end{aligned}$$

4.2 Translation to an NFAS

(1) Let $R = \alpha a \beta[f] \in \mathrm{RES}(\Sigma)$, $a \in \Sigma$, and f be in a form of $f(a)$. We then modify R by introducing a temporary variable T as

$$R = \alpha a[\mathrm{T} \leftarrow a]\beta[f(\mathrm{T})]$$

and modify the NFAS by adding $[\mathrm{T} \leftarrow a]$ to the a-transition, and by replacing $f(a)$ with $f(\mathrm{T})$. Here, $[\mathrm{T} \leftarrow a]$ is an assignment and is executed immediately after a is read. All these temporary variables are assigned different names. We call the set of these assignments $\Omega_t(\Omega_t \cap \Omega = \emptyset)$. For example, $np[\mathrm{prt}(n)]$ of Example 1 is changed to

$$\bigcirc \xrightarrow{n[\mathrm{T} \leftarrow n]} \bigcirc \xrightarrow{\mathrm{p}} \bigcirc \xrightarrow{\varepsilon[\mathrm{prt}(\mathrm{T})]} \bigcirc$$

In some cases, the temporary names should be changed. For example, when we combine q_1 and q_2 of

$$p \xrightarrow{n[\mathrm{T}_1 \leftarrow n]} q_1, \qquad p \xrightarrow{n[\mathrm{T}_2 \leftarrow n]} q_2$$

to make a DFAS, the names T_1 and T_2 should be changed so that they have the same name.

(2) For an expression $R = (\alpha_1 \mid \alpha_2)\beta[f] \in \mathrm{RES}(\Sigma)$, where f is

$$\begin{aligned} f = \textbf{case } & \alpha_1 : f_1 \\ & \alpha_2 : f_2 \end{aligned}$$

we introduce a temporary variable T and modify R as

$$(\alpha_1[\mathrm{T} \leftarrow 1] \mid \alpha_2[\mathrm{T} \leftarrow 2])\beta[f']$$

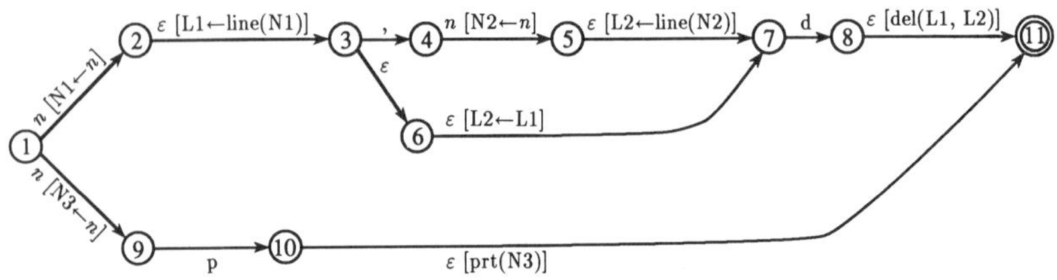

Fig. 4 NFAS for Example 1.

$$
\begin{aligned}
f' = \textbf{case}\ \mathrm{T}\ \textbf{of} \\
1 : f_1 \\
2 : f_2
\end{aligned}
$$

Moreover, we change

$$\bigcirc \xrightarrow{\overline{\alpha}_i} \bigcirc \qquad (i = 1, 2)$$

in the NFAS to

$$\bigcirc \xrightarrow{\overline{\alpha}_i} \bigcirc \xrightarrow{\varepsilon[\mathrm{T} \leftarrow i]} \bigcirc \qquad (i = 1, 2)$$

and replace f with f'. In the DFAS it is not necessary to execute [T← i] immediately after α_i has been read. In some cases it can be executed only after a part of β has been read. Therefore, we assume that [T← i] is in Ω (not in Ω_t). In (1), on the other hand, we assume that the value of a is available only immediately after a has been read, and this [T← a] should be executed in the DFAS immediately after a has been read.

(3) For an expression $R = \{\alpha\}\beta[f] \in \mathrm{RES}(\Sigma)$, where

$$
\begin{aligned}
f = \textbf{case}\ \text{number-of}\ \alpha\ \textbf{of} \\
0 : f_0 \\
1 : f_1 \\
\geq 2 : f_2
\end{aligned}
$$

we change the transitions ε_0, ε_1 and ε_2 of the NFAS shown in the translation algorithm 3.2(3) as follows, by introducing a temporary variable T:

$$\varepsilon_0[\mathrm{T} \leftarrow 0], \quad \varepsilon_1[\mathrm{T} \leftarrow 1], \quad \varepsilon_2[\mathrm{T} \leftarrow 2]$$

(we also let [T← i] $\in \Omega$ as in case (2)), and replace f with the following f':

$$
\begin{aligned}
f' = \textbf{case}\ \mathrm{T}\ \textbf{of} \\
0 : f_0 \\
1 : f_1 \\
2 : f_2
\end{aligned}
$$

The NFASs obtained by the above algorithm for Exs. 1 and 2 are shown in Figs. 4 and 5, respectively.

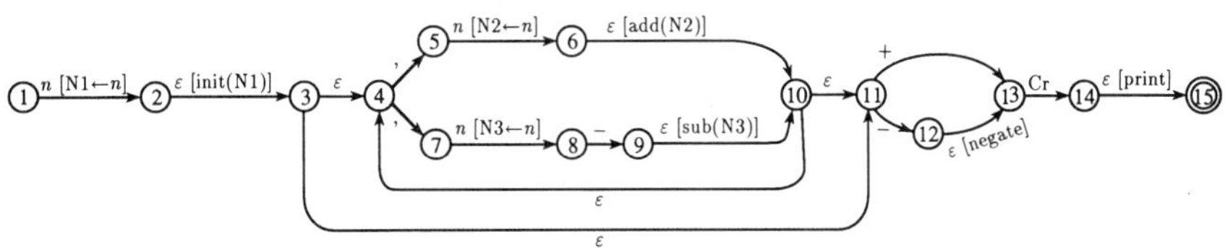

Fig. 5 NFAS for Example 2.

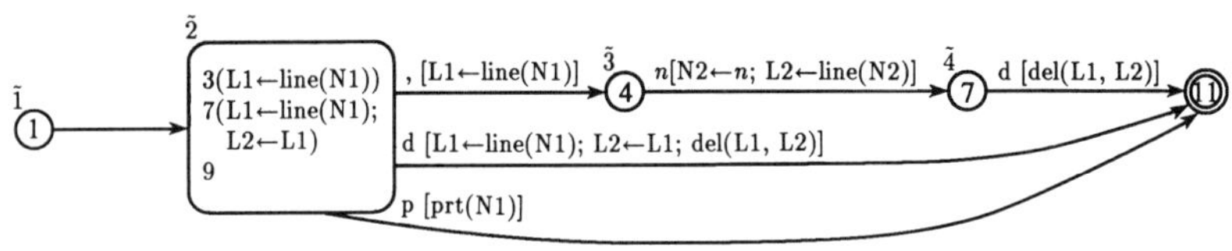

Fig. 6 DFAS for Example 1.

4.3 Translation from an NFAS to a DFAS

The assignment [T←a] $\in \Omega_t$ introduced in 4.2(1) should be executed when n has been read. It cannot be carried over to later states. Therefore, the algorithm in Section 3.3 should be modified as follows. First we define

$$\text{next}_1(R,a) = \{q(s) \mid \exists p(s) \in R : p \xrightarrow{a[f]} q \text{ or } p \xrightarrow{a} q\}$$

$$\text{assign}(\tilde{p},a) = \begin{cases} f & \text{if } \exists f \text{ such that } p(s) \in p : p \xrightarrow{a[f]} q \\ \varepsilon & \text{otherwise} \end{cases}$$

Notice that $f \in \Omega_t$ if $p \xrightarrow{a[f]} q (a \neq \varepsilon)$. This f, if it exists, is unique by 4.2(1). Using these definitions, the algorithm of 3.3 is modified as follows:

Algorithm 4. Algorithm for translation from an NFAS to a DFAS (modified parts only)

Replace next_0 with next_1.

Replace the transition indicated by (*) by

$$\tilde{p} \xrightarrow{a[s_h^1;\, \text{assign}(\tilde{p},a);\, s_h^2]} \tilde{q}$$

where $s_h = s_h^1; s_h^2$ and s_h^1 is the part of s_h that is carried over to $\tilde{p}$, and s_h^2 is added to s_h by the closure_0 operation for $\text{next}_1(\tilde{p},a)$. Either of these may possibly be ε.

The DFASs generated from the NFAS of Example 1 (Fig. 4) and from the NFAS of Example 2 (Fig. 5) by the above algorithm are shown in Figs. 6 and 7, respectively. The generation steps of the first half of Fig. 6 can be explained as follows:

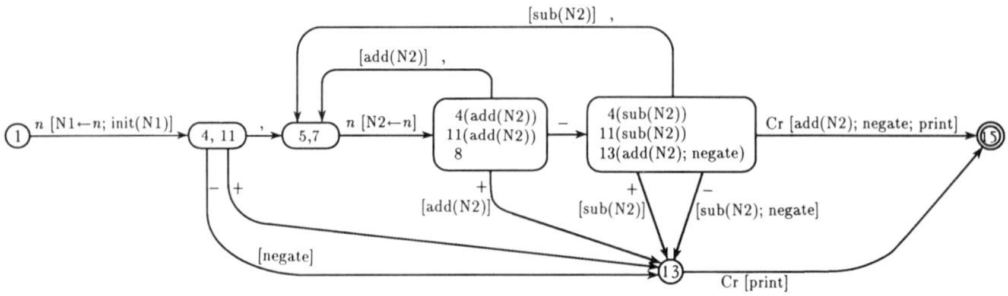

Fig. 7 DFAS for Example 2.

(1) $\tilde{1} = \text{closure}_0(\{1\}) = \{1\}, \tilde{Q} := \{\tilde{1}\}$

(2) For $\tilde{1} = \{1\} \in \tilde{Q}$,

$\text{next}_1(\{1\}, n) = \{2, 9\}$

$\text{assign}(\{1\}, n) = \text{N1} \leftarrow n$, N1 is replaced with N3.

Calculation of $\text{closure}_0(\text{next}_1(\{1\}, n))$:

{2,3(L1←line(N1)), 9}

⟶{3(L1←line(N1)), 6(L1←line(N1)), 9}

⟶{3(L1←line(N1)), 7(L1←line(N1);L2←L1), 9} $= \tilde{2}$

$\tilde{2}$ is added to $\tilde{Q}$. Because $s_h = \varepsilon$, the transition from $\tilde{1}$ to $\tilde{2}$ becomes

$\tilde{1} \xrightarrow{n[\text{N1}\leftarrow n]} \tilde{2}$

For $\tilde{2}$,

$\text{next}_1(\tilde{2}, ,) = \{4(\text{L1}\leftarrow\text{line(N1)})\}$, $\text{assign}(\tilde{2}, ,) = \varepsilon$

$\text{closure}_0(\text{next}_1(\tilde{2}, ,)) = \{4(\text{L1}\leftarrow\text{line(N1)})\}$

$s_h = s_h^1 = \text{L1}\leftarrow\text{line(N1)}$ is deleted from the above,

and the resultant $\{4\} = \tilde{3}$ is added to $\tilde{Q}$.

The transition from $\tilde{2}$ to $\tilde{3}$ becomes $\tilde{2} \xrightarrow{,[\text{L1}\leftarrow\text{line(N1)}]} \tilde{3}$

For $\tilde{3}$,

$\text{next}_1(\tilde{3}, n) = \{5\}, \text{assign}(3, n) = \text{N2} \leftarrow n$

$\text{closure}_0(\text{next}_1(\tilde{3}, n)) = \{7(\text{L2}\leftarrow\text{line(N2)})\}$

$s_h = s_h^2 = \text{L2}\leftarrow\text{line(N2)}$ is deleted from the above,

and the resultant $\{7\} = \tilde{4}$ is added to $\tilde{Q}$.

The transition from $\tilde{3}$ to $\tilde{4}$ becomes $\tilde{3} \xrightarrow{n[\text{N2}\leftarrow n;\text{L2}\leftarrow\text{line(N2)}]} \tilde{4}$

Suppose that $\tilde{p} \xrightarrow{a[s_h^1;f;s_h^2]} \tilde{q}$ is derived by the above algorithm, where $f = [\text{T}\leftarrow a] \in \Omega_t$. If s in $q(s) \in \tilde{q}$ has a function that has T as a parameter, and this function has been already carried over in $\tilde{p}$, then the given semantic rules cannot be implemented by our method, because a is assigned to T here, while T has some value yet to be processed. (This case cannot be handled by a static method like ours, in which the name of a temporary variable of $f \in \Omega_t$ is assigned statically to each state of NFAS.) For example,

$$\{a[f(a)]\}a[g(a)]b$$

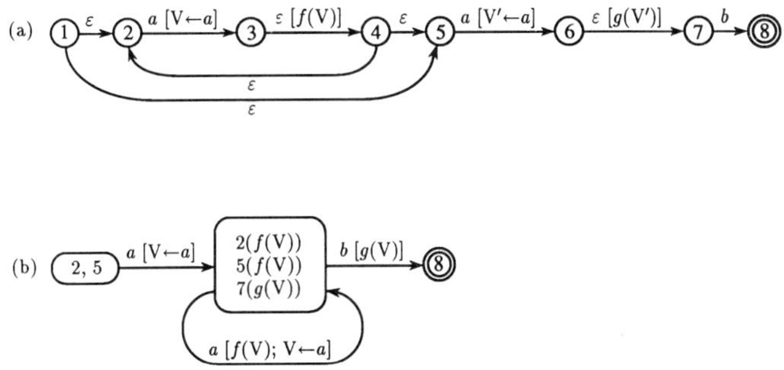

Fig. 8 (a) NFAS and (b) DFAS for $\{a[f(a)]\}a[g(a)]b$.

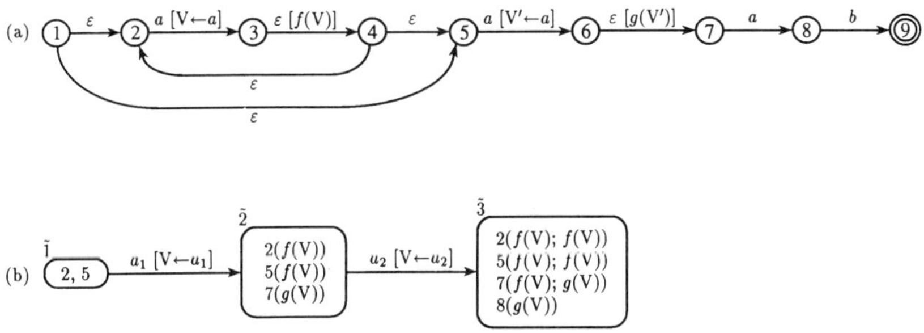

Fig. 9 (a) NFAS and (b) DFAS (first part) for $\{a[f(a)]\}a[g(a)]ab$.

causes no problem (Fig. 8), whereas

$$\{a[f(a)]\}a[g(a)]ab$$

cannot be implemented (Fig. 9), because $\mathrm{V}\leftarrow a_2$ is to be executed at the transition from $\tilde{2}$ to $\tilde{3}$, while $f(\mathrm{V})$ for $\mathrm{V}\leftarrow a_1$ has not yet been evaluated. (In this case, it can be implemented by increasing the number of variables, for example, by changing these assignments into $\mathrm{V1}\leftarrow a_1$ and $\mathrm{V2}\leftarrow a_2$, and $2(f(\mathrm{V});f(\mathrm{V}))$ in $\tilde{3}$ into $2(f(\mathrm{V1});f(\mathrm{V2}))$.)

5 Conclusion

We have proposed regular expressions with semantic rules, and algorithms that generate a finite automaton with semantic actions from such expressions. This means that from a given regular expression with semantic rules we can automatically generate a program that semantically manipulates the sentences defined by that expression. For example, if the structure of some data is defined by a regular expression, a program for manipulating these data can be generated by describing the semantic actions for these data within the description of their structure. Moreover, as we mentioned at the beginning of the paper, our method can be used to generate compilers by defining semantic rules for extended context-free grammars that have regular expressions in the right parts.

References

[1] Aho, A. V., Sethi, R., and Ullman, J. D. : *Compilers: Principles, Techniques, and Tools*, Addison-Wesley, 1986.

[2] Sassa, M. : Rie and Jun: Towards the Generation of all Compiler Phases, LNCS 477, Springer-Verlag, 1991.

[3] Kastens, U., Hutt, B., and Zimmermann, E. : *GAG: A Practical Compiler Generator*, LNCS 141, Springer-Verlag, 1982.

[4] Lorho, B. (ed.): *Methods and Tools for Compiler Construction*, Cambridge University Press, 1984.

[5] Nakata, I. : *Compiler*, Sangyo-Tosho, 1981 (in Japanese).

Initially published in "Computer Software", Vol. 3, No. 1, in Japanese.

Ikuo Nakata
Institute of Information Sciences and Electronics
University of Tsukuba
Tsukuba, Ibaraki
305 Japan

Masataka Sassa
Institute of Information Sciences and Electronics
University of Tsukuba
Tsukuba, Ibaraki
305 Japan

Misty: An Object-Oriented Programming Language with Multiple Inheritance and Strict Type-Checking

Yasushi Kuno

Summary. A strong type-checking facility is indispensable for an object-oriented programming language to be usable in large-scale software development. Misty is an object-oriented programming language with both multiple inheritance and strict type-checking facilities. Type-checking is applied not according to subtype relations between types, but according to strict equality between types. This principle differs markedly from that of other object-oriented programming languages with "strong" type-checking facilities, which incorporate subtype relations, and Misty's type-checking facility therefore termed a "strict" one. In spite of this strictness, Misty retains most of the flexibility seen in object-oriented programming languages without compile-time type checking. Moreover, experience of programming in Misty has revealed that program design and development using a class specification hierarchy along with a compiler to check its consistency will be a valuable and powerful tool for programming-in-the-large.

1 Introduction

The concept of object-orientation has recently become increasingly popular. One of the main reasons for this is that object-oriented programming languages allow the programmer to think and design in terms of real world analogies, which lead to simpler and more flexible program structures. However, earlier object-oriented programming languages such as Smalltalk-80 [3] and Flavors [10] do not possess a strong type-checking facility, and hence do not incorporate compile-time type checking. This presented no great problems as long as the main use of the languages were for small-scale prototyping, in which flexibility and short turnaround time after modification were the main objectives. But for large-scale software development, a compile-time type checking facility is indispensable. For this reason, I proposed Misty, an object-oriented programming language with both multiple inheritance and strict type checking ("strict" in the sense that type checking is done according to the strict type equality, not subtype relation). In this paper, the Misty language, the structure of the Misty compiler, and some observations based on experience of programming in Misty are reported.

The following ection (Section 2) discusses the merits of object-oriented programming languages and problems encountered in incorporating strong type checking in these languages. In Section 3, the Misty language itself is explained, with a description of how I solved the problems listed in Section 2. In Section 4, the structure

ISBN 0-12-037103-0

of the Misty compiler is briefly reviewed. In Section 5, an example of a window system is described and observations based on experience of programming in Misty are reported. Finally, Section 6 consists of a summary and some conclusions.

2 Object-Oriented Programming Languages and Types

No universally accepted definition of "object-oriented programming languages" exists, but I think that following four points are essential:

1. A *class* description contains structure and/or behavior definitions for a particular kind of data.
2. Multiple *instances* can be obtained from each class description.
3. An operation invocation specifies (one or more) instances as targets or arguments, and an actual *method* is called for, which is selected dynamically through the instances' class and the operation's name. Method definitions are also included in the class description.
4. A new class (subclass) can *inherit* definitions from some existing class (superclass), and only those definitions that differ in the superclass and subclass need be described explicitly in the subclass definition.

In the following paragraphs, we shall examine the way to introduce a compile-time type-checking facility into programming languages with the above characteristics.

Abstract data-type languages such as CLU [7] possess the characteristics outlined in points 1 and 2, along with the strong type-checking facility, so there are no difficulties.[1]

In the framework of strongly typed languages, however, the type of a variable is determined at compile time and does not change thereafter. On the other hand, point 3 requires that a single variable should be able to have instances of various classes dynamically. Somehow, we must resolve this conflict.

Moreover, in the framework of strongly typed languages, two types are either equal or not equal, and no other relations are defined. If we are to introduce inheritance, as described in point 4, we must also extend the concept of types to handle "similarity" (superclass-subclass relation); otherwise we cannot make full use of this extended concept.

One method of solving the above two problems is as follows: If a variable is declared to be of type A, it is allowed to hold an instance of type B as long as B is a (possibly indirect) subclass of A. In operation calls, methods defined in the class corresponding to the variable's current value (instance) are invoked. This is the approach adopted in Simula [1] and in most recent object-oriented programming languages with strong type-checking (such as Trellis/Owl [9] and C++ [11]).

But when this approach is chosen, type checking must be performed not according to type equality but according to type inclusion, and misuse of the instance of a type and its subtypes cannot be discovered by compile-time type-checking. My

[1] Types in strongly typed languages and classes in object-oriented languages are not strictly the same. But to merge these two kind of language, it is natural to regard types as corresponding to classes. I follow this line of reasoning and uses the words "type" and "class" interchangeably hereafter.

goal was to discover as many inconsistencies as possible in the compiler, and so instead of this approach, Misty follows the one outlined in the next section.

3 Design of the Misty Language

Misty is modeled on CLU [7], an abstract data type language developed at the Massachusetts Institute of Technology (MIT); this language's simplicity and compactness made it easy to extend. Basically, CLU was already strongly typed, so the main task was to add object-orientedness to it in a structured fashion.

3.1 Class Specification and Class Body

A Misty program consists of modules called *class*es. The role of classes is to define and establish (abstract data) types. A class without parameters corresponds to a type (we shall examine parameterized classes later, in Section 3.6).

A class is defined by means of two lexical units, a *class specification* and a *class body*. The class specification defines the name of the class, the names of the operations possessed by the class, and the specifications of these operations (that is, the number and types of these operations' arguments and return values). To compile a module that refers to a class, only the class specification for that class is required.

On the other hand, the class body defines the actual data representation of the class along with implementation of each operation. Therefore, if actual instances of a class are not required (as in the case of the "virtual class" of Smalltalk-80), the corresponding class body need not exist.

As an example, here is a simplified class specification for the "Boolean value" class:

```
bool = class spec
    defines and, or, not
  and = proc(x,y:self) returns(self)
  or = proc(x,y:self) returns(self)
  not = proc(x:self) returns(self)
end bool
```

The first line indicates the name of the class and the fact that this unit is a class specification. After the keyword `defines`, the names of the operations defined in this class are listed. Next, specifications for each of these operations are given. The above example declares that `and` and `or` receive two arguments, `not` receives one argument, and all three return one value, and that all arguments and return values are of the type bool (`self` means the type being defined in the enclosing class specification or body).

3.2 Inheriting Class Specifications

In Misty, the term "inheritance" indicates a facility for defining a new class specification in terms of existing class specifications. Hence, inheritance is related only to class specifications, and not to class bodies. As an example, let us define a class named `xbool`. This class is the same as `bool` except that the `xor` operation is added. The class specification of `xbool` is as follows:

```
xbool = class spec
    super bool
    defines xor
  xor = proc(x,y:self) returns(self)
end xbool
```

The line `super bool` directs the compiler to include operation specifications found in `bool`, so `xbool` possesses four operations, `and`, `or`, `not` and `xor`, all of which receive `xbool` type argument(s) (one for `not`, two for the others), and return one `xbool` result. Note that `self` here indicates `xbool`, even if operation specifications are included from the `bool` class.

After the keyword `super`, any number of types can be specified. However, to avoid the problem of circular dependency, no class can be a (possibly indirect) superclass of itself. When multiple superclasses are listed, all operation specifications found in those classes are corrected and merged together. If an operation name is found in more than two of those classes, all specifications under that operation name should match each other;[2] otherwise, an error is flagged. The order of types in the `super` list is not relevant, because inheritance of specifications is totally independent of the implementation part (class body). In most object-oriented programming languages, on the other hand, the order is used to resolve method name crashes from multiple superclasses (that is, if a multiple method definition exists, the class earlier in the superclass list takes precedence). Consequently, the modification of the superclass list may have unexpected results. Misty does not have such problems.

If no `super` declaration exists,

```
super object
```

is assumed, where `object` is a special built-in class. Hence, `object` is a (possibly indirect) superclass of every class, including itself.

If some of the operations need not be inherited, one may specify the fact by

`excludes` *list-of-operation-names*

or alternatively, one may explicitly specify only those that are needed by

`includes` *list-of-operation-names*

This facility is useful when operation specifications for a particular operation name do not match between superclasses. In creating a new class, to add new operation names that do not exist in any of its superclasses, `defines` clauses are used. To modify operation specifications inherited from its superclasses, one can use

`modifies` *list-of-operation-names*

This is semantically equivalent to the combination of `excludes` and `defines`.

3.3 Class Bodies

As stated above, a class body defines an actual data representation for that class, along with the implementation of each operation. As an example, here is the class body for `xbool` class:

---

[2] That is, the number and types of the arguments and the return values should be the same.

```
xbool = class body
    rep = bool
  and = proc(x,y:cvt) returns(cvt)
    return(x & y)
  end and
  or = proc(x,y:cvt) returns(cvt)
    return(x | y)
  end or
  not = proc(x:cvt) returns(cvt)
    return(~x)
  end not
  xor = proc(x,y:cvt) returns(cvt)
    return(x & ~y | ~x & y)
  end xor
end xbool
```

Note that `&`, `|`, and `~` indicate the operations `bool!and`, `bool!or`, and `bool!not`. In Misty, an operation under each class can be specified by the notation

type-name! *operation-name*

Misty also allows a notation of the form

expression! *operation-name*(...)

which is equivalent to

type-of(expression)! *operation-name*(*expression*,...)

This notation is modeled on Rekimoto's extended CLU [8]. Note also that *type-of(...)* denotes the type that the compiler recognizes at compile time. The Misty language does not actually have such a notation.

In the above example, "`rep =`" defines the actual data representation for this class. The external specification and the internal representation are totally independent, and therefore, one may, for example, use the integers 0 and 1 to represent values of the class `xbool`. Here we represent `xbool` values by ordinary Boolean values. The implementation of each of the operations in this class follows the representation definition. Here, `cvt` in the operation's header means that the argument or the return value should be regarded as of the type `self` from outside the module, and as of the type `rep` from inside the module. This notation is also modeled on CLU.

3.4 Borrowing Operation Implementations

In the `xbool` example above, all that `xbool!and`, `xbool!or`, and `xbool!not` do is to call `bool!and`, `bool!or`, and `bool!not`, respectively, with the same argument(s). In my experience with CLU, such "delegating" operations are very common in abstract data-type languages. These operations are tedious to write and impose an overhead of extra operation invocations. To overcome this problem, Misty provides a mechanism for "borrowing" operation implementations from other classes. With this facility, the example above can be written as follows:

```
xbool = class body
```

```
      rep = bool
      use bool for and, or, not
    xor = proc(x,y:cvt) returns(cvt)
      return(x & ~y | ~x & y)
    end xor
  end xbool
```

The `use` clause in the third line directs the system to invoke `bool!and`, `bool!or`, and `bool!not` directly if `xbool`'s `and`, `or`, and `not` are needed. For the `xor` operation, no appropriate operation to borrow exists, so the implementation is specified as before.

In Misty, this kind of "borrowing" is specified by using the following four types of `use` clause:

`use` *type* `for` *list-of-operation-names*
`use` *type*! *operation-name* `for` *list-of-operation-names*
`use id for` *list-of-operation-names*
`use (`*expression*`) for` *list-of-operation-names*

Hereafter, the term "borrowing operation" is used to indicate the operation being implemented through `use`, and the term "borrowed operation" to refer to the already existing operation, namely "borrowed."

As indicated in the example above, the first form borrows another class's operation with the same name. The class need not be the one corresponding to the `rep` type. In the above example, if yet another class, say `z`, has the operation

```
and = proc(x,y:bool) returns(bool)
```

then it is perfectly legal to borrow the `and` operation:

```
use z for and
```

The second form is functionally similar to the first one, but can borrow another class's operations under a different name.

The third form is used when no operation implementation is actually required. For example, `xbool` should possess operations that convert `bool` values to `xbool` values, and vice versa. We therefore add the following lines, along with the corresponding `defines`, to the `xbool` class specification:

```
b2x = proc(b:bool) returns(self)
x2b = proc(x:self) returns(bool)
```

In such cases, `xbool` values are represented in `bool` values, so one need do nothing to convert between them. It will suffice to specify

```
use id for b2x, x2b
```

in the `xbool` class body. These operations conceptually exist, but no code is generated to invoke them.

The fourth form is the most complicated one. In this form, *expression* should contain one or more occurrences of the pseudo-variable identifier `ref`. The semantics of this form is as follows:

1. Within the arguments of the borrowing operation `p`, select those that are specified as of type `self`. For each of these `self` arguments, bind its value to the pseudo-variable `ref` and evaluate the *expression*.

2. Invoke *type-of(expression)*`!p`, with the original arguments except that `self` arguments are substituted, with corresponding evaluated values.

This form is useful for classes in which `rep` is defined as a record type. Such classes are used frequently in practice.[3] Suppose a class has a `rep` definition

```
rep = record{ct:counter, ...}
```

and also an operation specification of the form

```
count_up = proc(x:self, n:int) returns(int)
```

whose only job is to `count_up` on the `ct` field. This can be specified, using fourth form, as:

```
use (ref.ct) for count_up
```

The ordinary implementation of this operation would be

```
count_up = proc(x:cvt, n:int) returns(int)
  return(counter!count_up(x.ct, n))
end count_up
```

which is rather lengthy, tedious to write, and difficult to understand.

3.5 Compatibility Condition for Borrowing

In the borrowing facility, a borrowing operation `p` and a borrowed operation `q` should be *compatible* to ensure type safety. For the first and second forms of the `use` clause, the following conditions are required:

a. The numbers of arguments of `p` and `q` should be the same, and `p`'s ith argument type should be assignable to `q`'s ith argument type.

b. The numbers of return values of `p` and `q` should be the same, and `q`'s ith return value type should be assignable to `p`'s ith return value type.

c. If `p` and `q` have any signals with the same name, then apply rule **b** for each such signal, substituting "signal argument" for "return value."

The definition of "assignable" is given later, in Section 3.7. In all the above conditions and in **d** below, when the arguments or return values are specified as of type `self`, they can be regarded as `rep` if necessary, because `self` and `rep` are exactly the same within one class.

The roles of `p` and `q` are exchanged between **a** and **b** because, in the case of arguments, values prepared for `p` should actually be accepted by `q`, and in the case of return values, values prepared by `q` should actually be received by the code that is expecting values from `p`. When condition **c** obtains, signals whose names exist solely on `p` or `q` are independent of each other, but for those signals whose names are shared by `p` and `q`, signal arguments should be handled as extended return values.

For the third form of the `use` clause, there are no borrowed operations at all, so the following condition is used instead of **a** and **b** above:

[3] In many object-oriented programming languages, representations of class values are implicit record types.

d. The number of arguments and the number of return values of `p` should be the same, and the ith argument's type should be assignable to the ith return value's type.

For the fourth form, the main line is same as that of the first and the second forms, but to handle `ref` substitution, **a** is modified as follows:

a': The numbers of arguments of `p` and `q` should be the same, and if `p`'s ith argument type was specified as `self` (i.e., `ref` substitution occurs), *type-of(expression)* should be assignable to `q`'s ith argument type. Otherwise, (i.e., no `ref` substitution), `p`'s ith argument type should be assignable to `q`'s ith argument type.

Note that, as the borrowing facility always requires the explicit specification of the borrowing operations, no ambiguity arises even if multiple superclasses include operations with the same name. Actually, the borrowing facility is totally independent of the superclass-subclass relation, as indicated previously.

3.6 Type Parameterization and Inheritance

A *type generator* is a kind of module with *type parameters.* Supplied with various types as argument(s), type generators generate actual types. Misty's built-in type generators include `record`, `oneof` (similar to C's union), and `array`:

`record`{$Field_1 : Type_1 , \ldots , Field_n : Type_n$}
`oneof`{$Tag_1 : Type_1 , \ldots , Tag_n : Type_n$}
`array`[*Type*]

As shown above, arguments enclosed in {} form a list of identifier-type pairs, and arguments enclosed in `[]` form a list of types. A type generator of the latter form can be defined by the user.

As an example, let us consider a data structure similar to `array`, but whose elements are always sorted in ascending order, so that the nth smallest element can be accessed quickly. A class specification for the module, named `linear_array`, is shown below:

```
linear_array = class spec[t:linear]
    super array[t]
    excludes store, addh, addl
    defines add1, del1, lookup
  add1 = proc(x:self, elt:t)
  del1 = proc(x:self, i:int) returns(t) signals(bounds)
  lookup = proc(x:self, elt:t) returns(int) signals(not_found)
end linear_array
```

The type `linear_array[t]` inherits most of its operations from `array[t]`. For example, the ith element can be accessed by the notation `a[i]` (which is a syntax-sugar of the `fetch` operation). But `linear_array[t]` excludes operations that store values in some specific location, because the location of each element is determined by its value. Instead, operations for inserting a value into the appropriate position, deleting the ith element, and (perhaps binary-) searching for the specific value's position are added.

The notation `[t:linear]` in the module header specifies that type parameter `t`'s *upper bound* is the type `linear`, which means that the actual type argument corresponding to `t` must be a (possibly indirect) subclass of the type `linear`. Here `linear` represents a class of values with linear order. This condition is required, because elements stored in `linear_array[t]` must be comparable with one another. For example, `linear_array`'s class body must have operation implementations for `add1` and `lookup`, and these should contain invocations of comparison predicates for `t`'s value, such as `t!gt` and `t!lt`. As `t` is guaranteed to be a (possibly indirect) subclass of `linear`, it should have those operations.[4] The compiler also knows the specifications of these operations from the class specifications of `linear`, so compile-time checking for these operations is possible.

In general, any type can be specified as an upper bound of a type parameter. But to avoid the problem of circular dependency, there is a prohibition against refering to the class currently being defined, or to other type parameters in the same header.

Programming languages such as CLU or Ada also have type parameterization facilities. But in these languages, the programmer must supply operation specifications for every type parameter explicitly. These descriptions are lengthy and tedious to write, and they do not give insights or hints for answering the question "What kinds of types are expected for this type parameter?" In Misty, all that is needed is to specify the upper bound for that type parameter. Information on operation specifications is automatically obtained from the class hierarchy. At the same time, this also gives useful hints on answering the above question.

3.7 Dynamic Operation Binding in Misty

As in other object-oriented programming languages, Misty's inheritance facility allows a programmer to group classes according to their "natural" hierarchy in the real world. For example, a class named `vehicle` might have an operation named `right_turn`. If other classes called `horse` and `car` are both subclasses of `vehicle`, they both inherit the `right_turn` operation by default. Thus, when variables `x` and `y` are of type `horse` and `car`, respectively, one can use both

```
x!right_turn(...)
y!right_turn(...)
```

in the same manner. On the other hand, point 3 in Section 2 specifies that, in this case, it should be possible to let a variable, say `z`, hold instances of `horse` or `car` arbitrarily in the course of execution, and

```
z!right_turn(...)
```

should invoke `horse!turn_right` or `car!turn_right` dynamically, corresponding to the type of instance currently held by `z`. However, in the framework of strict type checking, `horse` and `car` are different types, and instances of them cannot be held by one variable. (To understand the reason for this, consider how it is possible to determine the type of the variable `z`.)

[4] It is possible that somewhere between `linear` and `t` these operations might be `excluded` or `altered`. In this case, the compiler should flag an error.

In Misty, the above problem is solved by introducing a new built-in type generator, any[t]. Its class specification is as follows:

```
any = class spec[t:object]
    super t
    defines relax, force, is_type, isa_type
  relax = proc[t1:t](x:t1) returns(self)
  force = proc[t1:t](x:self) returns(t1) signals(wrong_type)
  is_type = proc[t1:t](x:self) returns(bool)
  isa_type = proc[t1:t](x:self) returns(bool)
end any
```

As any[t] is a subclass of type t, it has the same operation set as t. In addition, any[t] has four *procedure generators.* As in type generators, procedure generators supplied with type arguments correspond to actual procedures. Of these, relax[t1], where t1 should be a (possibly indirect) subclass of t, converts values of type t1 into values of type any[t]. In contrast, force[t1] converts values of type any[t] into values of type t1. In this case, if the value of any[t1] was not the one constructed from a value of type t1, the signal wrong_type is issued. The other two procedure generators is_type[t1] and isa_type[t1] test whether the value of type any[t] is the one previously constructed from the value of type t1, or t1 and its (possibly indirect) subclass in the case of isa_type[t1].

Thus, by declaring the variable z to be of type any[vehicle], one can legally write

```
z!right_turn(...)
```

As noted before, this is equivalent to

```
any[vehicle]!right_turn(z, ...)
```

and any[vehicle]!right_turn invokes horse!turn_right or car!turn_right, according to z's current instance. To assign the values horse or car, one should strictly write

```
z := any[vehicle]!relax[horse](x)
```

and so on, which is tedious. Assignment compatibility is therefore defined as follows:

Definition of Assignment Compatibility

Given arbitrary types t and t1, the following condition is necessary to assign a value of type t1 to a variable of type t, or to pass a value of type t1 to an argument specified as of type t.

a. t = t1. In this case, the value is assigned or passed as it is.

b. t ≠ t1, t possesses a procedure generator whose name is relax, and the specification of relax[t1] is proc(x:t1)returns(t). In this case, the given value is converted to type t by this procedure.

Thus, it is possible to write the same assignment as

```
z := x
```

The reverse assignment should still be written as

```
x := z!force[horse]()
```

because this case might result in the wrong_type signal.

Implementation of any[t]'s operations is supplied by the compiler and the runtime system. Its function is to manage the type tag of its current value along with the value itself, and in the case of inherited operations to invoke the operation of the actual type, according to the type tag. This requires a kind of type table, but the table need only contain the part actually used and can be kept small. Note also that this dynamic operation binding is used only when any[t] is used, and that all other operation bindings are done at compile time.

4 The Compiler

This section describes the structure of the Misty compiler and runtime system. The system currently runs on VAX/Unix 4.3bsd. Figure 1 shows the overall structure of the system. The sizes of the modules in source code lines are as follows:

```
Front-End (lex, yacc, C)     700 lines
Back-End (extended CLU)    4,500 lines
Run-Time (Common Lisp)       500 lines
```

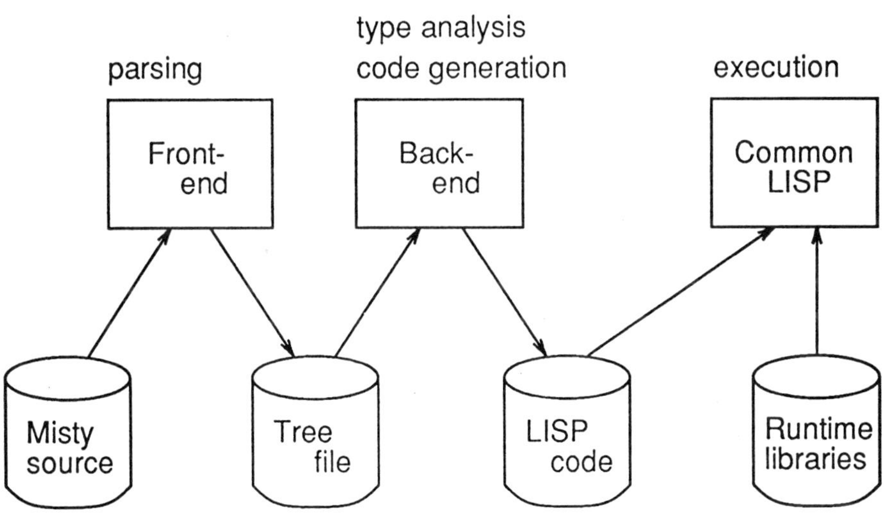

Fig. 1 Structure of the Misty compiler.

In this system, the front-end phase performs lexical and syntax analysis and outputs abstract syntax-tree code onto the file. All syntax-sugar notations are also expanded in this phase. The front-end phase was built by using lex and yacc.

The back-end phase constitutes the core of the compiler. In this phase, information about each class and its operations is extracted and managed. This phase is written in extended CLU [8]. This phase processes each Misty module in the following manner:

1. Read abstract syntax-tree code, and build an internal tree structure.
2. Scan the internal tree, extract class names and operation names/specifications, and record them in the symbol table.
3. When the module is a class specification, the processing is over.
4. For a class body, perform type-checking for the statement codes contained in the module.
5. If no error is found, generate codes and output the codes to the object file.
6. After all input modules have been processed, write information about built-in type usages (which is required by the runtime support).

The generated code is a collection of Common LISP functions and macros. These are loaded onto the KCL (Kyoto Common LISP) system, along with the runtime library, and executed. When the execution speed is important, these codes can be compiled by the KCL compiler. Common LISP codes are chosen for the following reasons:

- Run-time memory management can be entrusted on to the existing LISP system, which allows the system to be developed rapidly.
- Generated codes can be kept relatively high-level, which facilitates both code generation and runtime support development.
- Generated codes can be executed in various Common LISP execution environments.

5 Programming in Misty

In this section, we take an example of a toy window system and discuss the characteristics of programming in Misty.

5.1 An Example: A Toy Window System

Window systems are appropriate vehicles for demonstrating the expressive power of an object-oriented programming language, because such a system contains various kinds of object with similar characteristics (for example, they can all be displayed on the screen). The example below is a toy window system that uses character display terminals. As shown in Fig. 2, this system makes it possible to create multiple overlapped windows. There are two kind of windows: text-only windows, and windows that can contain multiple subwindows. Other kinds can be added easily.

In the design of the system, various components required for its functions are identified, and then described as Misty's class specifications. Once these specifications are fairly concrete, class bodies are written. Meanwhile, new components may again be identified and new classes may be introduced. In the following paragraphs, this process is briefly outlined and explained.

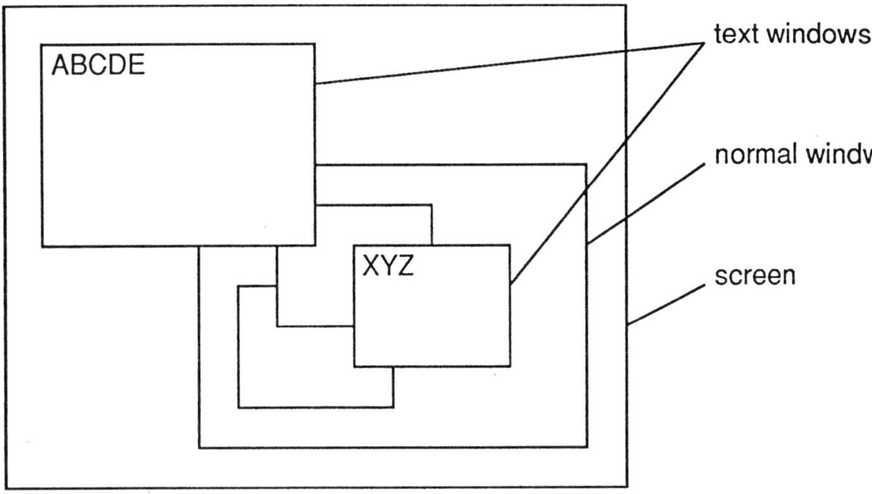

Fig. 2 Sample screen image of the toy window system.

First, window systems must "display" various objects on the screen, so we at least need a class corresponding to "something that can be displayed." We name it `display`. All that needs to be known about the `display` object is its appearance. The class specification of `display` is as follows:

```
display = class spec
    defines contents, get_area
  contents = iter(x:self) yields(point, char)
  get_area = proc(x:self) returns(rectangle)
end display
```

Here `contents` is an iterator [7] and yields multiple return values, each of which is a pair consisting of a point (relative to its origin) and a character that should be displayed at that point. `get_area` returns the bounding box of the `display` object.

To display objects on the screen, those objects should be *attached* to one of windows. We can add such operations to the `display` class, but it is desirable to distinguish them, and for this reason we made another class called `view`:

```
view = class spec
    super display
    defines attach_to, detach_from
  attach_to = proc(x:self, w:any_window) signals(already_attached)
  detach_from = proc(x:self, w:any_window) signals(not_attached)
end view
```

Moreover, some objects may optionally accept user input (such as keystrokes), and therefore so we made a corresponding class and named it `control`:

```
control = class spec
```

```
      super view
      defines select
    select = proc(x:self, f:stream)
  end control
```

To enable a control object to accept input, one calls the select operation, giving it a stream object from which to read input characters. Implementations of select should read as many characters as necessary to perform the task and return to the caller when the "unselect" command (also read from the stream) is found.

Finally, of course, we need windows:

```
window = class spec
    super control
    defines attach, detach, update
  attach = proc(x:self, v:any_view, p:point) signals(attach_twice)
  detach = proc(x:self, v:any_view) signals(not_attached)
  update = proc(x:self, v:any_view, r:rectangle)
                                    signals(not_attached)
end window
```

One can place view objects in the window by using attach and remove them by using detach. When the appearance of some view changes, one should call update to inform the window and have its screen image correctly modified. In the preceding codes, the following definition is also assumed:

```
any_view = any[view]
any_control = any[control]
any_window = any[window]
```

The reason for using any is that windows can accept various kinds of view, and one view might be attached to the bare screen, or to one window. As noted in Section 3.7, one should use any when several kinds of object are switched dynamically in one place.

Note also that control is a subclass of view, and therefore formal arguments specified as any_view can accept control objects. Among the various objects displayed in a window, only those that belong to the control class are allowed to be "selected." This can be expressed as follows:

```
if v!isa_type[control]() then
  v!force[any_control]()!select(f)
else
  % this does not belong to control class...
end
```

When a primary class structure is designed, we can proceed to design actual functionality classes (which are going to have class bodies). In this example, the followings classes were made:

- text_control : a text window.
- normal_window : a window that can have subwindows.
- screen_window : a window that corresponds to the terminal screen.

Of these, `text_control` is a subclass of `control`; the other two classes are subclasses of `window`. In addition, the following support classes were necessary:

- `point` : an (X, Y) coordinate pair.
- `rectangle` : a rectangular area.
- `form` : a two-dimensional array of characters.
- `crt` : a bare CRT terminal.

Figure 3 shows the complete class structure of the program.

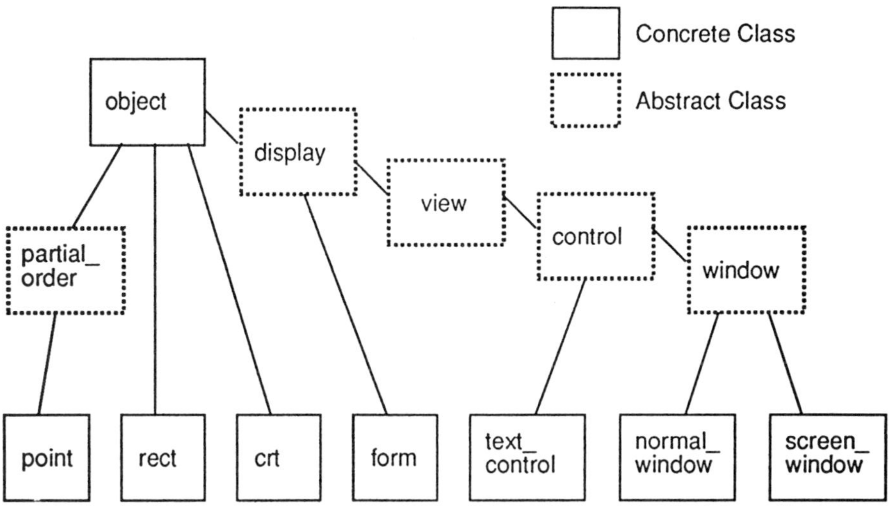

Fig. 3 Class hierarchy of the sample window system.

5.2 Experiences with Programming in Misty

In the process described in Section 5.1, abstract classes are designed first, in a top-down fashion, and followed by concrete (non-abstract) classes, enriching the class hierarchy structure. This "abstract class first" procedure was also natural and useful in developing other example programs. In some cases, the design process involved radical modification of the class hierarchy structure, but as the compiler detects inconsistency in the revised structure, fairly straightforward cycles of correction and recompilation led smoothly to a new consistent state.

Programming in Misty is similar to programming in abstract data-type languages such as CLU, in that specification of types are developed first. The main difference is that inheritance allows natural sharing of specification descriptions and makes relations between similar types explicit and clear. These are notable advantages.

Unlike other object-oriented programming languages without strong type checking, Misty imposes programmers the burden of designing the class structure first.

But for large-scale software development, this kind of design consideration is always necessary, and enforcing this process as the first stage of development can be viewed as a strong point. Moreover, the output of the design stage is explicitly left as separate class specifications, which is another merit in this respect.

6 Conclusions

To apply object-oriented programming to large-scale software development, a strong type-checking facility is indispensable. Misty is an object-oriented programming language for this purpose. Its main characteristics are as follows:

1. The description of a class is separated into two parts – a *specification* unit, in which all outside information referred to is collected, and a *body* unit, in which internal structures and implementations of instances are described.
2. The *inheritance* facility is defined as a mechanism for collecting specification information from multiple superclasses.
3. The *borrowing* facility delegates the implementation of each method to other classes (including superclasses).
4. Implementation of a class is guarded from outside, and also from its subclasses. This preserves the independence of each class's implementation and the merits of abstract data types.
5. Information on *type parameters* is supplied by specifying their *upper bounds*, which are related to the class structure hierarchy. This makes the description simple and easy to understand.
6. Dynamic type polymorphism is provided through the special built-in type generator `any[t]`, without disturbing the framework of *strict* type checking.

As a whole, Misty provides both a framework for strict type checking and flexibility almost equivalent to that of object-oriented programming languages without type checking. In comparison with these languages, Misty has a strong restriction in that subclasses are not allowed to access a superclass's internal structure, but in my opinion this is an advantage because it ensures the properties (and merits) of data abstraction.

References

[1] O-J. Dahl and C. A. R. Hoare: Hierarchical Program Structures, in O-J. Dahl, E. W. Dijkstra and C. A. R. Hoare: Structured Programming, Academic Press, 1972.

[2] Reference Manual for the Ada Programming Language, U.S. Department of Defence, 1980.

[3] A. Goldberg and D. Robson: Smalltalk-80 — The Language and Its Implementation, Addison-Wesley, 1983.

[4] Y. Kuno: Misty – A Language with Multiple Inheritance and Strict Type Checking, Proceedings of the 1st Annual Conference of the JSSST, pp. 73-76, 1984 (in Japanese).

[5] Y. Kuno: A Program Design Methodology for Abstract Data-Type Programming Languages, Proceedings of the IPSJ, Vol. 26, No. 11, pp. 515-523, 1985 (in Japanese).

[6] Y. Kuno: Object-Oriented Programming Languages with Type Hierarchy, Proceedings of the IPSJ, Vol. 29, No. 4, pp. 318-324, 1988 (in Japanese).

[7] B. Liskov, R. Atkinson, T. Bloom, E. Moss, J. C. Schaffert, R. Scheifler and A. Snyder: CLU Reference Manual, Springer, 1981.

[8] J. Rekimoto: An Extension of CLU Language's Syntax and Modification to the Compiler, personal communication, 1984.

[9] C. Schaffert, T. Cooper, B. Bullis, M. Kilian and C. Wilpolt: An Introduction to Trellis/Owl, Proc. OOPSLA' 86, pp. 9-16.

[10] D. Weinreb and D. Moon: Flavors: Message Passing in the Lisp Machine, MIT AI memo 602, 1980.

[11] B. Stroustrup: The C++ Programming Language, Addison-Wesley, 1984.

[12] A. Yonezawa: Current Status and Trends in Object-Oriented Computation, Proceedings of the IPSJ, Vol. 29, No. 4, pp. 290-294, 1988 (in Japanese).

Initially published in "Computer Software", Vol. 6, No. 3, in Japanese.

Yasushi Kuno
Graduate School of Systems Management
Univ. of Tsukuba, Tokyo
3–29–1, Otsuka, Bunkyo-ku, Tokyo
112 Japan

The Semantics of an Object-Oriented Concurrent Programming Language: Process Algebraic Approach

Yutaka Ishikawa Satoru Tomura Kokichi Futatsugi

Summary. In this paper, the formal semantics of an object-oriented concurrent programming language called `Mono` is given. `Mono` is a model language that includes key features of object-oriented concurrent languages, e.g., synchronous and asynchronous message passing, delegation mechanism, and so on. A process algebra called ECCS, which is an extension of CCS, is introduced. The semantics of ECCS is defined by inference rules. The transformation function that transforms `Mono` into ECCS gives the formal semantics of `Mono`.

1 Introduction

One of the recent requirements for modern programming languages is a facility for concurrent programming. It is widely known, however, that giving elegant and usable semantics to concurrent programming languages is one of the most challenging research themes in computer science. The advantages that are provided by such semantics should include: (1) programmers can understand the semantics of the language easily, and it helps them to write programs with high reliability and efficiency; (2) the programs in the language can be analyzed and manipulated in rigorous fashion based on the semantics.

Object-oriented modeling is one of the promising approaches for providing high-level semantics to concurrent programming languages and is effective for programmers to understand the semantics of the languages. In object-oriented modeling, an application is modeled as a set of cooperative objects according to the following ideas; (1) every object is an active entity; (2) concurrency is controlled by message-passing form, such as synchronous or asynchronous message-passing; and (3) an object may be defined using the inheritance or delegation mechanisms. Actor [1], ConcurrentSmalltalk [5], ABCL/1 [6], and Orient84/K [2] are examples of languages based on these concepts.

Milner introduced CCS (Calculus of Communicating Systems) [3] with the intention of establishing theoretical basis for concurrent programming. In CCS, the behavior of a process is modeled as a sequence of observable events. The sequence of events is specified using a few operators that obey several algebraic identities. The system, which is composed of operators that obey identities only, makes an algebra. This is why CCS-like formal systems are called process algebras.

In this paper, an algebraic approach to the formal semantics of an object-oriented concurrent programming language is employed. Because CCS is not capable of specifying a peer of communication dynamically, we propose ECCS, an

ISBN 0-12-037103-0

extension of CCS. In order to describe the key features of object-oriented concurrent languages, a model language called `Mono` is introduced, which has rich features of those languages. The transformation from `Mono` to ECCS is given by functions, and thus the formal semantics of `Mono` is given by the transformation.

The organization of this paper is as follows: The next section describes the general notation. In Section 3, `Mono` is informally defined with examples. ECCS is defined by inference rules in Section 4. Section 5 is devoted to specifying the transformation from `Mono` to ECCS.

2 Notation

The syntax of `Mono` and ECCS is described by BNF notation. A string surrounded by < and > is a nonterminal symbol, while a string enclosed by two "'s is a terminal symbol. $[\alpha]$ means that α may appear or not. $\alpha|\beta$ means that α or β may appear. $\left\{\alpha\right\}$ means that α may repeat more than 0 times.

The typewriter font, e.g., `Window`, is used to express a program written in `Mono`. A set of nonterminal symbols is written in the bold font, e.g., **Prog**. Meta variables over nonterminal symbol are written in the slanted font, e.g., *Def*.

A set of nonterminal symbols in ECCS is written in the small-capital font, i.e., NAME. Meta variables over nonterminal symbol in ECCS are written in the italic font, i.e., x. Behavior expressions of ECCS are written in sans serif font, e.g., nil.

$\left\{\alpha_i\right\}_{i=1}^{n}$ expresses empty "" or a sequence "$\alpha_1 \cdots \alpha_n$". For short notation, $\left\{\alpha_i\right\}_i$ or α^* is used.

$\left\{\left\{\alpha_i^j\right\}_{j=1}^{f(i)}\right\}_{i=1}^{n}$ expresses empty "" or a sequence "$\left\{\alpha_1^j\right\}_{j=1}^{f(1)} \cdots \left\{\alpha_n^j\right\}_{j=1}^{f(n)}$". For short notation, $\left\{\alpha_i^*\right\}_i$ or $\left\{\alpha_i^*\right\}$ is used.

A transformation function from `Mono` to ECCS is written in calligraph letters, e.g., $\mathcal{M}$. $\mathcal{A}[m]$ means that a transformation function $\mathcal{A}$ is applied to parameter m.

3 Concurrent Object-Oriented Language Mono

In this section an object-oriented concurrent programming language called `Mono` is informally described with examples. `Mono` has the key features of concurrent object oriented programming languages such as Actor [1], ConcurrentSmalltalk [5], ABCL/1 [6], and Orient84/K [2].

3.1 Syntax and Meta Notation

The syntax of `Mono` is shown in Fig. 1. The metavariables used in `Mono` are defined as follows: Let **Prog** be a set of programs and *prog* stand for a member of **Prog**. Let **SDef** be a set of *static object creation expressions* and *sdef* stand for a member of **SDef**. We use a set **Name** of object names and *v*, *d*, *O* range over **Name**. We use a set **Var** of variables and *i*, *a*, *t*, *x* range over **Var**. Let **Term** be a set of *object expressions* and *n*, *r* stand for members of **Term**. We use a set **Exp** of *action expressions* and *c* range over **Exp**. Let **Method** be a set of methods and *m* stand for a member of **Method**. We use a set **Sel** of selectors and *s* range over **Sel**. We now define metanotations for nonterminal symbols in `Mono` as shown in

```
<program> ::= {<static object creation expression>}
<static object creation expression> ::= <object name> "::" <new expression>
<new expression> ::=
        <object definition> "(" <delegate expression> {<object expression>} ")"
<object definition> ::=  "[" "(" { <local variable> } ")" {<method>}  "]"
<method> ::=
        "(" "(" <selector>  {<formal parameter>} ")"
              "(" {<temporary variable>} ")" {<action expression>} ")"
<action expression> ::= <message expression>
       | <dynamic object creation expression>
<message expression> ::= <synchronous message transmission expression>
       | <synchronous message communication expression>
       | <asynchronous message transmission expression>
       | <asynchronous message communication expression>
       | <reply message transmission expression>
<synchronous transmission expression> ::= <object expression> <message> "."
<synchronous message communication expression> ::=
       <variable> "←" <object expression> <message> "."
<asynchronous message transmission> ::= <object expression> <message> "&" "."
<asynchronous message communication> ::=
        <variable> "←" <object expression> <message> "&" "."
<reply message transmission expression> ::= "↑" <object expression> "."
<message> ::= <selector> {<actual parameter>}
<dynamic object creation expression> ::= <variable> "←" <new expression> "."
<local variable> ::= <variable>
<formal parameter> ::= <variable>
<temporary variable> ::= <variable>
<selector> ::= <lower case letter>
<actual parameter> ::= <object expression>
<delegate expression> ::= <object expression>
<object expression> ::= <variable> | <object name> | "delegate"
<object name> ::= <ustring>
<variable> ::= <lstring>
<lstring> ::= <lletter> {<letter>}
<ustring> ::= <uletter> {<letter>}
<letter> ::= <lletter> | <uletter>
<lletter> ::=  "a" |  "b" | ··· |  "z"
<uletter> ::=  "A" |  "B" | ··· |  "Z"
```

Fig. 1 The syntax of Mono.

Fig. 2. Metaexpressions of a program are shown in Fig. 3.

3.2 Object and Message

The interaction among objects is realized by means of message passing. A message m consists of a message selector s and a sequence of *object expressions* n^*.

A receiver object receives a message and performs for the message sequentially. In contrast to ABCL/1 and Orient84/K, there are no prioritized messages. The receiver object interprets a script corresponding with the message's selector. A script that consists of a sequence of *action expressions* is called a method. *Action expressions* are (1) the *dynamic object creation expression* that enables us to create an object at runtime, and (2) *message expressions* that specify sending a message to an object. A method name is equivalent to a selector's name. For example, the

<program> : $\mathit{prog} \in \mathbf{Prog}$
<static object creation expression> : $\mathit{sdef} \in \mathbf{SDef}$
<object definition> : $\mathit{def} \in \mathbf{Def}$
<method> : $m \in \mathbf{Method}$
<action expression> : $c \in \mathbf{Exp}$
<local variable> : $i \in \mathbf{Var}$
<formal parameter> : $a \in \mathbf{Var}$
<temporary variable> : $t \in \mathbf{Var}$
<object name> : $O \in \mathbf{Name}$
<variable> : $x \in \mathbf{Var}$
<selector> : $s \in \mathbf{Sel}$
<actual parameter> : $n \in \mathbf{Term}$
<delegate expression> : $d \in \mathbf{Name}$
<object expression> : $v \in \mathbf{Term}$

Fig. 2 Metavariables in `Mono`.

$$
\begin{aligned}
\mathit{prog} &\equiv \mathit{sdef}^* \\
\mathit{sdef} &\equiv O\texttt{::}\mathit{def}\texttt{(}d\ v^*\texttt{)} \\
\mathit{def} &\equiv \texttt{[(}i^*\texttt{)}\ \left\{m_i^*\right\}_i\texttt{]} \\
m_i &\equiv \texttt{((}s_i\ a_i^*\texttt{)}\ \texttt{(}t_i^*\texttt{)}\ c_i^*\texttt{)}
\end{aligned}
$$

Fig. 3 Metaexpressions of a program.

selector `new`'s method is method `new`.

In an object, a method can refer to its instance variables i^*, the method's formal parameters a^*, and temporary variables t^*. The object's instance variables are referred to by all methods in the object. The execution of a method means that message parameters are assigned to the method's formal parameters and *action expressions* are executed.

It should be emphasized that a variable keeps the object name of an object instead of keeping the object itself, and a message may contain object names. However, we sometimes say a variable keeps an object or keeps a value informally.

3.3 Delegation

One of the key features in object-oriented language is the inheritance or delegation mechanisms. Those mechanisms allow a programmer to program reusable software. In the inheritance and delegation mechanisms, if the method for a message is not defined in a class or an object, another class named a superclass or object named a delegation object is responsible for that message.

In the inheritance mechanism, a subclass can directly refer to and assign a value to a variable defined in its superclass. However, a variable defined in a delegated object cannot be directly referred to by the delegation object in the delegation mechanism. Instead, it can be realized by passing messages. In the delegation mechanism, a delegation object can be changed dynamically and some objects may share the same delegation object.

`Mono` provides the delegation mechanism because it is a more basic mechanism than the inheritance mechanism. A virtual variable `delegate` is introduced in order to point to a delegation object. If an object receives a message whose method is not defined in the object, the message is automatically forwarded to a delegation object denoted by the `delegate` variable.

3.4 Execution of a Program

Program *prog* is a sequence of *static object creation expressions*, *sdef**. A program includes a *static object creation expression* that creates object `Start`. The execution is started when the `init` message is sent to the `Start` object by the runtime routine.

3.5 Object Creation

There are two means of the object creation: *static object creation expressions* and *dynamic object creation expressions.* A *static object creation expression* is only evaluated at compile time, whereas a *dynamic object creation expression* is evaluated at runtime.

Both *static* and *dynamic object creation expressions* have the object creation form:

$$def\ (d\ v^*)$$

When this form is evaluated, a new object is created based on the object definition *def*. The new object has a delegation variable where an object name specified by *d* is stored and instance variables whose initial values are specified by v^*.

3.5.1 Static Object Creation

The following form is a *static object creation expression:*

$$O::def(d\ v^*)$$

When this expression is evaluated at compile time, an object is created with an object name *O*.

3.5.2 Dynamic Object Creation

The following form is a *dynamic object creation expression:*

$$x \leftarrow def\ (d\ v^*)\ .$$

After the execution of this expression, an object name that denotes an object created is stored in variable *x*.

3.6 Message Expression

In terms of message expressions, Mono provides (1) synchronous message transmission, (2) asynchronous message transmission, (3) synchronous message communication, and (4) asynchronous message communication.

In asynchronous message transmission and asynchronous message communication, it is significant whether or not the order of messages sent is preserved at the receiver. Communication that preserves the order is called *ordered communication*, while communication that does not preserve the order is called *arbitrarily ordered communication* in this paper.

For example, an object sends another object message M_2 after sending M_1. In *ordered communication*, the receiver object receives message M_2 after receiving M_1, while in *arbitrarily ordered communication*, the receiver object receives messages in arbitrary order.

In Mono, *arbitrarily ordered communication* is employed. The semantics of message expressions based on *ordered communication* is presented in the appendix.

3.6.1 Synchronous Message Transmission

In synchronous message transmission, the sender object has to wait until the receiver object receives the message. As shown below, a message whose selector is s and its parameters are n^* is sent to object r synchronously. More precisely, the message is sent to an object indicated by an object name stored in r because r denotes an object name. In short, we denote object r in the rest of this paper:

$$r\ s\ n^*\ .$$

3.6.2 Synchronous Message Communication

Synchronous message communication allows us to send a message to a receiver object and get a result from the receiver. The sender has to wait until the result is available. In the following example, the sender object sends object r a message whose selector is s and whose parameters are n^*, and stores the return value in variable x:

$$x \leftarrow r\ s\ n^*\ .$$

3.6.3 Asynchronous Message Transmission

In asynchronous message transmission, after sending a message to a receiver the sender object can execute the subsequent expressions regardless of the receiver receiving the message. In the following example, a message whose selector is s and whose arguments are n^* is sent to object r asynchronously:

$$r\ s\ n^*\ \&\ .$$

3.6.4 Asynchronous Message Communication

Asynchronous message communication allows us to send a message asynchronously to a receiver object and receive asynchronously its reply message. An example is the following:

$$x \leftarrow r\ s\ n^*\&\ .$$

This example shows that a message, in which a selector is s and its parameters are n^*, is sent to object r asynchronously. After sending the message, the sender object executes the subsequent expressions regardless of the receiver receiving the message. When a return message arrives from the receiver object r, the return value is stored in variable x.

The sender object may send a message to an object that will be the result value from the receiver even when the result message has not been received by the sender. When the sender object has not received the result message, all messages to the result object are enqueued into a message queue corresponding with variable x. After the return object is established, the messages enqueued are sent to the return object.

3.6.5 Reply Message Transmission

In the reply message transmission, the receiver object sends back an object to the sender object. The following example shows that an object name stored in x is sent back to the sender:

$$\uparrow x \, .$$

3.7 Example

A program example is shown in Fig. 4. In this example, object `Object` is predefined by the system. Object `Window` has a method `new` where an object that has methods `put` and `get` is created, and the object name of the created object is sent back to the sender.

In object `Obj`, methods `init`, `loopback`, `put`, and `get` are defined. When a message whose selector is `init` is received by object `Obj`, `Obj` initializes its internal state where the result value from `Window` is set to `w`.

When a message whose selector is `loopback` is received, the message's parameter is returned to the sender. When a message whose selector is `put` is received, the `put` message is synchronously sent to an object denoted by `w`. When a message whose selector is `get` is received, the `get` message is sent to an object denoted by `w`, and the result value is received synchronously. Then the result value is sent back to the sender.

Object `Text` only accepts the message `init`.

4 Process Algebra Model ECCS

In this section, process algebra model ECCS is defined. ECCS is an extension of CCS (Calculi of Communicating System) [3], and it specifies the execution of programs written in `Mono`.

The concurrent execution model of CCS is that each process has its own state and produces events. There are two types of events: external and internal events. External events are classified into two types: input and output events. Suppose that a process produces an input event and another process produces an output event where both event names are the same. The two processes may synchronize, and the value may be passed from the output event to the input event. Thus, an event is a unit of synchronized communication. Event names are constants in CCS,

```
;;; The definition of Window
Window :: [()
          ((new) (t)
            t ← [()
                  ((put x ) ···    )
                  ((get) (y) ···
                      ↑ y .)]  (Object)
            ↑ t .)]  (Object)
;;; The definition of Obj.
Obj :: [(w)
        ((init) ()
         w ← Window new .)
        ((loopback x) ↑ x .)
        ((put x) () w put x & .)
        ((get) (y)
         y ← w get.
         ↑ y .)]  (Object Object)
;;; The definition of Text.
Text :: [(v)
         ((init) () ... )](Object)
;;; The definition of Start
Start ::  [()
          ((init) ()
            Obj init.
            Obj loopback Text.
            ··· )] (Object)
```

Fig. 4 Simple example.

so that a process cannot communicate with a specified process dynamically though a process can communicate with an unspecified process. In other words, when a process produces an input event and other processes produce an output event where event names are the same, which of these other processes can communicate with the process producing the input event is nondeterministic.

The characteristics of communication of Mono different from CCS are (1) an object communicates with another object which is dynamically decided by the sender, (2) a message may contain objects in Mono while a message can not contain a process in CCS, and (3) an object may communicate with another object that comes via a message. Mono is not capable of communication with an unspecified object but is capable of communication with any specified object dynamically.

Let us consider the relation between Mono and CCS. While we can map an object in Mono to a process in CCS, communication cannot be mapped because of the semantics gap. Thus, we introduce ECCS, an extension of CCS, in order to define the semantics of Mono. In ECCS, an event name in CCS is extended so that an event name has parameters.

4.1 Syntax and Metanotation

The syntax of ECCS is shown in Fig. 5. Let us define metanotations used in ECCS. We use a set BExp of behavior expressions and B as a member of BExp. Let Rec be a set of recursion definitions and p be a member of Rec. We use a set EventExp of event expressions and F as a member of EventExp. We use a set Name of event names and e as a member of Name. Let Event be a set of events

```
<event> ::= <external event> | <internal event>
<external event> ::= <input event> | <output event>
<internal event> ::= tau
<input event> ::= <extended event name> "?" <event parameter>
<output event> ::= <extended event name> "!" <event parameter>
<event mode> ::= "!" | "?"
<event parameter> ::= [ "(" {<constant>} ")" ]
<extended event name> ::= <event name> <extended event name parameter>
<extended event name parameter> ::= [ "[" {<constant>} "]" ]

<program> ::= <behavior expression>
<behavior expression> ::= nil | <event expression> "." <behavior expression>
          | <behavior expression> "+" <behavior expression>
          | <behavior expression> "|" <behavior expression>
          | <recursive behavior expression>  | <recursion call expression>
<recursive behavior expression> ::= <recursion definition> "(" {<term>}")"
<recursion definition expression> ::=
          "[" "rec " "P" "(" {<variable>} ")" <behavior expression> "]"
<recursion call expression> ::= "P" "(" {<term>} ")"
<event expression> ::= <internal event expression> | <external even expression>
<internal event expression> ::= tau
<external event expression> ::= <output event expression> | <input event expression>
<output event expression> ::= <event expression> "!" [ "(" {<term>} ")" ]
<input event expression> ::= <event expression> "?" [ "(" {<variable>} ")" ]
<event expression> ::= <event name> [ "[" {<term>} "]" ]
<event name> ::= <letter> {<letter>}
<term>     ::= <constant> | <variable>
<constant> ::= "#" <letter> {<letter>}
<variable> ::= <letter> {<letter>} [ {<number>} ]
<letter> ::= <lowercase letter> | <uppercase letter>
<number> ::= "0" | "1" | ··· | "9"
<lowercase letter> ::= "a" | "b" | ··· | "z"
<uppercase letter> ::= "A" | "B" | ··· | "Z"
```

Fig. 5 The syntax of ECCS.

and E be a member of EVENT. Let VAL be a set of constants and c be a member of VAL. We use a set VAR of variables and x and y as members of VAR. We use a set TERM of terms and t as a member of TERM.

Now we can define metavariables for nonterminal symbols shown in Fig. 6.

4.2 Event and Event Expression

A behavior expression specifying an event is called an event expression. An event expression is an internal or external event expression. An internal event expression is specified by tau. An extended event expression consists of an event name expression, an event mode, and event parameters. An event mode is an input event

<behavior expression>	: $B \in \text{BEXP}$
<recursion definition>	: $p \in \text{REC}$
<event expression>	: $F \in \text{EVENTEXP}$
<event name>	: $e \in \text{NAME}$
<event>	: $E \in \text{EVENT}$
<constant>	: $c \in \text{VAL}$
<variable>	: $x, y \in \text{VAR}$
<term>	: $t \in \text{TERM}$

Fig. 6 Metavariables.

mode "?" or output event mode "!". An example of an external event expression is "put[x]!(y)" where "put[x]" is an extended event name expression, "!" is the input event mode, and "(y)" is an event parameter.

If an extended event name expression contains variables, those variables must be replaced with constants when that event name expression is evaluated. An extended event name expression such that variables are replaced with constants is called an extended event name. For example, "put[#a]" is an extended event name.

Parameters in an input event expression must be variables while parameters in an output event expression must be terms. If a term in an output event expression is a variable, the variable must be replaced with a constant before the expression is evaluated.

An event expression where all variables are replaced with constants is an event. For example, "put[#a]!(#b)" is an event.

If there are input and output events whose extended event names are the same, those events are called complement events. When complement events occur at the same time, processes that produce those events may be synchronized with passing values. At the synchronization, the internal event tau is observed.

4.3 Behavior Expression

A behavior expression specifies a process's action. A behavior expression may consist of event expressions, null expressions "nil", sequence operators ".", choice operators "+", parallel operators "|", recursive behavior expressions, and recursion call expressions. Precedence of three operators is "." "+" "|" in that order. For example,

$$F_1 \,.\, B_1 + F_2 \,.\, B_2 \mid F_3 \,.\, B_3$$

is equivalent to the following expression:

$$((F_1 \,.\, B_1) + (F_2 \,.\, B_2)) \mid (F_3 \,.\, B_3)$$

The semantics of those operators is given in terms of inference rules on event observation. The event observation is expressed as relations between behavior expressions. The transition relation

$$B_1 \xrightarrow{E} B_2$$

means that behavior expression B_1 may produce event E and then become behavior expression B_2.

4.3.1 Scope Rule

The meaning of a variable depends on the occurrence of the variable. Assume the following behavior expressions:

(a) $e[t^*]?(x^*).B$

(b) $e[t_1^*]!(t_2^*).B$

(c) $[\mathsf{rec}\ \mathsf{P}(x^*)B](t^*)$

(d) $\mathsf{P}(t^*)$

In expression (a), variables of terms t^* are references. That is, those variables are replaced with values before the evaluation of the expression. Variables x^* are declarations of variables that are visible within B. That is, those are free variables.

In expression (b), variables of both t_1^* and t_2^* are references. In expression (c), variables of t^* are references, while x^* is declaration of variables that are visible within B. In expression (d), variables of terms t^* are references.

For example, a behavior expression

$$e_1?(\mathsf{x})\ .\ e_2[\mathsf{x}]?(\mathsf{x}\ \ \mathsf{y})\ .\ e_3[\mathsf{x}]!(\mathsf{y}).\mathsf{nil}$$

is equivalent to the following expression:

$$e_1?(\mathsf{a})\ .\ e_2[\mathsf{a}]?(\mathsf{b}\ \ \mathsf{c})\ .\ e_3[\mathsf{b}]!(\mathsf{c}).\mathsf{nil}$$

4.3.2 Null Expression

The "nil" is a behavior expression. When a behavior expression reaches "nil", no events are produced. The "nil" expression specifies either the end of execution or a deadlock.

4.3.3 Sequence Operator

The sequence operator "." : EVENTEXP, BEXP → BEXP defines a sequence of events. For example, the behavior expression "e.nil" is to produce event "e" and then become behavior expression "nil". The semantics of the sequence operator is given by the following inference rule:

$$e[c_1^*]!(c_2^*)\ .\ B \xrightarrow{e[c_1^*]!(c_2^*)} B \qquad (1)$$

$$e[c_1^*]?(x^*)\ .\ B \xrightarrow{e[c_1^*]?(x^*)\{c_2^*/x^*\}} B\{c_2^*/x^*\} \qquad (2)$$

where $\{c_2^*/x^*\}$ is equivalent to $\{c_2^1/x_1, \cdots, c_2^n/x_n\}$, which expresses the substitution of constants $c_2^1, \cdots, c_2^n$ for free variables $x_1, \cdots, x_n$. For example, $e?[c_1^*](x^*)\{c_2^*/x^*\}$ is equivalent to $e?[c_1^*](c_2^*)$.

(1) defines the occurence of behavior expression B after producing event $e[c_1^*]!(c_2^*)$. In (2), an event where constants are substituted for variables x^* is produced and then becomes $B\{c_2^*/x^*\}$, where variables x^* appearing in B are substituted by c_2^*.

4.3.4 Choice Operator

The choice operator "+" is an operator : BExp, BExp → BExp that defines producing alternative events. For example, the behavior expression "$E_1.E_2.\mathsf{nil} + E_1.E_3.\mathsf{nil}$ " means that the event sequence "$E_1.E_2$" or "$E_1.E_3$" is produced and the behavior expression becomes "nil".

The inference rule for the choice operator is as follows:

$$\frac{B_1 \xrightarrow{E} B_1'}{B_1 + B_2 \xrightarrow{E} B_1'} \qquad \frac{B_2 \xrightarrow{E} B_2'}{B_1 + B_2 \xrightarrow{E} B_2'}$$

Let $\sum B_i$ express $B_1 + B_2 + \cdots$.

4.3.5 Parallel Operator

The parallel operator is a function : BExp, BExp → BExp that expresses parallel execution of processes. Let us consider the following behavior expression:

$$e_1[c_1]?(x_1).e_2[c_2]?(x_1).\mathsf{nil} \mid e_1[c_1]!(c_2).e_3[c_2]?(x_2).\mathsf{nil}$$

Let the left-hand side of "|" be process 1 and the right-hand side of "|" be process 2. Assume that there are only constants c_1 and c_2. Then both processes may produce the following events independently:

$$e_1[c_1]?(x_1).e_2[c_2]?(x_1).\mathsf{nil} \xrightarrow{e_1[c_1]?(c_1)} e_2[c_2]?(c_1).\mathsf{nil} \tag{3}$$

$$e_1[c_1]?(x_1).e_2[c_2]?(x_1).\mathsf{nil} \xrightarrow{e_1[c_1]?(c_2)} e_2[c_2]?(c_2).\mathsf{nil} \tag{4}$$

$$e_1[c_1]!(c_2).e_3[c_2]?(x_2).\mathsf{nil} \xrightarrow{e_1[c_1]!(c_2)} e_3[c_2]?(x_2).\mathsf{nil} \tag{5}$$

In (3), process 1 produces event $e_1[c_1]?(c_1)$, which is the result of the substitution of c_1 for x_1 in $e_1[c_1]?(x_1)$. In (4), process 1 produces event $e_1[c_1]?(c_2)$, which is the result of the substitution of c_2 for x_1 in $e_1[c_1]?(x_1)$. In (5), process 2 produces event $e_1[c_1]!(c_2)$.

Thus, there are four possible transitions in the example:

$$e_1[c_1]?(x_1).e_2[c_2]?(x_1).\mathsf{nil} \mid e_1[c_1]!(c_2).e_3[c_2]?(x_2).\mathsf{nil}$$
$$\xrightarrow{\mathsf{tau}} e_2[c_2]?(c_2).\mathsf{nil} \mid e_3[c_2]?(x_2).\mathsf{nil} \tag{6}$$

or

$$\xrightarrow{e_1[c_1]?(c_1)} e_2[c_2]?(c_1).\mathsf{nil} \mid e_1[c_1]!(c_2).e_3[c_2]?(x_2).\mathsf{nil} \tag{7}$$

or

$$\overset{e_1[c_1]?(c_2)}{\longrightarrow} e_2[c_2]?(c_2).\mathsf{nil} \;|\; e_1[c_1]!(c_2).e_3[c_2]?(x_2).\mathsf{nil} \tag{8}$$

or

$$\overset{e_1[c_1]!(c_2)}{\longrightarrow} e_1[c_1]?(x_1).e_2[c_2]?(x_1).\mathsf{nil} \;|\; e_3[c_2]?(x_2).\mathsf{nil} \tag{9}$$

In (6), both processes 1 and 2 are synchronized. That is, processes 1 and 2 produce events such as (4) and (5) simultaneously and the internal event tau is observed. (7), (8), and (9) are cases in which processes are not synchronized.

The parallel operator is defined by the following inference rule:

$$\frac{B_1 \overset{e[c_1^*]?(c_2^*)}{\longrightarrow} B_1' \quad B_2 \overset{e[c_1^*]!(c_2^*)}{\longrightarrow} B_2'}{B_1|B_2 \overset{\mathsf{tau}}{\longrightarrow} B_1'|B_2'}$$

$$\frac{B_1 \overset{e[c_1^*]!(c_2^*)}{\longrightarrow} B_1' \quad B_2 \overset{e[c_1^*]?(c_2^*)}{\longrightarrow} B_2'}{B_1|B_2 \overset{\mathsf{tau}}{\longrightarrow} B_1'|B_2'}$$

$$\frac{B_1 \overset{e[c_1^*]!(c_2^*)}{\longrightarrow} B_1'}{B_1|B_2 \overset{e[c_1^*]!(c_2^*)}{\longrightarrow} B_1'|B_2} \qquad \frac{B_2 \overset{e[c_1^*]!(c_2^*)}{\longrightarrow} B_2'}{B_1|B_2 \overset{e[c_1^*]!(c_2^*)}{\longrightarrow} B_1|B_2'}$$

$$\frac{B_1 \overset{e[c_1^*]?(c_2^*)}{\longrightarrow} B_1'}{B_1|B_2 \overset{e[c_1^*]?(c_2^*)}{\longrightarrow} B_1'|B_2} \qquad \frac{B_2 \overset{e[c_1^*]?(c_2^*)}{\longrightarrow} B_2'}{B_1|B_2 \overset{e[c_1^*]?(c_2^*)}{\longrightarrow} B_1|B_2'}$$

4.3.6 Recursive Behavior Expression

The recursive behavior expression expresses the repeated execution of a process. For example, the following behavior expression expresses an event put[#a]!(#b) being produced repeatedly:

[rec P(x y) put[x]!(y) . P(x y)](#a #b)

In this expression, the part [rec P(x y) put[x]!(y) . P(x y)] is called a recursion definition expression, where the last expression P(x y) is called a recursion call expression. The part (#a #b) is called the initialization part of the recursive behavior expression.

It should be emphasized that the recursion call expression is a member of BExp and the sequence operator is an operator : EventExp, BExp → BExp. Thus, the recursive call expression only appears at the tail of a sequence of behavior expressions.

The inference rule of the recursion form is as follows:

$$\frac{B\{c_1/x_1, \cdots, c_n/x_n, [\mathsf{rec}\ \mathsf{P}(x_1, \cdots, x_n)B]/\mathsf{P}\} \overset{E}{\rightarrow} B'}{[\mathsf{rec}\ \mathsf{P}(x_1, \cdots, x_n)B](c_1, \cdots, c_n) \overset{E}{\rightarrow} B'}$$

4.4 Execution of Behavior Expression

A behavior expression defines the sequence of events of a process. The program execution is defined by the transition of the behavior expression in which taus are only observed. In other words, the transition of a behavior expression in which all events are synchronized defines the program execution.

Let us consider the following behavior expressions where three processes concurrently execute:

$$(e_1? \,.\, e_2? \,.\, \mathsf{nil}) \;|\; (e_1! \,.\, e_3! \,.\, \mathsf{nil}) \;|\; (e_2! \,.\, e_3? \,.\, \mathsf{nil})$$

The execution of the behavior expression is the following state transition:

$$\begin{array}{l} (e_1? \,.\, e_2? \,.\, \mathsf{nil}) \;|\; (e_1! \,.\, e_3! \,.\, \mathsf{nil}) \;|\; (e_2! \,.\, e_3? \,.\, \mathsf{nil}) \\ \stackrel{\mathsf{tau}}{\rightarrow} (e_2? \,.\, \mathsf{nil}) \;|\; (e_3! \,.\, \mathsf{nil}) \;|\; (e_2! \,.\, e_3? \,.\, \mathsf{nil}) \\ \stackrel{\mathsf{tau}}{\rightarrow} (\mathsf{nil}) \;|\; (e_3! \,.\, \mathsf{nil}) \;|\; (e_3? \,.\, \mathsf{nil}) \\ \stackrel{\mathsf{tau}}{\rightarrow} (\mathsf{nil}) \;|\; (\mathsf{nil}) \;|\; (\mathsf{nil}) \end{array}$$

5 Transformation from `Mono` to ECCS

In this section the transformation from a program in `Mono` to a behavior expression in ECCS is described. First, we describe an overview of the transformation. Then, the transformation is defined by functions.

5.1 Overview of the Transformation

The basic idea of the transformation is that message communication in `Mono` is expressed by events in ECCS. For example, let us consider the following action in `Mono`: Object `Start` sends object `Obj` a message in which the selector is `loopback` and parameter is `Text`. Object `Obj` receives the message and sends back a reply message containing `Text` to object `Start`.

In ECCS, the action: "Object `Start` receives a message where the selector is `loopback` and parameter is `Text`." is expressed as follows:

loopback[#Obj]!(#Start #Text)

The extended event name loopback[#Obj] expresses the message selector and the receiver name while event parameters #Start and #Text express the sender object name and the message argument.

The action: "Object `Obj` received a message from object `Start`. The message contains the `loopback` selector and the `Text` parameter," is expressed as follows:

loopback[#Obj]?(#Start #Text)

The action: "Object `Obj` sends back a reply message to the object `Start`. The reply message contains `Text` ," is translated into the following ECCS expression:

reply[#Start #Obj]!(#Text)

and the action: "Object `Start` receives the reply message from object `Obj`," is translated into the following ECCS expression:

reply[#Start #Obj]?(#Text)

In summary, the following observation specifies the execution of all examples in this subsection:

$$\begin{array}{ll} \text{Object } \texttt{Start}: & \mathsf{loopback[\#Obj]!(\#Start\ \#Text)\ .\ reply[\#Start\ \#Obj]?(\#Text)} \\ \text{Object } \texttt{Obj}: & \mathsf{loopback[\#Obj]?(\#Start\ \#Text)\ .\ reply[\#Start\ \#Obj]!(\#Text)} \end{array} \quad (10)$$

Now we define the `loopback` method in object `Obj`:

(`(loopback x)` () ↑ `x` .)

The possible event sequence produced by the translated expression must include the event sequence in (10). Thus, we define the following expression:

loopback[r]?(s x0) . reply[s r]!(x0)

Indeed, if the variable r is bound with #Obj, the expression may produce the event sequence in (10).

In `Mono` an object performs for one incoming message repeatedly. In order to express such a capability in ECCS, an object is defined by the recursion definition expression and each behavior expression corresponding to a method contains tail recursion. Instance variables are translated into parameters of a recursion definition expression. The translation of the delegation mechanism is realized as follows: Each undefined method is translated into an expression that receives a message, sends it to the delegation object, and calls its own recursion definition expression.

Let us consider the program in Fig. 4. Object `Obj` has the delegation object `Object` and has methods `init`, `loopback`, `put`, and `get`, but the `new` method is not defined in the object `Obj`. The following recursive behavior expression expresses object `Obj`:

[rec P(r d w0)
  init[r]?(s x0) . ⋯ . P(r d w0) (11)
 + loopback[r]?(s x0) . ⋯ . P(r d w0) (12)
 + put[r]?(s x0) . ⋯ . P(r d w0) (13)
 + get[r]?(s) . ⋯ . P(r d w0) (14)
 + new[r]?(s x) .new[d]!(s x) . P(r d w0) (15)
 ](#Obj #Object #Object)

where the **Sel** set of selectors in Fig. 4 is

$$\mathbf{Sel} \equiv \{\texttt{init}, \texttt{loopback}, \texttt{put}, \texttt{get}, \texttt{new}\}$$

Variables r, d, and w0 specify the receiver object, delegation object, and instance variable, respectively. (11), (12), (13), and (14) specify methods `init`, `loopback`, `put`, and `get`, respectively. (15) expresses that when a `new` message is received, the message is sent to a delegation object specified by the d variable.

5.2 Transformation Details

In the previous subsection, an overview of the transformation from `Mono` to ECCS is described informally. Here, we define the whole transformation formally. The basic elements in `Mono` corresponding with ECCS are as follows:

`Mono`		ECCS
Variable	$\rightarrow$	Variable
Object Name	$\rightarrow$	Constant
Selector	$\rightarrow$	Event Name
Method	$\rightarrow$	Behavior Expression
Object Creation Expression	$\rightarrow$	Recursion Definition Expression
Program	$\rightarrow$	Behavior Expression

The above transformations are defined as the following functions:

$$\begin{aligned}
\mathcal{N} &: \textbf{Name} \rightarrow \textrm{VAL} \\
\mathcal{S} &: \textbf{Sel} \rightarrow \textrm{NAME} \\
\mathcal{H} &: \textbf{Var} \rightarrow \textrm{VAR} \\
\mathcal{G} &: \textrm{VAR} \rightarrow \textrm{VAR} \\
\mathcal{L}_j &: \textbf{Method} \times \textbf{Var} \rightarrow \textrm{VAL} \\
\mathcal{R}_j &: \textbf{Method} \times \textbf{Var} \rightarrow \textrm{VAR} \\
\mathcal{T}_j &: \textbf{Method} \times \textbf{Term} \rightarrow \textrm{TERM} \\
\mathcal{O} &: \textbf{Def} \rightarrow \textrm{REC} \\
\mathcal{D} &: \textbf{SDef} \rightarrow \textrm{BEXP} \\
\mathcal{M} &: \textbf{Method} \rightarrow \textrm{BEXP} \\
\mathcal{M}_j &: \textbf{Method} \rightarrow \textrm{BEXP} \\
\mathcal{P} &: \textbf{Prog} \rightarrow \textrm{BEXP} \\
\mathcal{C}_j &: \textbf{Method} \rightarrow \textbf{Exp}
\end{aligned}$$

We use the following short notation:

$$\begin{aligned}
\mathcal{N}^*[O^*] &= \left\{\mathcal{N}[O_i]\right\}_i \\
\mathcal{H}^*[\mathrm{x}^*] &= \left\{\mathcal{H}[\mathrm{x}_i]\right\}_i \\
\mathcal{L}_j^*[m, \mathrm{x}^*] &= \left\{\mathcal{L}_j[m, \mathrm{x}_i]\right\}_i \\
\mathcal{R}_j^*[m, \mathrm{x}^*] &= \left\{\mathcal{R}_j[m, \mathrm{x}_i]\right\}_i \\
\mathcal{T}_j^*[m, \mathrm{v}^*] &= \left\{\mathcal{T}_j[m, \mathrm{v}_i]\right\}_i
\end{aligned}$$

Function $\mathcal{C}_i$ is a function that returns the ith expression in a method, i.e.,

$$\mathcal{C}_i[m] = c_i$$

5.2.1 Transformation

Transformations for object names, selectors, variables, and object expressions are given as follows:

[**Object Name** O]

Transformation function $\mathcal{N}$ is to transform an object name in `Mono` to a constant in ECCS. The transformed constant is the object name followed by #. For example,

$$\mathcal{N}[\![\texttt{Window}]\!] = \#\mathsf{Window}$$

[**Selector** s]

Transformation function $\mathcal{S}$ is to transform a selector in `Mono` into an event name in ECCS. The transformed event name has the same letters in the selector, but in a different font. For example,

$$\mathcal{S}[\![\texttt{new}]\!] = \mathsf{new}$$

[**Variable** x]

A variable in `Mono` is dynamically bound to an object, while a variable in ECCS cannot be bound after the value bounds the variable. In other words, the assignment of a variable in ECCS satisfies the single assignment rule.

In order to explain the transformation for a variable, let us consider the following program:

$$\texttt{x} \leftarrow \texttt{Window new.} \tag{16}$$

$$\texttt{x} \leftarrow \texttt{x get.} \tag{17}$$

$$\texttt{x init.} \tag{18}$$

Variable `x` in (16) (we call such a variable a "left-hand-side variable") must keep the same object of variable `x` in the right-hand side of "←" (we call such a variable a "right-hand-side variable") in (17), while variable `x` in (16) may keep the different object of variable `x` in the left-hand side in (17). Variable `x` on the left-hand side of "←" in (17) must keep the same object as variable `x` in (18). Thus, the following program is equivalent to the previous program and satisfies the single assignment rule:

```
x1 ← Window new.
x2 ← x1 get.
x2 init.
```

In order to generate such variables to keep the single assignment rule for ECCS, functions $\mathcal{L}_j$ and $\mathcal{R}_j$ are defined. $\mathcal{L}_j$ is a function that generates a left-hand-side variable of the jth action expression in a method m, while $\mathcal{R}_j$ is a function that generates a right-hand-side variable of the jth action expression in a method m.

Auxiliary functions $\mathcal{H}$ and $\mathcal{G}$ are defined. Function $\mathcal{H}$ generates an ECCS variable such that the letters are the same letters of a variable in `Mono`, but the number "0" is added. For example, `x` is transformed as follows:

$$\mathcal{H}[\![\texttt{x}]\!] = \mathsf{x0}$$

Function $\mathcal{G}$ generates a new ECCS variable from a variable generated by $\mathcal{H}$. For example,

$$\mathcal{G}[\mathsf{v314}] = \mathsf{v315}$$

$\mathcal{R}_j$ and $\mathcal{L}_j$ are defined as follows:

$$\begin{aligned}
\mathcal{L}_0[m,x] &= \mathcal{H}[x] \\
\mathcal{L}_j[m,x] &= \begin{cases} \mathcal{G}[\mathcal{L}_{j-1}[m,x]] & \text{if } x \text{ appears at the left hand side of ``}\leftarrow\text{'' in } \mathcal{C}_j(m) \\ \mathcal{L}_{j-1}[m,x] & \text{otherwise} \end{cases} \\
\mathcal{R}_j[m,x] &= \mathcal{L}_{j-1}[m,x]
\end{aligned}$$

[**Object Expression** v]

The $\mathcal{T}_j$ is a transformation function that transforms an object expression of the jth action expression in a method into a term in ECCS:

$$\mathcal{T}_j[m,x] = \begin{cases} \mathcal{N}[x] & \text{if } x \in \textbf{Name} \\ \mathcal{R}_j[m,x] & \text{if } x \in \textbf{Var} \end{cases}$$

5.2.2 From Object Definition to Recursion Definition Expression

In this subsection, we first define function $\mathcal{O} : \textbf{Def} \rightarrow \text{REC}$, which transforms an object definition into a recursion definition expression. Then, function $\mathcal{D} : \textbf{SDef} \rightarrow \text{BEXP}$, which transforms a static object definition expression into a behavior expression, is given.

Function $\mathcal{O}$ is defined as follows:

$$\mathcal{O}[\ \texttt{[(}i^*\texttt{)}\ \left\{\texttt{((}s_i\ \ a_i^*\texttt{)(}t_i^*\texttt{)}\ \ c_i^*\texttt{)}\right\}_i\texttt{]}] =$$

$$[\mathsf{rec\ P(r\ d}\ \mathcal{H}^*[i^*])$$

$$\sum_i \mathcal{M}[m_i] \tag{19}$$

$$+ \sum_{e \in \text{NAME} - \cup_i \{\mathcal{S}[s_i]\}} \left\{e[\mathsf{r}]?(\mathsf{s}\ \mathcal{H}^*[\mathsf{a}^*])\ .\ e[\mathsf{d}]!(\mathsf{s}\ \mathcal{H}^*[\mathsf{a}^*])\ .\ \mathsf{P(r\ d}\ \mathcal{H}^*[i^*])\right\}] \tag{20}$$

In $(\mathsf{r\ d}\ \mathcal{H}^*[i^*])$ of the recursion definition expression, the first parameter r is a variable that expresses an object name, the second parameter d is a variable expressing a delegation object name, and the rest of the parameters $\mathcal{H}^*[i^*]$ specify instance variables of an object.

(19) specifies behavior expressions that are transformed from methods. Function $\mathcal{M}$ is defined later.

(20) expresses the delegation mechanism. All events except for events specified in (19) are specified so that the messages corresponding to those events are received. The expression denotes the fact that those messages are sent to the delegation object.

Now we can define $\mathcal{D}$: **SDef** $\to$ BEXP by using $\mathcal{O}$:

$$\mathcal{D}[O :: def \quad (d\ v^*)] = \mathcal{O}[def](\mathcal{N}[O]\ \mathcal{N}[d]\ \mathcal{N}^*[v^*])$$

where the recursion definition expression is given by applying $\mathcal{O}$, and the initialization part in the recursive behavior expression is given by $(\mathcal{N}[O]\ \mathcal{N}[d]\ \mathcal{N}^*[v^*])$.

5.2.3 From Method to Behavior Expression

Transformation function $\mathcal{M}$: **Method** $\to$ BEXP is to transform a method to a behavior expression. The auxiliary function $\mathcal{M}_j$: **Method** $\to$ BEXP is defined so that the expressions from the jth action expression in a method are transformed into behavior expressions. Functions $\mathcal{M}$,$\mathcal{M}_j$ are defined as follows:

$$\mathcal{M}[m_i] = \mathcal{S}[s_i][\mathsf{r}]?(\mathsf{s}\ \mathcal{H}^*[a_i^*])\ .\ \mathcal{M}_1[m_i] \tag{21}$$

$$\mathcal{M}_j[m_i] = \begin{cases} \mathcal{S}[s][\mathcal{T}_j[m_i, r]]!(\mathsf{r}\ \mathcal{T}_j^*[n^*])\ .\ \mathcal{M}_{j+1}[m_i] & \text{if } \mathcal{C}_j[m_i] \equiv r\ \ s\ n^*\ . \quad (M1) \\ \mathcal{S}[s][\mathcal{T}_j[m_i, r]]!(\mathsf{r}\ \mathcal{T}_j^*[n^*])\ .\ \mathsf{reply}[\mathsf{r}\ \mathcal{T}_j[m_i, r]]?(\mathcal{L}_j[m_i, x])\ .\ \mathcal{M}_{j+1}[m_i] & \text{if } \mathcal{C}_j[m_i] \equiv x\ \leftarrow\ r\ s\ n^*\ . \quad (M2) \\ \mathcal{S}[s][\mathcal{T}_j[m_i, r]]!(\mathsf{r}\ \mathcal{T}_j^*[n^*])\ .\ \mathsf{nil}\ \mid\ \mathcal{M}_{j+1}[m_i] & \text{if } \mathcal{C}_j[m_i] \equiv r\ \ s\ n^*\ \&. \quad (M3) \\ \mathsf{getid}?(\mathcal{L}_j[m_i, x])\ . \\ (\ \ (\mathcal{S}[s][\mathcal{T}_j[m_i, r]]!(\mathcal{L}_j[m_i, x]\ \mathcal{T}_j^*[n^*])\ . \\ \quad \mathsf{reply}[\mathcal{L}_j[m_i, x]\ \mathcal{T}_j[m_i, r]]?(\mathsf{c}). \\ \quad \mathcal{O}[[\ ()\ \ ]](\mathcal{L}_j\ [m_i\ , x]\ \mathsf{c})) \\ \ \mid\ \mathcal{M}_{j+1}[m_i]) & \text{if } \mathcal{C}_j[m_i] \equiv x\ \leftarrow\ r\ s\ n^*\ \&\ . \quad (M4) \\ \mathsf{reply}[\mathsf{s\ r}]!(\mathcal{T}_j[m_i, y])\ .\ \mathcal{M}_{j+1}[m_i] & \text{if } \mathcal{C}_j[m_i] \equiv\uparrow y\ . \quad (M5) \\ \mathsf{getid}?(\mathcal{L}_j[m_i, x])\ .\ (\mathcal{M}_{j+1}[m_i]\ \mid\ \mathcal{O}[def](\mathcal{L}_j[m_i, x]\ \mathcal{N}[d]\ \mathcal{N}^*[v^*])) & \text{if } \mathcal{C}_j[m_i] \equiv x \leftarrow def\ \ (d\ v^*)\ . \quad (M6) \\ \mathsf{P}(\mathsf{r\ d}\ \mathcal{R}_j^*[i^*]) & \text{if } \mathcal{C}_j[m_i] \equiv \phi \quad (M7) \end{cases}$$

In (21), extended event expression $\mathcal{S}[s_i][\mathsf{r}]?(\mathsf{s}\ \mathcal{H}^*[a_i^*])$ specifies receiving a message whose selector is specified by s_i and whose parameters are specified by s and $\mathcal{H}^*[a_i^*]$. In the expression, r is a variable specifying a receiver object and s is a variable bound by the object name of a sender object.

(M1) to (M6) in $\mathcal{M}_j$ are the transformations for behavior expressions in a method. (M7) specifies a tail recursion at the end of the transformed expression so that an object performs for another message.

[**Synchronous Message transmission** $r\ s\ n^*$.]

The transformation for a synchronous message transmission expression is specified in (M1). The transformed expression includes a behavior expression that produces an event corresponding to the selector of the message.

[**Synchronous Message Communication** $x \leftarrow r\ s\ n^*$.]

(M2) specifies the transformation for a synchronous message communication. The reply event is added in order to specify receiving a reply message.

[**Asynchronous Message transmission** $r\ s\ n^*$ & .]

(M3) is defined for an asynchronous message transmission expression. This transformation tells us that two processes are created so that the left-hand-side process is responsible for message transmission while the right-hand-side process is responsible for the subsequent actions in Mono.

[**Asynchronous Message Communication** $x \leftarrow r\ s\ n^*$& .]

The transformation for an asynchronous message communication expression is specified in (M4). In order to explain the transformation, we extract (M4) and apply function $\mathcal{O}$ to the expression

$$\mathsf{getid}?(\mathcal{L}_j[m_i, \mathrm{x}]) \ . \tag{22}$$

$$(\ \mathcal{S}[s][\mathcal{T}_j[m_i, \mathrm{r}]]!(\mathcal{L}_j[m_i, \mathrm{x}]\ \mathcal{T}_j^*[n^*])\ .\ \mathsf{reply}[\mathcal{L}_j[m_i, \mathrm{x}]\ \mathcal{T}_j[m_i, \mathrm{r}]]?(\mathrm{c})\ . \tag{23}$$

$$[\mathsf{rec}\ \mathsf{P}(\mathsf{r}\ \mathsf{d})\ \sum_{e \in \mathrm{NAME}} \{e[\mathsf{r}]?(\mathsf{s}\ \mathsf{a}^*)\ .\ e[\mathsf{d}]!(\mathsf{s}\ \mathsf{a}^*)\ .\ P(\mathsf{r}\ \mathsf{d})\}](\mathcal{L}_j[m_i, \mathrm{x}]\ \mathsf{c}) \tag{24}$$

$$|\ \mathcal{M}_{j+1}[m_i]\ ) \tag{25}$$

We assume that there is a process that produces getid!(c) such that a new constant c is generated. When event getid is synchronized in (22), a new constant is given.

A new constant at (22) is used as an object name for a return value from object r. Processes expressed by expressions (23) and (25) are created. Expression (23) specifies that message s is sent to object r and the reply message is received at variable c. (24) shows that all messages are received as if it is a return object from object r, and then those are sent to the object specified by variable c.

The process specified in (25) is responsible for the rest of the execution of the method.

[**Reply Message Transmission** $\uparrow\ y$.]

(M5) is for the reply message expression.

[**Dynamic Object Creation** $x \leftarrow$ *def* $(d\ v^*)$.]

(M6) specifies the transformation for a dynamic object creation expression. A recursion definition expression is generated by applying function $\mathcal{O}$.

5.2.4 From Program to Behavior Expression

We can now define the function from a program in Mono to a behavior expression in ECCS, $\mathcal{P}$: **Prog** $\rightarrow$ BEXP:

$$\mathcal{P}[prog] = \begin{cases} \mathcal{O}[sdef] | \mathcal{P}[sdef^*] & \text{if } prog \equiv sdef \ \ sdef^* \\ (\mathsf{init}[\#\mathsf{Start}]!(\#\mathsf{System})\ .\ \mathsf{nil}) & \text{if } prog \equiv \phi \end{cases}$$

The $\mathcal{P}$ defines the formal semantics of `Mono`.

6 Summary

In this paper, first, the model language `Mono` for object-oriented concurrent programming languages was introduced. Second, the algebraic model ECCS was proposed to define the semantics of `Mono`. Then, the full transformations from `Mono` to ECCS were described. The formal semantics of `Mono` was defined as the transformation from `Mono` to ECCS.

The contribution of this paper is defining the full transformation functions from an object-oriented concurrent programming language with rich features into a process algebra model.

Acknowledgments. The authors wish to express their thanks to the anonymous referees for their valuable comments that have greatly improved this paper.

References

[1] G. A. Agha. *ACTORS*. MIT Press, 1986.

[2] Y. Ishikawa and M. Tokoro. A Concurrent Object-Oriented Knowledge Representation Language Orient84/K: Its Features and Implementation. In *Proc. of OOPSLA-86* (1986), pp. 232–241.

[3] R. Milner. *A Calculus of Communicating Systems*. Lecture Notes in Computer Science, Vol. 92 (1980).

[4] S. Tomura, Y. Ishikawa, K. Futatsugi. Inter Process Communication in a Process Algebraic Language. In Annual Meet. of the Inst. Electronics, Inf. & Comm. Eng. Japan, SD-4-5 (1989)

[5] Y. Yokote and M. Tokoro. Experience and Evolution of ConcurrentSmalltalk. In *Proc. of OOPSLA-87* (1987), pp. 406–415.

[6] A. Yonezawa, J-P Briot, and E. Shibayama. Object-Oriented Concurrent Programming in ABCL/1. In *Proc. of OOPSLA-86* (1986), pp. 258–268.

[7] A. Yonezawa and M. Tokoro, editors. *Object-Oriented Concurrent Programming*. MIT Press, 1987.

Appendix

The Semantics of Ordered Communication

Communication that preserves the arrival order of messages sent is called *ordered communication*, while communication that does not preserve the order is called *arbitrarily ordered communication*. Message communication in `Mono` is *arbitrarily ordered communication*. For example, when an object executes "`Obj init & . Obj loopback Text .`", message `loopback` may be received before `init` is received.

```
[rec P (r d v0)
 (getid?(a) .
    ;;;; Recipient Process
  ([rec P (r a)
     put[#a r]?(s x0) . getid?(b) . ( put[#a r a]!(b s x0) . nil | P(r b))
   + put[#s r]?(s x0) . getid?(b) . ( put[#s r a]!(b s x0) . nil | P(r b))
     ...
   ] (r a)
     ;;;; Arbiter Process
 | [rec P (r a)
     put[#a r a]?(b s x0) . put[r]!(s x0) . P(r b)
   + put[#s r a]?(b s x0) . put[r]!(s x0) . ack[s r]! . P(r b)
     ...
   ] (r a)))
   ;;;; Interpreter Process
 | [rec P (r d v0)
     init[r]?(s) . ··· P(r d v0)
   + loopback[r]?(s x0) . loopback[d]!(s x0) . P(r d v0)
   + new[r]?(s x0) . new[d]!(s x0) . P(r d v0)
   + put[r]?(s x0) . put[d]!(s x0) . P(r d v0)
   + get[r]?(s) . get[d]!(s) . P(r d v0)]]
 (#Text #Object #Object)
```

Fig. 7 The semantics of `Text` in $\texttt{Mono}_{oc}$.

In this appendix, we show the semantics of another `Mono` that is based on *ordered communication* by using ECCS. The `Mono` based on *ordered communication* is called $\texttt{Mono}_{oc}$. In $\texttt{Mono}_{oc}$, the syntax of message expressions is identical with that in the original `Mono`. The informal semantics of $\texttt{Mono}_{oc}$ can be described as follows: A sender object synchronously communicates with a receiver object in order to achieve the ordered communication. To realize asynchronous communication, the receiver object has a communication buffer.

An overview of the transformation from $\texttt{Mono}_{oc}$ to ECCS is described. An object is mapped to three processes, i.e., interpreter, arbiter, and recipient processes. The interpreter process is the same as a process representing an object in the original `Mono`. The recipient process is responsible for receiving messages in the order that the messages were sent. The arbiter process gets a message from the recipient process and passes it to the interpreter process as if the arbiter process represents a buffer. The basic idea is presented in [4].

For example, the semantics of object `Text` is shown in Fig. 7. Assume that the put message is sent. The sender and recipient processes are synchronized at put[#a r] or put[#s r], where #a and #s are constants and are not equal to other constants of objects. #a and #s stand for asynchronous and synchronous types, respectively.

The recipient and arbiter processes are synchronized at put[#a r a] or put[#s r a], where variable a denotes a constant value that represents a ticket. At the synchronization, the recipient gives the arbiter the sender object s, message argument x0, and a constant value b that represents the next ticket. After the arbiter process communicates with the interpreter process, it will be synchronized with the recipient process at put[#a r a] or put[#s r a], where variable a denotes the next ticket. That is, the ticket guarantees the execution order of messages sent.

The arbiter and interpreter processes are synchronized at extended event name put[r], which is the same event in the original `Mono`. In the ordered synchronous message transmission, the arbiter process has to wait for acknowledgment from the interpreter process where extended event name ack[s r] is used after the synchronization. This acknowledgment is not needed in the ordered asynchronous message transmission.

In this way, we can give the semantics of $\mathtt{Mono}_{oc}$. First, function $\mathcal{O}$ is redefined as follows:

$$\mathcal{O}[\ [(i^*)\ \left\{((s_i\ \ a_i^*)(t_i^*)\ \ c_i^*)\right\}_i]] =$$

$$
\begin{array}{l}
[\mathsf{rec\ P(r\ d}\ \mathcal{H}^*[i^*])\\
\quad(\mathsf{getid?(a)}\ .\\
\quad\ (\ [\mathsf{rec\ P(r\ a)}\\
\qquad\qquad \sum\limits_{e\in \text{NAME}} \{e[\mathsf{\#a\ r}]?(\mathsf{s}\ \mathcal{H}^*[\mathsf{a}^*])\ .\ \mathsf{getid?(b)}\ .\ (e[\mathsf{\#a\ r\ a}]!(\mathsf{b\ s}\ \mathcal{H}^*[\mathsf{a}^*])\ .\ \mathsf{nil}|\mathsf{P(r\ b)})\}\\
\qquad\ +\ \sum\limits_{e\in \text{NAME}} \{e[\mathsf{\#s\ r}]?(\mathsf{s}\ \mathcal{H}^*[\mathsf{a}^*])\ .\ \mathsf{getid?(b)}\ .\ (e[\mathsf{\#s\ r\ a}]!(\mathsf{b\ s}\ \mathcal{H}^*[\mathsf{a}^*])\ .\ \mathsf{nil}|\mathsf{P(r\ b)})\}\\
\qquad](\mathsf{r\ a})\\
\quad\ |\ [\mathsf{rec\ P(r\ a)}\\
\qquad\qquad \sum\limits_{e\in \text{NAME}} \{e[\mathsf{\#a\ r}]?(\mathsf{s}\ \mathcal{H}^*[\mathsf{a}^*])\ .\ e[\mathsf{r}]!(\mathsf{s}\mathcal{H}^*[\mathsf{a}^*])\ .\ \mathsf{P(r\ b)}\}\\
\qquad\ +\ \sum\limits_{e\in \text{NAME}} \{e[\mathsf{\#s\ r}]?(\mathsf{s}\ \mathcal{H}^*[\mathsf{a}^*])\ .\ e[\mathsf{r}]!(\mathsf{s}\mathcal{H}^*[\mathsf{a}^*])\ .\mathsf{ack[s\ r]!}\ .\ \mathsf{P(r\ b)}\}\\
\qquad](\mathsf{r\ a})\ )\ )\\
\ |\ [\mathsf{rec\ P(r\ d}\ \mathcal{H}^*[i^*])\\
\qquad(\sum\limits_i \mathcal{M}[m_i]\\
\qquad +\ \sum\limits_{e\in \text{NAME}-\cup_i\{\mathcal{S}[s_i]\}} \left\{e[\mathsf{r}]?(\mathsf{s}\ \mathcal{H}^*[\mathsf{a}^*])\ .\ e[\mathsf{d}]!(\mathsf{s}\ \mathcal{H}^*[\mathsf{a}^*])\ .\ \mathsf{P(r\ d}\ \mathcal{H}^*[i^*])\right\})\\
\qquad]\ ]
\end{array}
$$

The auxiliary function $\mathcal{M}_j$ is redefined, i.e., (M1) to (M4) in $\mathcal{M}_j$ are replaced with the following (m1) to (m4):

[**Synchronous Message Transmission:** $r \quad s \; n^*$.]

After synchronization with the recipient process, event ack[s r] is produced to confirm that the interpreter process has received the message.

$\mathcal{S}[s]$[#s $\mathcal{T}_j[m_i, r]$]!(r $\mathcal{T}_j^*[n^*]$) . ack[s r]? . $\mathcal{M}_{j+1}[m_i]$ (m1)

[**Synchronous Message Communication:** $x \leftarrow r \; s \; n^*$.]

Because the sender process is synchronized with the interpreter process by reply[r $\mathcal{T}_j[m_i, r]$], the arbiter process does not need to be synchronized with the interpreter process by ack[s r]. The sender and recipient processes are synchronized at $\mathcal{S}[s]$[#a $\mathcal{T}_j[m_i, r]$].

$\mathcal{S}[s]$[#a $\mathcal{T}_j[m_i, r]$]!(r $\mathcal{T}_j^*[n^*]$) . reply[r $\mathcal{T}_j[m_i, r]$]?($\mathcal{L}_j[m_i, x]$) . $\mathcal{M}_{j+1}[m_i]$ (m2)

[**Asynchronous Message Transmission:** $r \quad s \; n^*$ &.]

The $\mathcal{S}[s]$[#a $\mathcal{T}_j[m_i, r]$] is used to synchronize with the recipient process.

$\mathcal{S}[s]$[#a $\mathcal{T}_j[m_i, r]$]!(r $\mathcal{T}_j^*[n^*]$) . $\mathcal{M}_{j+1}[m_i]$ (m3)

[**Asynchronous Message Communication:** $x \leftarrow r \; s \; n^*$ & .]

The sender process is synchronized with the recipient process of the receiver by using $\mathcal{S}[s]$[#a $\mathcal{T}_j[m_i, r]$]. Then, two processes are created, i.e, a proxy process to receive the result and a process to continue the execution of the method.

getid?($\mathcal{L}_j[m_i, x]$) .
$\mathcal{S}[s]$[#a $\mathcal{T}_j[m_i, r]$]!($\mathcal{L}_j[m_i, x]$ $\mathcal{T}_j^*[n^*]$) .
(reply[$\mathcal{L}_j[m_i, x]$ $\mathcal{T}_j[m_i, r]$]?(c) .
$\mathcal{O}$[[()]]($\mathcal{L}_j[m_i, x]$ c)
| $\mathcal{M}_{j+1}[m_i]$) (m4)

Initially published in "Computer Software", Vol. 7 No. 2, in Japanese.

Yutaka Ishikawa
Electrotechnical Laboratory
1–1–4 Umezono, Tsukuba
Ibaraki, 305 Japan

Satoru Tomura
Electrotechnical Laboratory
1–1–4 Umezono, Tsukuba
Ibaraki, 305 Japan

Kokichi Futatsugi
Electrotechnical Laboratory
1–1–4 Umezono, Tsukuba
Ibaraki, 305 Japan

Floating-Point Numbers and Real Numbers II

Hiroshi Horiguchi Tsutomu Tayama

1 Introduction

The 8-tuple $(F(M,E), +, -, \cdot, ^{-1}, 0, 1, <)$ (where $F(M,E)$: the set of all binary floating-point numbers, $+, -, \cdot, ^{-1}, 0, 1$: floating-point operations and constants, $<$: total order relation on $F(M,E)$) shall be called the structure of binary floating-point arithmetic. This structure determines the holding probabilities of all axioms for real numbers through probability interpretation. These probabilities serve as one of the indicators that measure the degree that the floating-point numbers of a computer can faithfully represent real numbers in mathematics.

In [1], all axioms for real numbers were interpreted by probability interpretation using the structure of floating-point arithmetic $\boldsymbol{F}(M,E)$, where the M–bit is the length of the mantissa and the E–bit is the length of the exponent. In $\boldsymbol{F}(M,E)$, all operations were entirely introduced by truncation.

In this thesis, all axioms for real numbers are attempted to be interpreted by the structure $\boldsymbol{F_2}(M,E)$ in which all operations are introduced by rounding off on the same underlying set $F(M,E)$. Let us see the effects of changing truncation to round off.

2 The Structure of Floating-Point Round-off Arithmetic

The underlying set $F(M,E)$ is defined as

$$F(M,E) \stackrel{\text{def}}{=} \{\pm(m/2^M) \times 2^\varepsilon \mid -2^{E-1} \leq e < 2^{E-1} \wedge 2^{M-1} \leq m < 2^M\} \cup \{\bar{0}\}$$

On $F(M,E)$, addition, inversion of sign, multiplication, inverse operation when other than zero, zero element, unit element, and order are defined rounding off the $(M+1)$st decimal place.

Addition: The exponents of two numbers are compared. If they are the same, the two mantissas are added as is, and this is then taken to be the mantissa portion. When they are different, the smaller exponent is subtracted from the larger one, and the mantissa portion of the number having the smaller exponent is shifted to the right by the amount of that difference (divided by 2^n when the difference of the exponents is n). At this time, the $(M+1)$st decimal place is rounded off. The sum of the mantissas is then calculated. The exponent portion is taken to be the larger exponent. When the sum of the mantissa portions becomes zero, the sum of the floating-point numbers is taken to be $\bar{0}$. When the sum of the mantissa portions is not zero, this sum is normalized in consideration of rounding off, and if there is no overflow in the exponent portion, that amount is the sum of the two floating-point numbers. When there is overflow, the sum is taken to be the maximum absolute value and is either the maximum value or minimum value, depending on the sign of the mantissa. $\bar{0}$ results when there is underflow in the exponent portion.

ISBN 0–12–037103–0

Inversion of sign: If the sign in front of the mantissa is +, the sign of the floating-point number changes to −, and if the sign in front of the mantissa is −, the sign of the floating-point number changes to +.

Multiplication: Adding the exponents and calculating the product of the mantissas of the two numbers. This is normalized in consideration of rounding off. When there is no overflow in the exponent, this is the product of the two floating-point numbers. The treatment of overflow or underflow in the exponent is the same as above.

Inverse operation: When $(2^{M-1}/2^M) \times 2^1$ exists within $F(M, E)$, this is called a unit element and is represented with $\bar{1}$. When this unit element is present, the inverse element is defined in the following manner: To begin with, $(2^{M-1}/m)$ is calculated and taken to be the mantissa with respect to a positive element $(m/2^M) \times 2^e$, and the exponent is taken to be $1 - e$. The normalized result in consideration of rounding off is the inverse element of that positive element. Overflows and underflows in the exponent are treated as previously mentioned. The inverse element of a negative element is the result of determining the inverse element by inverting the sign and then inverting that sign. An inverse element is not defined for $\bar{0}$.

Zero element: This is the element $\bar{0}$ of $F(M, E)$.

Unit element: This is the element $\bar{1}$ of $F(M, E)$ in case $F(M, E)$ has $\bar{1}$.

Order: As $F(M, E)$ is embedded in the field of rational numbers, the order within that field is used as is.

Therefore,

$$F(M, E) \stackrel{\text{def}}{=} (F(M, E), +, -, \cdot, {}^{-1}, 0, 1, <)$$

is called the structure of (M, E) binary floating-point number round off arithmetic.

Let us examine the probability interpretation of all axioms of real numbers using $F_2(M, E)$. Probability interpretation of an axiom, in the case of Ax. 5 for example, considers the set of all ordered triples (a, b, c) $(a, b, c \in F(M, E))$. The number of those ordered triples n is $|F(M, E)|^3$. Both sides of Ax. 5 are calculated with these ordered triples, and let the number of triples (a, b, c) for which both sides coincide be r. At this time, r/n is the holding probability of Ax. 5. When there are conditional statements within an axiom, these axioms are interpreted with conditional probabilities. For example, in the case of Ax. 15, let n' be the number of ordered triples (a, b, c) that satisfy the condition $a < b$, and let r' be the number of ordered triples (a, b, c) from among those ordered triples for which $a + c < b + c$ holds true, the holding probability of Ax. 15 is r'/n'.

Axioms for the real numbers that are used are described as follows:

Ax. 1. $a \leq a$
Ax. 2. $a \leq b \wedge b \leq a \Rightarrow a = b$
Ax. 3. $a \leq b \wedge b \leq c \Rightarrow a \leq c$
Ax. 4. $a \leq b \vee b \leq a$
Ax. 5. $(a + b) + c = a + (b + c)$
Ax. 6. $a + 0 = a$
Ax. 7. $a + (-a) = 0$
Ax. 8. $a + b = b + a$
Ax. 9. $(ab)c = a(bc)$

Ax. 10. $a1 = a$
Ax. 11. $a \neq 0 \Rightarrow aa^{-1} = 1$
Ax. 12. $ab = ba$
Ax. 13. $(a + b)c = ac + bc$
Ax. 14. $0 \neq 1$
Ax. 15. $a < b \Rightarrow a + c < b + c$
Ax. 16. $a < b \wedge 0 < c \Rightarrow ac < bc$
Ax. 17. Every nonempty subset X that has a lower bound has a greatest lower bound; dually, every nonemply subset X that has an upper bound has a least upper bound.

The axioms that are of issue in this thesis are Ax. 5, 9, 11, 13, 15, and 16 only. The reason for the other axioms have a holding probability of 1 is the same as that described in [1].

3 Research Results

Similar to that stated in [1], we will adopt total inspections within the range of $M + E \leq 6$. Before doing this, let us look at two or three points of discussion. In the binary system, since $0.1 \times 0.1 = 0.01$ and $0.1/0.1 = 1$, when $M = 1$, the result is the same whether the second decimal place is truncated or whether it is rounded off after normalization. Therefore, there is no change in multiplication and inverse operations. Moreover, since $0.10 \times 0.10 = 0.0100$, $0.10 \times 0.11 = 0.0110$, and $0.11 \times 0.11 = 0.1001$, the results are also the same whether the third decimal place is truncated or whether it is rounded off after normalization.

Therefore, the multiplication arithmetic for both agree when $M = 2$. For this reason, the holding probabilities of Ax. 9, Ax. 11, and Ax. 16 when $M = 1$ and the holding probabilities of Ax. 9 and Ax. 16 when $M = 2$ are the same as when operations are introduced by rounding off. Let us now try to determine the value of $F(M, E)\|\text{Ax. } n\|$ $(n = 5, 9, 11, 13, 15, 16)$ (Table 1).

Next, the graphs of the results of random sampling are shown in Figs. 1–6.

4 Conclusion

When comparing Figs. 1–6 and the graphs that correspond to these of [1], overall they are nearly the same, with the exception of the holding probability of Ax. 11. (There may be some places in which their probabilities rise by 5 or 6%.)

Next, the limit values are as indicated below:

$$\lim_{M=E\to\infty} F_2(M, E)\|\text{Ax. } 5\| = 1.00$$
$$\lim_{M=E\to\infty} F_2(M, E)\|\text{Ax. } 9\| = 0.61$$
$$\lim_{M=E\to\infty} F_2(M, E)\|\text{Ax. } 11\| = 0.85$$
$$\lim_{M=E\to\infty} F_2(M, E)\|\text{Ax. } 13\| = 0.98$$
$$\lim_{M=E\to\infty} F_2(M, E)\|\text{Ax. } 15\| = 0.67$$
$$\lim_{M=E\to\infty} F_2(M, E)\|\text{Ax. } 16\| = 0.92$$

Table 1 Total inspection $E + M \leq 6$ (omitting 0.1)

(M, E)	Ax. 5	Ax. 9	Ax. 11	Ax. 13	Ax. 15	Ax. 16
(1,1)	6,800	1.00	—	8,720	7,600	3,500
(2,1)	6,872	1.00	—	6,927	8,086	5,139
(3,1)	5,693	9,674	—	5,587	8,106	6,434
(4,1)	4,860	9,581	—	4,742	8,069	6,723
(5,1)	4,367	9,423	—	4,213	8,037	7,012
(1,2)	6,927	1.00	2,500	8,683	7,654	7,639
(2,2)	6,792	9,609	3,750	6,442	8,789	8,116
(3,2)	6,678	8,758	4,375	5,216	9,231	8,466
(4,2)	6,298	8,305	4,688	4,671	9,425	8,562
(1,3)	8,046	9,056	6,250	9,544	7,716	8,778
(2,3)	8,041	8,753	6,875	8,009	8,563	8,941
(3,3)	7,650	7,953	7,188	6,905	9,116	9,053
(1,4)	9,003	8,473	8,125	9,777	7,397	9,139
(2,4)	9,225	8,303	8,438	8,900	7,905	9,204
(1,5)	9,511	8,185	9,063	9,812	7,093	9,272

If we are willing to overlook the value of Ax. 11, no significant differences can be observed in these values, either.

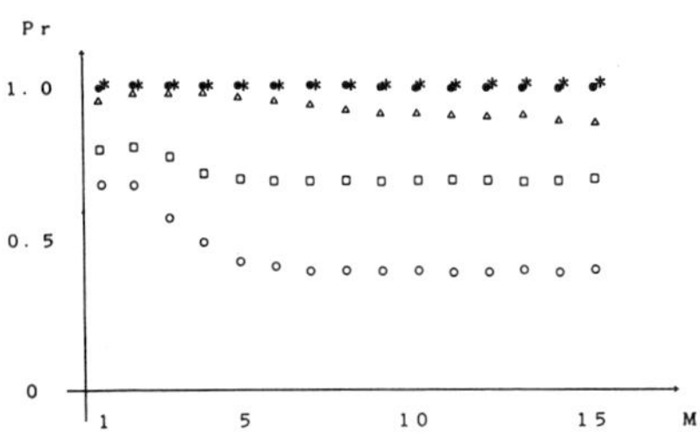

○ : $E = 1$, □ : $E = 3$, △ : $E = 5$,
• : $E = 7$, $*$: $E = 12$.

Fig. 1 The holding probability of Ax. 5.

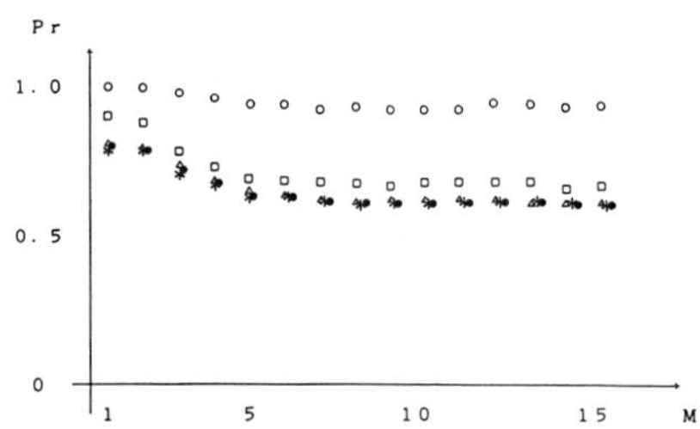

○ : $E = 1$, □ : $E = 3$, △ : $E = 5$,
• : $E = 7$, $*$: $E = 12$.

Fig. 2 The holding probability of Ax. 9.

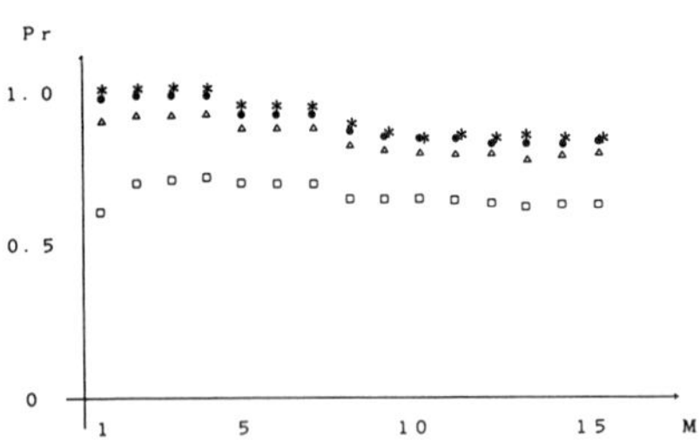

○ : $E = 1$, □ : $E = 3$, △ : $E = 5$,
• : $E = 7$, $*$: $E = 12$.

Fig. 3 The holding probability of Ax. 11.

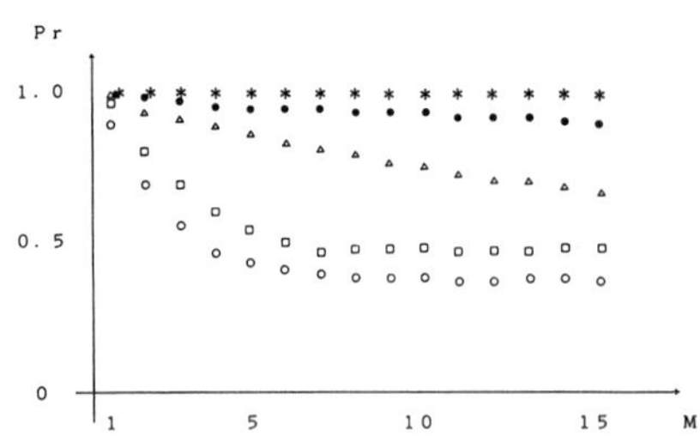

○ : $E = 1$, □ : $E = 3$, △ : $E = 5$,
• : $E = 7$, $*$: $E = 12$.

Fig. 4 The holding probability of Ax. 13.

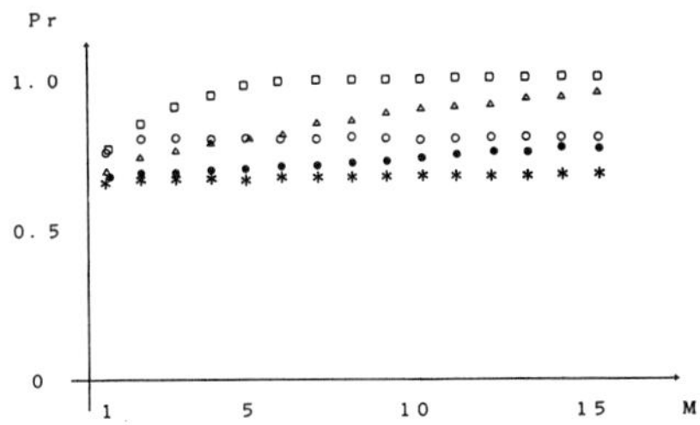

○ : $E = 1$, □ : $E = 3$, △ : $E = 5$,
• : $E = 7$, ∗ : $E = 12$.

Fig. 5 The holding probability of Ax. 15.

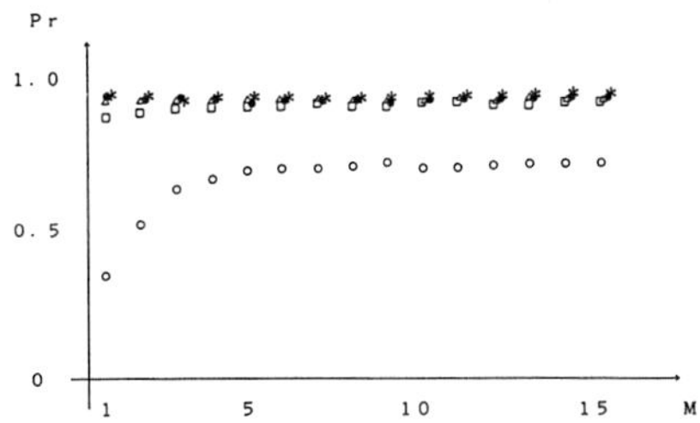

○ : $E = 1$, □ : $E = 3$, △ : $E = 5$,
• : $E = 7$, ∗ : $E = 12$.

Fig. 6 The holding probability of Ax. 16.

Acknowledgments. We must thank Prof. T. Simauti (the Department of Mathematics, Rikkyo University, Tokyo, Japan) for helpful suggestions.

References

[1] Horiguchi, Hiroshi: Floating-Point Numbers and Real Numbers, *Advances in Software Science and Technology*, Vol. 1 (1989), pp. 165–182.

[2] Simauti, Takakazu: On the Computer and Its Mathematical Theory, *Konpyuta to Suugaku 5, Nihon-hyouronsha*, pp. 161–164 (in Japanese).

Initially published in "Computer Software", Vol. 6, No. 1, in Japanese.

Hiroshi Horiguchi
Department of Mathematics
Tokyo Denki University
2–2 Nishiki-cho Kanda
Chiyoda-ku, Tokyo
101 Japan

Tsutomu Tayama
Department of Mathematics
Tokyo Denki University
2–2 Nishiki-cho Kanda
Chiyoda-ku, Tokyo
101 Japan

Constraint Dependency Grammar and Its Weak Generative Capacity

Hiroshi Maruyama

Summary. In order to represent a combinatorial number of syntactically ambiguous parse trees efficiently, we have developed a grammatical theory called *constraint dependency grammar*. In this paper, the formal definition of constraint dependency grammar and its weak generative capacity are discussed. We show that the weak generative capacity of constraint dependency grammars with $arity = 2, degree = 2$ is strictly greater than that of context-free grammars.

1 Introduction

It is known that "every-way" ambiguous constructs, such as prepositional attachment in English, have a Catalan number of ambiguous parses [3], which grows at a faster than exponential rate. A parser should be provided with a packed data structure that does not involve such a combinatorial number of parse trees explicitly. *State set* [4] and *chart* [9] are examples of packed data structures for parse trees. A problem of *state sets* and *charts* is that they can only represent parsing results of purely context-free grammars and lack enough descriptive power for complex grammars of real applications. For example, they were not used for nontrivial augmented context-free grammars such as [8] and [16]. There have been attempts to represent augmented context-free parse trees in a single data structure [1, 14, 16, 15], but the formal descriptive power and computational complexity of these approaches are not known.

We have developed a parsing method in which an intermediate parsing result is represented as a single constraint network over a finite domain [10]. Every solution that satisfies all the constraints simultaneously corresponds to an individual parse tree. No explicit parse trees are generated until ultimately necessary. Parsing and successive disambiguation are performed by adding new constraints to a data structure called a *constraint network*. Newly added constraints are efficiently propagated over the network by *constraint propagation* [17, 12] to make the network locally consistent. We have already shown that both (1) the computational complexity of forming an initial constraint network and (2) the computational complexity of constraint propagation are bounded by n^4, where n is the length of the input sentence [10].

Constraint dependency grammar (CDG for short) is a formal grammatical theory developed for this parsing technique. In this paper, we investigate the weak generative capacity of CDG. We will show that, under certain conditions, the set of languages generated by CDG properly includes the set of languages generated

ISBN 0-12-037103-0

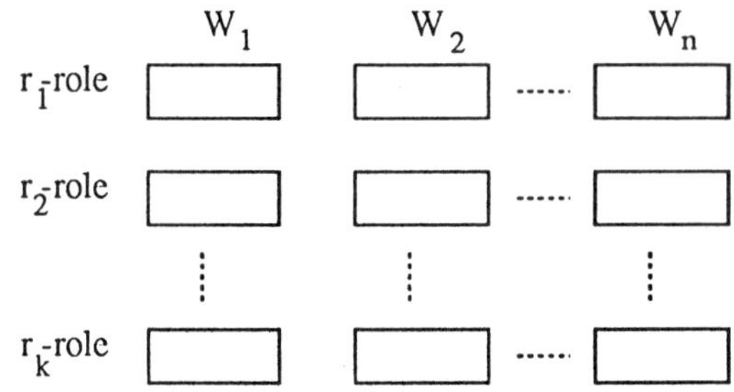

Fig. 1 Words and their *roles*.

by context-free grammar (CFG). As a result, there are non-context-free languages that are generated by a CDG.

We give the definition of CDG in the next section. Then, in Section 3, we prove that the weak generative capacity of CDG is strictly greater than that of CFG.

2 Constraint Dependency Grammar: Definition

Let a sentence $s = w_1 w_2 \dots w_n$ be a finite string on a finite alphabet Σ. Let $R = \{r_1, r_2, \dots, r_k\}$ be a finite set of *role-ids*. Suppose that each word i in a sentence s has k-different roles $r_1(i), r_2(i), \dots, r_k(i)$. Roles are like variables, and each role can have a pair `<a,d>` as its value, where the *label* a is a member of a finite set $L = \{a_1, a_2, \dots, a_l\}$ and the *modifiee* d is either $1 \leq d \leq n$ or a special symbol `nil`. An analysis of the sentence s is obtained by assigning appropriate values to the $n \times k$ roles (we can regard this situation as one in which each word has a frame with k slots, as shown in Fig. 1).

An *assignment* A of a sentence s is a function that assigns values to the roles. Given an assignment A, the label and the modifiee of a role x are determined. We define the following four functions to represent the various aspect of the role x, assuming that x is an r_j-role of the word i:

- $pos(x) \stackrel{\text{def}}{=}$ the position i of x
- $rid(x) \stackrel{\text{def}}{=}$ the role id r_j of x
- $lab(x) \stackrel{\text{def}}{=}$ the label of x
- $mod(x) \stackrel{\text{def}}{=}$ the modifiee of x

We also define $word(i)$ as the terminal symbol occurring at the position i.[1] Note that the domain of the first four functions is the set of roles, while the domain of $word()$ is a subset of integers. Therefore, $word(mod(x))$ is a valid term while $mod(mod(x))$ is not.

[1] In this paper, when referring to a word, we purposely use the *position* (1,2,...,n) of the word rather than the word itself ($w_1, w_2, \dots, w_n$), because the same word can occur in many different positions in a sentence. For readability, however, we sometimes use the notation $word_{position}$.

An individual grammar G in the CDG theory determines a set of possible assignments of a given sentence. G is represented as a four-tuple:

$$G = < \Sigma, R, L, C >$$

where

- Σ is a finite set of terminal symbols,
- R is a finite set of role-ids,
- L is a finite set of labels, and
- C is a constraint that an assignment A should satisfy.

A constraint C is a logical formula in a form

$$\forall x_1 x_2 ... x_p : role; P_1 \& P_2 \& ... \& P_m \qquad (p \geq 1)$$

where the variables $x_1, x_2, ..., x_p$ range over the set of roles in an assignment A and each subformula P_i consists only of the following vocabulary:

- Variables: $x_1, x_2, ..., x_p$
- Constants: elements of $\Sigma \cup L \cup R \cup \{\texttt{nil}, 1, 2, \ldots\}$
- Function symbols: $word(), pos(), rid(), lab()$, and $mod()$
- Predicate symbols: $=, <$, and $>$
- Logical connectors: $\&, |$, and $\neg$.

Specifically, we call a subformula P_i a *unary constraint* when P_i contains only one variable, and a *binary constraint* when P_i contains exactly two variables.

The semantics of the functions have been defined above. The semantics of the predicates and the logical connectors are defined as usual, except that comparing `nil` with another value by the inequality predicates $<$ and $>$ always yields the truth value **false**.

These conditions guarantee that, given an assignment A, it is possible to compute whether the values of $x_1, x_2, \ldots, x_p$ satisfy C in a constant time, regardless of the sentence length n.

Definition

- The *degree* of a grammar G is the size of the role-id set R.
- The *arity* of a grammar G is the number of variables in the constraint C.

  Unless otherwise stated, we deal with only $arity = 2$ cases.
- A nonnull string s over the alphabet Σ is *generated* iff there exists an assignment A that satisfies the constraint C.
- $L(G)$ is a *language* generated by the grammar G iff $L(G)$ is the set of all sentences generated by a grammar G.

In the following discussion, we consistently ignore the null string ϵ. The null string has no roles and is always generated by any grammar.

$$X_* \to a\ Y_1{}^*\ Y_2{}^*\ \cdots\ Y_m{}^*$$

Fig. 2 Annotated rule.

3 Weak Generative Capacity of CDG

We show that the weak generative capacity of CDG with $arity = 2$ and $degree = 2$ is strictly greater than that of CDG. This is done by proving the following two propositions:

- *For any context-free language, there exists a CDG with arity=2 and degree=2 that generates the language (i.e., $L(CFG) \subset L(CDG)$).*
- *There exists a non-context-free language that is generated by a CDG (i.e., $L(CDG) \not\subset L(CFG)$).*

3.1 $L(CFG) \subset L(CDG)$

We prove $L(CFG) \subset L(CDG)$ by (1) constructing a constraint dependency grammar G_{CDG} from an arbitrary context-free grammar G_{CFG} in Greibach Normal Form, (2) showing $L(G_{\text{CFG}}) \subset L(G_{\text{CDG}})$, and (3) showing $L(G_{\text{CDG}}) \subset L(G_{\text{CFG}})$.

3.1.1 Constructing G_{CDG} from G_{CFG}

Let $G_{\text{CFG}} =< \Sigma, V, P, S >$ be a context free grammar in Greibach Normal Form [5] where Σ is an alphabet, V is a set of nonterminal symbols, P is a set of production rules, and S is the start symbol. We construct $G_{\text{CDG}} =< \Sigma, R, L, C >$ with degree=2 and arity=2 from G_{CFG} as described below.

Let R be $\{head, body\}$. The analysis of a sentence by G_{CDG} is, therefore, to assign a *head-role* and a *body-role* to each word.

In G_{CDG}, any nonterminal symbol $X \in V$ can appear only a finite number of times in the production rules P. Let $X_1, X_2, \ldots$ be occurrences of the nonterminal symbol X on the left-hand side of the production rules. They are called a *left occurrence* of the nonterminal X. The set of all left occurrences of X is written X_H. Similarly, let X^1, $X^2, \ldots$ be occurrences of X on the right-hand side of the production rules. They are called a *right occurrence*, and the set of all right occurrences is written X^B. Let

- $V_H = \cup X_H (X \in V)$,
- $V^B = \cup X^B (X \in V)$.

Every production rule can be rewritten as shown in Fig. 2 by replacing each occurrence of a nonterminal symbol by the indexed one, so that every X_* or Y^* appears only once in all the production rules in P (superscript and subscript asterisks represent appropriate indices), where $a \in \Sigma, X_* \in V_H$, and $Y_i{}^* \in V^B (1 \le i \le m)$. We call the indexed version of a production rule an *annotated rule.* The set of labels L of G_{CDG} is defined as

- $L = V_H \cup V^B \cup \{\#\}$

The constraint C of G_{CDG} is the conjunction of the following seven types of formulas (x, y are roles and universally quantified):

1. (*Lexical*)

   For every nonterminal symbol $a \in \Sigma$,

$$\begin{aligned} &word(pos(x)) = a, rid(x) = head \Rightarrow \\ &\quad lab(x) \in \{X_{0*} \mid X_{0*} \rightarrow a\ X_1{}^*\ X_2{}^*\ \cdots\ X_m{}^*\} \qquad (0 \le m) \end{aligned}$$

   (The label of the head-role of word a must be a left-occurrence of a nonterminal symbol from which a string beginning with a can be derived.)

2. (*Head-role – body-role consistency*)

   For every nonterminal symbol $X \in V$,

$$\begin{aligned} &pos(x) = pos(y), rid(x) = head, rid(y) = body, lab(x) \in X_L \Rightarrow \\ &\quad lab(y) \in X^R \cup \{\#\} \end{aligned}$$

   (If the head-role label is X_*, the label of the body-role of the same word must be either X^* or $\#$.)

3. (*Loop*)

   For every annotated rule

$$X_{0*} \rightarrow a\ X_1{}^*\ X_2{}^*\ \cdots\ X_m{}^* \qquad (1 \le m),$$

$$\begin{aligned} &lab(x) = X_{0*}, mod(x) = pos(y), rid(y) = body \Rightarrow \\ &\quad pos(x) < pos(y), lab(y) = X_m{}^*, \\ &lab(x) = X_m{}^*, mod(x) = pos(y), rid(y) = body \Rightarrow \\ &\quad pos(x) < pos(y), lab(y) = X_{m-1}{}^*, \\ &\quad \vdots \\ &lab(x) = X_2{}^*, mod(x) = pos(y), rid(y) = body \Rightarrow \\ &\quad pos(x) < pos(y), lab(y) = X_1{}^*, \\ &lab(x) = X_1{}^*, mod(x) = pos(y), rid(y) = head \Rightarrow \\ &\quad pos(x) < pos(y), lab(y) = X_{0*}, \\ &lab(x) = X_1{}^*, pos(y) < pos(x) \Rightarrow \\ &\quad pos(y) \le mod(x) \end{aligned}$$

   (These constraints are introduced so that, for each application of the production rule p, there exists a loop as shown in Fig. 3. That is, if there is a role with any one of the labels $X_{0*}, X_1{}^*, X_2{}^*, ...,$ or $X_m{}^*$, the other roles are determined uniquely. In the figure, the upper half of each box represents a head-role, and the lower half of the box represents a body-role. Whether this sequence is really a loop will be made clear later by the *looping lemma*.)

4. (*Terminal*)

$$lab(x) \in \{X_* \mid X_* \rightarrow a \in P'\} \Leftrightarrow mod(x) = \texttt{nil}, rid(x) = head$$

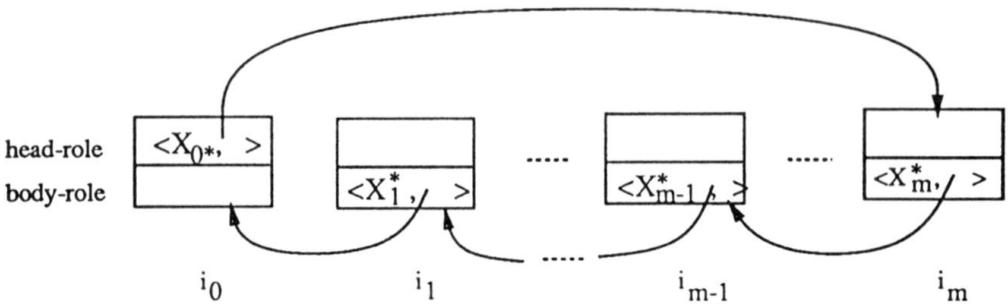

Fig. 3 Loop of modification links.

(This is the $m = 0$ case of Constraint 3, that is, the modifiee of head-role x with the label X_* is $\texttt{nil}(mod(x) = \texttt{nil})$ if and only if the corresponding annotated rule is in the form

$$X_* \rightarrow a.$$

5. (*Start symbol*)

$$rid(x) = head, pos(x) = 1 \Rightarrow \\ lab(x) \in \{S_* \mid S_* is a left-occurrence of the start symbol S of G_{\mathrm{CFG}}\}$$

(The head-role label of the leftmost word is a left-occurrence of the start symbol S of G_{CFG}.)

$$rid(x) = body \Rightarrow (pos(x) = 1 \Leftrightarrow lab(x) = \# \Leftrightarrow mod(x) = \texttt{nil})$$

(Let x be a body-role. Then, $pos(x) = 1$, $lab(x) = \#$, and $mod(x) = \texttt{nil}$ are equivalent.)

6. (*No crossing*)

- $pos(x) < pos(y) < mod(x) \Rightarrow pos(x) \leq mod(y) \leq mod(x)$
- $pos(x) < mod(y) < mod(x) \Rightarrow pos(x) \leq pos(y) \leq mod(x)$
- $mod(x) < pos(y) < pos(x) \Rightarrow mod(x) \leq mod(y) \leq pos(x)$
- $mod(x) < mod(y) < pos(x) \Rightarrow mod(x) \leq pos(y) \leq pos(x)$.

(These conditions assure that no two modifications cross each other.)

7. (*Uniqueness of modifiee with the same label*)

$$x \neq y, mod(x) = mod(y) \neq \texttt{nil} \Rightarrow lab(x) \neq lab(y)$$

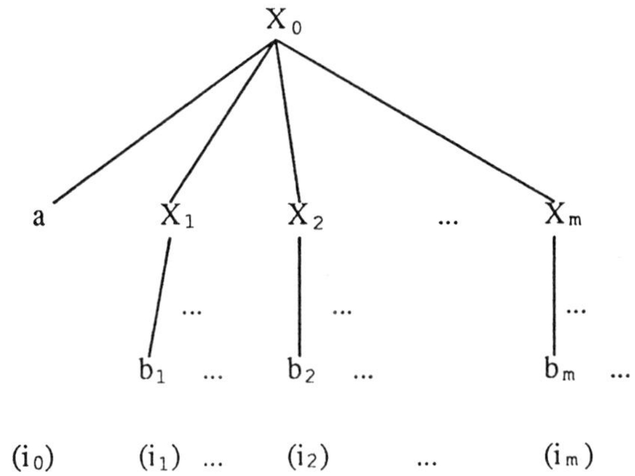

Fig. 4 A rule application in a derivation tree of G_{CFG}.

All of the preceding seven types of constraints are in the form of CDG constraints discussed earlier, and their arity is two. Although in the preceding definition we strictly distinguished a word and its roles, in the following discussion we sometimes refer to a role x by its word position $i = pos(x)$ when it is clear from the context which role, head-role or body-role, we are referring to. In addition, we use the shorthand notation $i \xrightarrow{H} j$ to show that the modifiee of the head-role of word i is j (i.e., $pos(x) = i$ & $rid(x) = head$ & $mod(x) = j$) and $i \xrightarrow{B} j$ to show that the modifiee of the body-role of word i is j (i.e., $pos(x) = i$ & $rid(x) = body$ & $mod(x) = j$).

3.1.2 $L(G_{\mathrm{CFG}}) \subset L(G_{\mathrm{CDG}})$

Let s be an arbitrary sentence generated by G_{CFG}. There is a derivation of G_{CFG} such that $S \overset{*}{\Longrightarrow} s$. We construct an assignment A by using this derivation D. Since G_{CFG} is in Greibach Normal Form, an application of a production rule p

(p) $X_0 \rightarrow a\ X_1\ X_2\ \cdots\ X_m \qquad (0 \leq m)$

is as shown in Fig. 4.

Let the annotated rule p' corresponding to p be

(p') $X_{0*} \rightarrow a\ X_1{}^*\ X_2{}^*\ \cdots\ X_m{}^* \qquad (0 \leq m)$,

and the position of the first word of the string derived from X_j be i_j $(0 \leq j \leq m)$. We assign to the head-role of word i_0

$<X_{0*}, i_m>$ when $m \leq 1$,

$<X_{0*}, \texttt{nil}>$ when $m = 0$,

and to the body-role of word $i_m (1 \leq j \leq m)$

$<X_j{}^*, i_{j-1}>$.

In the derivation tree, a word always appears on the leftmost branch of some node; hence, its head-role is uniquely determined. Every word except the first is derived from some node, which in turn appears on some branch other than the leftmost one of its parent node, so the body-roles are also uniquely determined except for the first word. We define the body-role of the first word to be `<#,nil>`.

It is trivial to show that the assignment A defined earlier, because of the way in which we constructed it, satisfies the constraint C of $G_{\rm CDG}$. Therefore, $s \in L(G_{\rm CDG})$.

□

3.1.3 $L(G_{\rm CDG}) \subset L(G_{\rm CFG})$

From $s \in L(G_{\rm CDG})$, there is an assignment A that satisfies C (1 to 7). First we study various properties of the assignment A. After that, we will show the existence of a derivation D of $G_{\rm CFG}$ such that $S \stackrel{*}{\Longrightarrow} s$.

Because of the constraints 1 (*lexical*) and 2 (*head-role – body-role consistency*), the following conditions hold for any role x:

$$x \text{ is a body-role} \Rightarrow lab(x) \in V^R \cup \{\#\}$$

$$x \text{ is a head-role} \Rightarrow lab(x) \in V_L$$

Considering this property and the constraints 3 (*loop*) and 4 (*terminal*), we can derive the following property:

If $j \neq$ `nil`,

$i \xrightarrow{H} j \Rightarrow i < j$ (a head-role modifies a word on the right)

$i \xrightarrow{B} j \Rightarrow j < i$ (a body-role modifies a word on the left)

Lemma 1 (Looping Lemma) *Every head-role has a left occurrence of some non-terminal symbol as its label. Let the annotated rule corresponding to the label X_{0*} of the head-role of word i_0 be*

$$(p)\ X_{0*} \rightarrow a\ X_1{}^*\ X_2{}^*\ \cdots\ X_m{}^* \qquad (0 \leq m).$$

If $m \geq 1$, there is a unique word sequence $i_1, i_2, \cdots, i_m, j_0$ such that

1. $i_0 \xrightarrow{H} i_m \xrightarrow{B} i_{m-1} \xrightarrow{B} \ldots \xrightarrow{B} i_1 \xrightarrow{B} j_0 \qquad (i_0 < i_m, j_0 < i_1 < \ldots < i_m)$

and

2. $i_0 = j_0$.

(In other words, this lemma says that the loop described in Fig. 3 certainly exists for each rule application where $m \leq 1$.)

Proof. From constraint 3, it is trivial to show that there is a unique word sequence

$$i_1, i_2, \ldots, i_m, j_0$$

that satisfies the first of the conditions. So it suffices to prove $i_0 = j_0$.

Assume that there is at least one word i_0 such that $i_0 \neq j_0$. We consider the minimum i_0 among them. Since the label of the head-role of word j_0 is also X_{0*} (by constraint 3), there exists another sequence

$$j_0 \xrightarrow{H} j_m \xrightarrow{B} j_{m-1} \xrightarrow{B} \ldots \xrightarrow{B} j_1 \xrightarrow{B} k_0 \qquad (j_0 < j_m, k_0 < j_1 < \ldots < j_m).$$

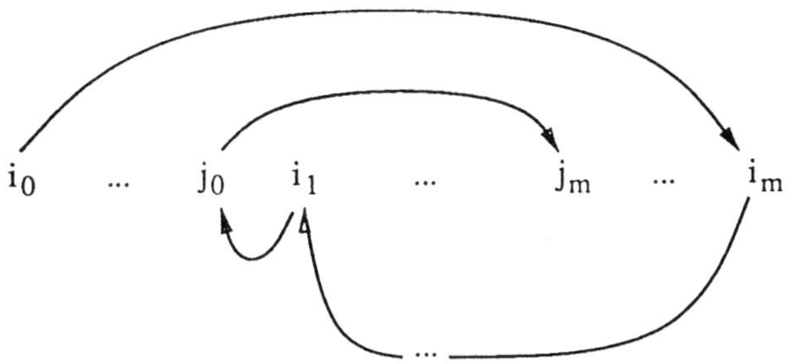

Fig. 5 When $i_0 < j_0$ is assumed.

By the assumption, i_0 and j_0 are distinct. Both have the same head-role label X_{0*}. Therefore, by constraint 7 (*uniqueness of modifiee with the same label*), $i_m \neq j_m$. Similarly, since both i_m and j_m have the same body-role label $X_m{}^*$, $i_{m-1} \neq j_{m-1}$. Repeating the same argument, we can show that $i_{m-2} \neq j_{m-2}, ..., i_1 \neq j_1, j_0 \neq k_0$.

If $j_0 < i_0$, then $j_0 \xrightarrow{H} ... \xrightarrow{B} k_0$ form a loop (i.e., $j_0 = k_0$) by the minimality of i_0. This is contradictory.

Therefore, let us assume that $i_0 < j_0$. Consider two modifications, $i_0 \xrightarrow{H} i_m$ and $j_0 \xrightarrow{H} j_m$. Because $i_0 < j_0 < i_m$, by constraint 6 (*no crossing*), $j_m < i_m$. Since we have already shown that $j_m \neq i_m$, it must be true that $j_m < i_m$.

On the other hand, i_1 is different from any one of $j_1, j_2, ..., j_m$, because we have already shown that $i_1 \neq j_1$ and that the body-role label of i_1, which is $X_1{}^*$, is different from the body-role labels of $j_2, j_3, ..., j_m$.

The arguments up to here are summarized in Fig. 5.

We now show that $j_0 < k_0$. By the same reasoning as above, we know that $j_0 \neq k_0$, so let us assume that $k_0 < j_0$. Then, since i_1 is between k_0 and j_0 ($k_0 < i_1 < j_0$), the modification of the body-role of some j_l ($1 \leq l \leq m$) jumps over i_1 (i.e. $j_l \xrightarrow{B} p$ and $p < i_1 < j_l$) (notice that i_1 should be different from either j_l or p). This modification crosses some modification in the $i_m \xrightarrow{B} i_{m-1} \xrightarrow{B} ... \xrightarrow{B} i_1$ loop. This contradicts constraint 7 (*no crossing*). Therefore, it must be true that $j_0 < k_0$.

By the same reasoning, we can generate the loop beginning from k_0 as

$$k_0 \xrightarrow{H} k_m \xrightarrow{B} k_{m-1} \xrightarrow{B} ... \xrightarrow{B} k_1 \xrightarrow{B} k'_0,$$

the loop beginning from k'_0 as

$$k'_0 \xrightarrow{H} k'_m \xrightarrow{B} k'_{m-1} \xrightarrow{B} ... \xrightarrow{B} k'_1 \xrightarrow{B} k''_0,$$

and so on. Thus, there should be an infinite increasing sequence

$$i_0 < j_0 < k_0 < k'_0 < k''_0 < ...,$$

but in fact there are only n words in the sentence s. Therefore, the assumption that $i_0 \neq j_0$ is contradictory.

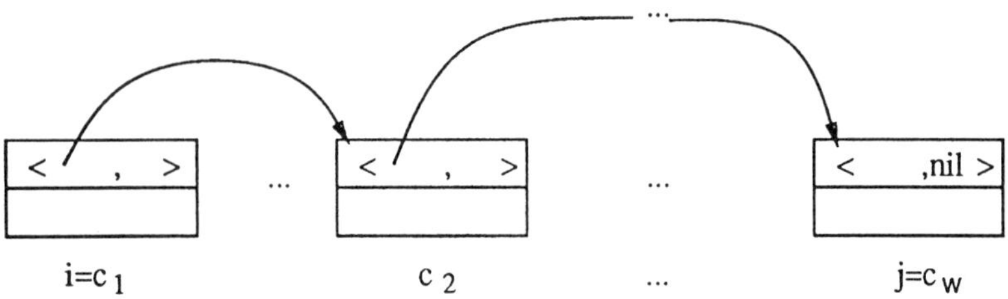

Fig. 6 Closure.

□

Corollary 1.

Let the body-role label of word j be $X_k{}^*$, and the annotated rule that contains $X_k{}^*$ be

(p) $X_{0*} \to a\ X_1{}^*\ X_2{}^*\ \cdots\ X_m{}^* \qquad (1 \leq m).$

Then, there exists a unique sequence

$$i < i_1 < i_2 < ... < j < ... < i_m$$

that forms a loop in the sense of the looping lemma.

Proof. By following the body-role modification links starting from word j, we will reach word i with the head-role $< X_{0*}, i_m >$. From the looping lemma, there is a loop beginning from word i. Applying constraint 7 iteratively, it is clear that word j actually participates in this loop.

□

From the looping lemma and its corollary, it is guaranteed that, provided that $mod(x) \neq \texttt{nil}$, any modification of role x participates in exactly a single loop. Next, we will introduce a notion that corresponds to a phrase of context-free grammar.

Definition

Given an assignment A, the substring α that spans from word i to word j in the sentence s is called a *closure* if and only if there is a sequence of words

$$c_1 \overset{H}{\rightarrow} c_2 \overset{H}{\rightarrow} ... \overset{H}{\rightarrow} c_w \overset{H}{\rightarrow} \texttt{nil}$$

where $c_1 = i$ and $c_w = j$. That is, the head-role modification chain begins with word i ends exactly at the end of word j (see Fig. 6).

If the head-role label of the first word of some closure α is X_*, α is called *X-closure* $(X \in V)$.

Property 1. *Let $\alpha = w_i w_{i+1} ... w_j$ be a closure. If the modifiee of some word p is one of $i+1, i+2, ..., j$ (i.e., $p \overset{H}{\rightarrow} q$ or $p \overset{B}{\rightarrow} q$ and $i+1 \leq q \leq j$), where i is the position of the first word of α and j is the position of the last word of α, then $i \leq p \leq j$. That is, no word outside α can modify a word within α except for the first word of α. We call the string satisfying this condition closed.*

Proof. We employ an induction on the length of α l.

1. When $l = 1$ (i.e., $i = j$), there is no p such that $i + 1 \leq q \leq j$. Hence, the proposition holds.

2. Assume that the proposition holds for any closure whose length is less than l.

   Let the head-role modification chain of α be $c_1(= i)\xrightarrow{H}c_2\xrightarrow{H}...\xrightarrow{H}c_w(= j)\xrightarrow{H}\texttt{nil}$. Because $1 < l, 2 \leq w$. The substring $c_2...c_w$ is also a closure and its length is less than l, so by the assumption of induction, it is closed. Therefore, we only need to investigate the cases where $c_1 < q \leq c_2$. By $c_1\xrightarrow{H}c_2$ and the *no crossing* constraint, $c_1 \leq p \leq c_2$ when $c_1 < q < c_2$. So let us assume that $q = c_2$.

   (a) If $p\xrightarrow{H}q(= c_2)$, the loop that involves this modification begins from c_1. Hence, $p = c_1$.

   (b) If $p\xrightarrow{B}q(= c_2)$, this modification participates in either the loop containing $q\xrightarrow{B}r$ or the loop containing $q\xrightarrow{H}r$. The former is the loop $c_1\xrightarrow{H}c_w(= q)\xrightarrow{B}...\xrightarrow{B}c_1$, so it is impossible that $p\xrightarrow{B}q$ participates in it. Therefore, p must be in the latter loop $c_2(= q)\xrightarrow{H}c_3\xrightarrow{B}...\xrightarrow{B}c_2(= q)$, which means that $p \leq c_3$.

   Thus, p must be within α.

□

Property 2. *Let A be an assignment of a sentence s. Then, s is an S-closure, where S is the start symbol of G_{CFG}.*

Proof. By constraint 5 (*start symbol*), it suffices to show that s is a closure.

Assume that s is a non-closure. Let the length of the sentence s be n. Consider the closure α which starts from the leftmost word of s. Let the head-role modification chain of this closure be $c_1\xrightarrow{H}...\xrightarrow{H}c_w\xrightarrow{H}\texttt{nil}$. Let the length of α be $i - 1 (2 \leq i \leq n, c_1 = 1, c_w = i - 1)$. Since $\alpha \neq s$, there is at least one word on the right of α. Let the word that follows immediately after α be i. The word i is not the leftmost word of s, and therefore there exists k such that $i\xrightarrow{B}k$ and $k < i$. Because α is closed, it must be true that $k = 1$. However, the loop involving this modification $i\xrightarrow{B}k(= 1)$ starts off from the leftmost word and hence, every word in this loop must be between $c_1(= 1)$ and $c_2(< i)$. This is contradictory.

□

Lemma 2. *Given an assignment A to a sentence s, for any V-closure α, there exists a derivation of G_{CFG} such that*

$$V\overset{*}{\Longrightarrow}\alpha.$$

Proof. We prove it by an induction on the length l of closure α.

1. When $l = 1$.

   Let the only word that constitutes α be i. Since α is a closure, the modifiee of the head-role of i is `nil`, and by constraint 4 (*terminal*), there exists an annotated rule

   $$V_* \rightarrow a.$$

   By constraint 1 (*lexical*), the actual symbol of the position i must be a.

2. Assume that the proposition holds for $1 < |\alpha| < l$.

   Let the head-role modification chain of α be $c_1 \xrightarrow{H} c_2 \xrightarrow{H} ... \xrightarrow{H} c_w \xrightarrow{H} \mathtt{nil}$, and the annotated rule corresponding to the head-role label of c_1 be

   $$V_* \rightarrow a\ X_1{}^*\ X_2{}^*\ \cdots\ X_m{}^* \qquad (1 \leq m).$$

   By the looping lemma, there exists a loop starting from c_1,

   $$i_0 (= c_1) \xrightarrow{H} i_m (= c_2) \xrightarrow{B} i_{m-1} ... \xrightarrow{B} i_1 \xrightarrow{B} i_0.$$

   Let α_k be the closure starting from i_k for $1 \leq k \leq m$. We will show that

   $$\alpha = a \alpha_1 \alpha_2 \cdots \alpha_m.$$

   (a) α_k and $\alpha_{k+1} (1 \leq k \leq m-1)$ are disjoint.

   If $|\alpha_k| = 1$, it is trivial to show this by $i_{k+1} \xrightarrow{B} i_k$. We therefore study the case in which $|\alpha_k| > 1$. Assume that the closure α_k that starts from i_k contains the first word of α_{k+1}, namely, i_{k+1}. By $i_m \xrightarrow{B} ... \xrightarrow{B} i_{k+2} \xrightarrow{B} i_{k+1} \xrightarrow{B} i_k$ and closedness of a closure, all $i_{k+2} ... i_m$ are also within α_k. Since α_k is a closure, there is some head-role modification $p \xrightarrow{H} q$ in the head-role modification chain of α_k such that $p < i_m \leq q$. Because of $i_0 \xrightarrow{H} i_m$ and the *no crossing* constraint, $q = i_m$. Considering the loop involving $i_0 \xrightarrow{H} i_m (= q)$ and the one involving $p \xrightarrow{H} q$, these two should be the same loop, but this contradicts $i_0 < p$.

   (b) α_k and α_{k+1} $(1 \leq k \leq m-1)$ are adjacent.

   Assume that there is a string $b\gamma$ (γ may be null) between α_k and α_{k+1}.

   $$\alpha = a ... \alpha_k b \gamma \alpha_{k+1} ...$$

   Let the position of word b be p, the position of the word a be i_0, ... the position of the first word of the string α_k be i_k, the position of the first word of the string α_{k+1} be i_{k+1}, and so on. Because p is not the first word of the sentence, there exists a p such that $p \xrightarrow{B} q$ and $q < p$. By the closedness of α_k and $i_{k+1} \xrightarrow{B} i_k$, $q = i_k$. However, $p \xrightarrow{B} i_k$ cannot participate in either the loop starting from the head-role of i_k or the loop $i_0 \xrightarrow{H} i_m \xrightarrow{B} ... \xrightarrow{B} i_1 \xrightarrow{B} i_0$.

(c) a and α_1 are adjacent.
Similarly, let us assume that α is $a\ b\ \gamma\ \alpha_1 \cdots$, and the position of a is i_0, the position of b is $p = i_0 + 1$, and the position of α_1 is i_1. Because of $i_1 \overset{B}{\rightarrow} i_0$ and the *no crossing* constraint, $p \overset{B}{\rightarrow} i_0$. Since the loop that goes through this $p \overset{B}{\rightarrow} i_0$ cannot participate in the loop beginning with $i_0 \overset{H}{\rightarrow} i_m$, it must be a part of the loop beginning with $i_0 \overset{B}{\rightarrow} r$, where r is outside of closure α. However, this loop cannot come back to position p because of the closedness of closure α. This is contradictory.

Since $|\alpha_k| < l$, by the assumption used in the induction, for every $k (1 \leq k \leq m)$

$$X_k \overset{*}{\Longrightarrow} \alpha_k.$$

Therefore,

$$V \Longrightarrow a X_1 X_2 \cdots X_m \overset{*}{\Longrightarrow} a \alpha_1 \alpha_2 \cdots \alpha_m = \alpha.$$

□

By applying Property 2 and Lemma 2, it can be shown that for any s in L(G_{CDG}), there exists a derivation of $G_{\mathrm{CFG}} S \overset{*}{\Longrightarrow} s$, which means that $s \in L(G_{\mathrm{CFG}})$. Thus, we have proved $L(G_{\mathrm{CDG}}) \subset L(G_{\mathrm{CFG}})$.

□

3.2 $L(CDG) \not\subset L(CFG)$

Next, we show that there is a simple non-context-free language that is generated by a CDG. Consider the language $Lww = \{ww | w \in (a+b)^*\}$, the language of strings that are obtained by concatenating the same arbitrary string over an alphabet {a,b}. Lww is known to be non-context-free [7] and is frequently mentioned when discussing the non-context-freeness of the "respectively" construct (e.g. "A, B, and C do D, E, and F, respectively") of various natural languages (e.g., [13]). Although there is no context-free grammar that generates Lww, a simple constraint dependency grammar can generate it.

Let us consider a constraint dependency grammar $Gww = < \Sigma, L, R, C >$ where

- $\Sigma = \{a, b\}$
- $L = \{l\}$
- $R = \{partner\}$.

Since L and R are singleton sets, we can always ignore the labels and role-ids. The constraint C is a conjunction of the following conditions (x and y are universally quantified):

1. (*Reflexive*)

   - $word(pos(x))$=a $\Rightarrow$ $word(mod(x))$=a
   - $word(pos(x))$=b $\Rightarrow$ $word(mod(x))$=b

- $mod(x) = pos(y) \Rightarrow mod(y) = pos(x)$
- $mod(x) \neq pos(x)$
- $mod(x) \neq \texttt{nil}$

2. (*Right modification*)

   - $pos(x) < pos(y) < mod(y) \Rightarrow pos(x) < mod(x) < mod(y)$

   This constraint specifies that for any word i $(= pos(x))$, if some word j $(= pos(y))$ on the right modifies a word on the right, i should also modify a word on the right. In addition, the ordering of the modifiees is preserved.

3. (*Left modification*)

   - $mod(y) < pos(y) < pos(x) \Rightarrow mod(y) < mod(x) < pos(x)$

   Similarly, this constraint specifies that for any word i, if some word j on the left modifies some other word on the left, i should also modify a word on the left, and the ordering is preserved.

We will prove that the non-context-free language Lww is generated by Gww.

We consider the $Lww \subset L(Gww)$ part first. For any $s \in Lww$, we assign the following values to the only role of each word of s. Let the length of s be $2n$. We assign $i+n$ to the first n roles, where i is the position of the word $(1 \leq i \leq n)$. For the latter half of the sentence, we give $i - n$, where i is the position of the word and $n < i \leq 2n$. This situation is shown in Fig. 7.

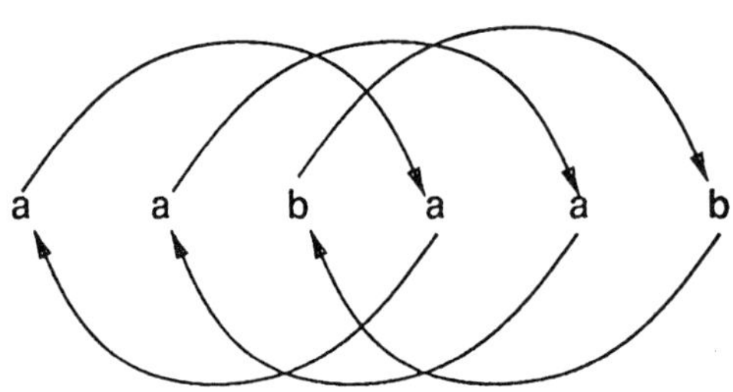

Fig. 7 Assignment to a sentence of Lww.

It is trivial to show that this assignment fulfills all the constraints.

Now let us consider the $L(Gww) \subset Lww$ part. Notice that the number of words in any sentence s in $L(Gww)$ is even, because from constraint 1, every word is paired with a unique word. Let the sentence length be $2n$. In the following discussion, we sometimes use the word positions i and j to refer to the roles x and y where $i = pos(x)$ and $j = pos(y)$.

Lemma 3. *For any i, if $i < mod(i)$ (i modifies a word on the right),*

(a) $i \leq n$,

(b) for any j such that $j < i, i < mod(j)$
(i.e., words on the left of i modify words on the right of i).

Similarly, if $mod(i) < i$ (i modifies a word on the left),

(a) $i > n$,
(b) for any j such that $i < j, mod(j) < i$.

Proof. We prove the $i < mod(i)$ case only. The $mod(i) < i$ case can be proved by the same logic. We use an induction on i.

1. When $i = 1$.

   Since $1 \leq n$, (a) is true. There is no j such that $j < i(= 1)$, so (b) is also true.

2. When $i > 1$.

   Assume that (a) and (b) hold for $1, 2, ..., i - 1$. Let j be an arbitrary word where $j < i$.

   - If $j < i - 1$, then by the assumption, $i - 1 < mod(j)$, which means that $i \leq mod(j)$. However, it cannot be true that $i = mod(j)$ because if so, $j = mod(i)$ (by the *reflexive* constraint), which contradicts the assumption that $i < mod(i)$. Thus, $i < mod(j)$.
   - If $j = i - 1$, then since $j < i < mod(i)$, it follows from constraint 2 that $j = i - 1 < mod(j)$. The $i = mod(j)$ case is rejected by the same reasoning as above, and therefore $i < q$.

   Thus, (b) holds.

   From constraint 1, $i \neq j$ implies that $mod(i) \neq mod(j)$. For this reason and from property (b), there should be at least i different words on the right of the word i. Therefore, $i \leq 2n - 1$. This entails (a).

□

Corollary 3.

- *For any i, $i \leq n \Rightarrow i < mod(i)$*

  (A word in the first half modifies the word on its right).

- *For any i, $n < i \Rightarrow mod(i) < i$.*

  (A word in the second half modifies the word on its left).

Proof. Assume that $i \leq n$. If i modifies the left ($mod(i) < i$), then $i > n$ from Lemma 3. This is contradictory. The same reasoning is used for the second half of the corollary.

□

Property 3. *For any i, if $i \leq n$, $mod(i) = i + n$. Otherwise, $mod(i) = i - n$.*

Proof. Any word i where $1 \leq i \leq n$ modifies the right because of Corollary 3. It follows that $n + 1 \leq mod(i)$, because $mod(i)$ should modify the left. By constraint 2, all right-modifications preserve their ordering, so $mod(1) < mod(2) <$

... $< mod(n)$. These modifiees must take different values of $n+1, n+2, ..., 2n$. Thus, $mod(1) = n+1, mod(2) = n+2, ..., mod(n) = 2n$. Similar reasoning is used for the latter half of the property.

□

By Property 3 and the *reflexive* constraint, it follows that $word(i) = word(i + n)(i \leq n)$. Thus, we have proved $Lww = L(Gww)$.

It is interesting to observe that such a simple language as Lww is not context-free and therefore is classified, according to Chomsky's hierarchy, as a member of the class of context-sensitive languages, for which it is believed that there are no general recognition algorithms running in polynomial time. Consider another language, $Lww^T = \{ww^T | w \in (a+b)^*\}$, which is a set of palindromes over the alphabet {a,b}, and which is known to be context-free. Lww^T is very similar to Lww; for example, it is possible to write special algorithms to recognize these two languages, where the only difference between these algorithms may be the order in which they compare the left and right halves of the string. This similarity is not captured by the context-freeness. In CDG, the language Lww^T is generated by simply replacing the consequent parts of constraints 2 and 3 of Gww by $pos(x) < mod(y) < mod(x)$ and $mod(x) < mod(y) < pos(x)$, respectively.

4 Conclusion

We have proposed a formal grammar that allows efficient structural disambiguation. Grammar rules are constraints on word-to-word modifications, and parsing is done by adding the constraints to a data structure called a constraint network. We showed that the weak generative capacity of CDG is strictly greater than that of CFG.

Although the weak generative capacity of CDG has been shown to be more than context-free, it is not known whether it exceeds the weak generative capacity of context-sensitive grammar (CSG). It can be shown that any language generated by CDG is a member of the language class DSPACE($n$log$n$), but whether DSPACE($n$log$n$) is equal to CSL is an open problem.

CDG is actually being used for an interactive Japanese parser of a Japanese-to-English machine translation system for a newspaper domain [11]. A parser for such a wide domain should make use of any kind of information available to the system, including syntactic, semantic, and pragmatic information, and even information obtained through human interaction. CDG allows, as its rule, any type of knowledge supplied in any order as long as it can be expressed as a constraint between word-to-word modifications.

Formally, a constraint of a CDG is given as a logical formula. However, logical formulas are usually bulky and are difficult to maintain. We are designing a rule language that has a more readable notation and is compiled into logical formulae before parsing.

Acknowledgments. The author wishes to thank the following people for their helpful discussions, suggestions, and encouragement: Hideo Watanabe, Shin'ichi Morishita, and the members of the Japanese Processing Group of Tokyo Research Laboratory, IBM Japan.

References

[1] Barton, G. E. and Berwick, R. C.: "Parsing with Assertion Sets and Information Monotonicity," *Proc. of IJCAI '85* (1985), pp. 769–771.

[2] Barton, G. E., Berwick, R. C., and Ristad, E. S.: *Computational Complexity and Natural Language,* MIT Press, 1987.

[3] Church, K. and Patil, R.: "Coping with Syntactic Ambiguity, or How to Put the Block in the Box on the Table," *American Journal of Computational Linguistics*, Vol. 8, No. 3–4 (1982), pp. 139–149.

[4] Earley, J.: "An Efficient Context-Free Parsing Algorithm," *Comm. ACM,* Vol. 13, No. 2, pp. 94–102 (1970).

[5] Greibach, S. A.: "A New Normal Form Theorem for Context-Free Phrase Structure Grammars," *J. ACM*, Vol. 12, No. 1 (1965), pp. 42–52.

[6] Hays, D. E.: "Dependency Theory: A Formalism and Some Observations," *Language*, Vol. 40 (1964), pp. 511–525.

[7] Hopcroft, J. E. and Ullman, J. D.: *Introduction to Automata Theory, Languages, and Computation*, Addison-Wesley, 1979.

[8] Jensen, K., Heidorn, G. E., Richardson, S. D., and Haas, N.: "PLNLP, PEG, and CRITIQUE: Three Contributions to Computing in the Humanities," *Proc. the Conference on Computing in the Humanities,* University of Toronto (1986), pp. 183–193.

[9] Kaplan, R. M.: "A general Syntactic Processor," in: Rustin, R. (ed.): *Natural Language Processing*, Algorithmics Press, 1973.

[10] Maruyama, H.: "Structural Disambiguation with Constraint Propagation," *Proc. of Annual Meeting of ACL '90*, Pittsburgh, to appear.

[11] Maruyama, H., Watanabe, H., and Ogino, S.: "An Interactive Japanese Parser for Machine Translation," *Proc. of COLING '90*, Helsinki, to appear.

[12] Montanari, U.: "Networks of Constraints: Fundamental Properties and Applications to Picture Processing," *Information Science*, Vol. 7 (1976).

[13] Savitch, W. J., Bach, E., Marsh, W., and Safran-Naveh, G. (eds.): *The Formal Complexity of Natural Language*, Reidel, 1987.

[14] Rich, E., Wittenburg, K., Barnett, J., and Wroblewski, D. : "Ambiguity Procrastination," *Proc. AAAI '87* (1987), pp. 571–576.

[15] Seo, J. and Simmons, R.: "Syntactic Graphs: A Representation for the Union of All Ambiguous Parse Trees," *Computational Linguistics*, Vol. 15, No. 7 (1988), pp. 19–32.

[16] Tomita, M.: "An Efficient Augmented-Context-Free Parsing Algorithm," *Computational Linguistics*, Vol. 13 (1987), pp. 31–46.

[17] Waltz, D. L.: "Understanding Line Drawings of Scenes with Shadows," in: Winston, P. H. (ed.): *The Psychology of Computer Vision*, McGraw-Hill (1975).

Initially published in "Computer Software", Vol. 7 No. 3, in Japanese.

Hiroshi Maruyama
IBM Research, Tokyo Research Laboratory
IBM Japan
5–11 Sambancho, Chiyoda-ku, Tokyo
102 Japan

Rules for Submission of English Papers and English Paper Style Guidelines

1 Rules for Submission of English Papers

"Advances in Software Science and Technology" will publish articles in the following areas of research:

1. software foundation
2. algorithms
3. programming languages
4. operating systems
5. programming methodology
6. software engineering
7. database
8. human factors in software
9. computer architecture
10. artificial intelligence
11. understanding and processing natural languages
12. knowledge engineering
13. recognition and learning models
14. other computer software related themes

1.1 Submission of Papers

The following papers will be published in "Advances in Software Science and Technology":

1. Papers that are reports of academic research by members of the Society, and are original, novel, and useful.

2. Papers that contain thought on academic or technical problems based on the thought of the author, can be sufficiently understood by members outside of the author's field, and bring about debate on points of dispute and thought.

3. Papers that investigate comprehensively the historical development of a particular field, and stimulate debate on technolgy.

4. Papers that announce research results as short notes.

5. Others.

1.2 Procedure for Submission

1. Submission of papers is, as a rule, limited to honorary, regular, and student members of the Society. If there is more than one author, at least one must

ISBN 0-12-037103-0

be an honorary, regular, or student member of the Society. Manuscripts may be solicited by the Editorial Board. These manuscripts are treated in the same manner as contributed manuscripts.

2. Manuscripts should be written according to the English Paper Style Guidelines.

3. Six copies of the manuscript should be made, and the author should retain one. Five copies should be sent to the Editor-in-Chief.

4. The final version of the accepted paper should be prepared according to the Author's Guide as determined by the Editorial Board, and sent to the Editor-in-Chief.

5. Papers should be sent to the following address:

   Editor-in-Chief
   Japan Society for Software Science and Technology
   World Trade Center Building, Box 104
   4–1 Hamamatsu-cho 2-chome, Minato-ku
   Tokyo, 105 Japan

1.3 Handling of Papers

1. The Editor-in-Chief will record the date of reception of the manuscript, give it a receipt number, and inform the author of these.

2. The paper will be refereed by persons determined by the Japan Society for Software Science and Technology. Accepted papers will be published in the journal "Advances in Software Science and Technology." Papers solicited by the Editorial Board will be refereed in the same manner. As a rule, papers will not be returned.

3. A final copy of the manuscript of an accepted paper prepared according the English Paper Style Guidelines will be requested.

2 English Paper Style Guidelines

2.1 Submission of Papers

As a rule, the following papers are contributed by members of the Japan Society for Software Science and Technology:

1. Unpublished papers.

2. Papers which have been published in the Japanese-language journal, "Computer Software," but have not appeared in English.

3. Papers solicited by the Editorial Board.

2.2 Structure of the Paper

1. Beginning from page one, the following should appear, in this order: title, author, author's affiliated institution, abstract, the body of the paper, bibliography.

2. Figures or tables: These should appear at appropriate places in the paper. However, illustrations which must be traced should appear on a separate page.
3. A separate page with the following information should accompany the manuscript:

   Title
   Author and affiliated institution
   Submission date
   Address for inquiries to the author (address, telephone number, and when available, fax number and electronic mail address)

The title should indicate clearly the content of the paper. The abstract should be limited to 100–150 words, and the main points should be made clear.

The manuscript should consist of an introduction and the body. The introduction should situate the problem and state the aims of the paper. The body of the paper should make clear what is being argued and how. The body should not be merely a display of facts, but should present methods for solving problems and hypotheses. It should further describe conclusions, evaluation, and future prospects.

2.3 Bibliography

1. As a rule the bibliography should be in alphabetical order by the author's last name, preceded by a number.

   Examples:

   [1] Codd, E. F. : A Relational Model ...
   [2] Doi, N. : ...
   [3] Liskov, B. H. and Zilles, S. N. : ...

2. When a reference is cited in the paper, it should be indicated by the bibliography number.

   Example:

   ... shows the transition among the three modes [2] ...

3. Generally accepted bibliographic abbreviations (ISO 4, ISO 833) should be used (see Table 1). In addition, Table 2 contains English abbreviations for representative Japanese journals.

   Examples:

   IEEE Trans. Comput.
   IEEE Trans. Softw. Eng.
   Comm. ACM
   ACM Trans. Math. Softw.

4. References should be formatted as follows:

(a) As a rule, the names of all connected persons should appear, with "and" appearing before the name of the last person.

(b) In the case of a paper, items should appear in the following order: author, title, journal (in italics), volume, number, year, pages.

Examples:

[1] Codd, E. F. : A Relational Model of Data for Large Shared Data Banks, *Comm. ACM*, Vol. 13, No. 6 (1970), pp. 377–383.

[2] Liskov, B. H. and Zilles, S. N. : Specification Technique for Data Abstraction, *IEEE Trans. Softw. Eng.*, Vol. SE–1, No. 1 (1975), pp. 7–19.

[3] Nakajima, R., Honda, M., and Nakahara, H. : Hierarchical Program Specification and Verification — A Many-sorted Logical Approach, *Acta Informatica*, Vol. 14 (1980), pp. 135–155.

(c) When the citation is a collection, items should appear in the following order: author (ed.), title (in italics), (volume), publisher, year.

Examples:

[1] Stoy, J. E. (ed.) : *Denotational Semantics — The Scott-Strachey Approach to Programming Language Theory*, MIT Press, 1977.

[2] Yeh, R. (ed.) : *Current Trends in Programming Methodology*, Vols. 1–4, Prentice Hall, 1977.

[3] Yoneda, N. (ed.) : *Programming Languages*, Joho-Kagaku 9, Iwanami Shoten, 1983 (in Japanese).

2.4 Figures and Tables

Figures which must be traced should be about 1.5 times the size which they will appear in the journal, clearly drawn with necessary accuracy. Figures consisting of computer output such as programs and execution results will be reduced in size and appear as they are, so they should be as clear as possible. Consult the Author's Guide concerning figures and tables of the final version.

2.5 Footnotes

Use footnotes to give information not directly related to the main topic. However, they should be neither numerous nor excessively long. The footnote should be indicated by a small superscript in the body of the paper.

Table 1 Abbreviated journal names.

journal names	abbreviated names
ACLS Newsletter	*ACLS Newsl.*
ACM Transactions on Database Systems	*ACM Trans. Database Syst.*
ACM Transactions on Mathematical Software	*ACM Trans. Math. Softw.*
ACM Transactions on Programming Languages and Systems	*ACM Trans. Prog. Lang. Syst.*
Acta Informatica	*Acta Inf.*
AEDS Journal	*AEDS J.*
AEDS Monitor	*AEDS Monit.*
ALGOL Bulletin	*ALGOL Bull.*
American Journal of Computational Linguistics	*Am. J. Comput. Linguist.*
American Scientist	*Am. Sci.*
Annals	*Ann.*
The Annals of the American Academy of Political and Social Science	*Annals AAPSS*
Applied Mathematics and Computation	*Appl. Math. Comput.*
Artificial Intelligence	*Artif. Intell.*
Association for Literary and Linguistic Computing-Bulletin	*Assoc. Lit. Linguist. Comput. Bull.*
The Australian Computer Journal	*Aust. Comput. J.*
Bell System Technical Journal	*Bell Syst. Tech. J.*
BIT	*BIT*
Communications of the ACM	*Comm. ACM*
Computer	*Computer*
Computer Aided Design	*Comput. Aided Des.*
Computer Bulletin	*Comput. Bull.*
Computer Design	*Comput. Des.*
Computer Educator	*Comput. Educ.*
Computer Graphics and Art	*Comput. Gr. Art*
Computer Graphics and Image Processing	*Comput. Gr. Image Process.*
Computer Graphics Newsletter	*Comput. Gr. Newsl.*
Computer Journal	*Comput. J.*
Computer Languages	*Comput. Lang.*
Computer Methods in Applied Mechanics and Engineering	*Comput. Methods Appl. Mech. Eng.*
Computers and Biomedical Research	*Comput. Biomed. Res.*
Computers & Graphics	*Comput. Gr.*
Computers and Humanities	*Comput. Hum.*
Computing	*Computing*
Computing Newsletter	*Comput. Newsl.*
Computing Surveys	*Comput. Surv.*
Datamation	*Datamation*
Education Technology	*Educ. Tech.*
Engineering and Instrumentation	*Eng. Instrum.*
IBM Journal of Research and Development	*IBM J. Res. Dev.*
IBM Systems Journal	*IBM Syst. J.*
IEEE Spectrum	*IEEE Spectrum*
IEEE Transactions on Computers	*IEEE Trans. Comput.*
IEEE Transactions on Software Engineering	*IEEE Trans. Softw. Eng.*
Industrial Engineering	*Ind. Eng.*

Table 1 Abbreviated journal names (continued).

journal names	abbreviated names
Information and Control	*Inf. Control*
Information Processing and Management	*Inf. Process. Manage.*
Information Processing Letters	*Inf. Process. Lett.*
Information Science	*Inf. Sci.*
The Information Scientist	*The Inf. Sci.*
Information Systems	*Inf. Syst.*
Instrumentation Technology	*Instrum. Technol.*
International Journal of Bio-Medical Computing	*Int. J. Bio-Med. Comput.*
International Journal of Computer and Information Sciences	*Int. J. Comput. Inf. Sci.*
International Journal of Computer Mathematics	*Int. J. Comput. Math.*
International Journal of General Systems	*Int. J. General Syst.*
International Journal of Man-Machine Studies	*Int. J. Man-Mach. Stud.*
Journal of the ACM	*J. ACM*
Journal of the American Society for Information Science	*J. Am. Soc. Inf. Sci.*
Journal of the American Statistical Association	*J. Am. Stat. Assoc.*
Journal of Chemical Information & Computer Sciences	*J. Chem. Inf. Comput. Sci.*
Journal of Clinical Computing	*J. Clin. Comput.*
Journal of Computational Physics	*J. Comput. Phys.*
Journal of Computer and System Sciences	*J. Comput. Syst. Sci.*
Journal of Cybernetics and Information Sciences	*J. Cybern. Inf. Sci.*
Journal of the Franklin Institute	*J. Franklin Inst.*
Journal of Symbolic Logic	*J. Symbolic Logic*
Journal of Systems Management	*J. Syst. Manage.*
Law and Computer Technology	*Law Comput. Technol.*
Management Information Systems Quarterly	*Manage. Inf. Syst. Q.*
Management Science	*Manage. Sci.*
Mathematical Programming	*Math. Program.*
Mini-Micro Systems	*Mini-Micro Syst.*
Nachrichtentechnische Zeitschrift	*Nachrichtentech. Z.*
Operations Research	*Oper. Res.*
Pattern Recognition	*Pattern Recogn.*
Popular Computing	*Pop. Comput.*
Proceedings of the IEEE	*Proc. IEEE*
Proceedings of the SID	*Proc. SID*
Science	*Science*
Scientific American	*Sci. Am.*
SIAM Journal on Applied Mathematics	*SIAM J. Appl. Math.*
SIAM Journal on Computing	*SIAM J. Comput.*
SIAM Journal on Control	*SIAM J. Control*
SIAM Journal on Mathematical Analysis	*SIAM J. Math. Anal.*
SIAM Journal on Numerical Analysis	*SIAM J. Num. Anal.*
SIAM Review	*SIAM Rev.*
SID Journal	*SID J.*
Simulation	*Simulation*
Software—Practice & Experience	*Softw. Prac. Exper.*
Soviet Cybernetics Review	*Sov. Cybern. Rev.*
Theoretical Computer Science	*Theor. Comput. Sci.*

Table 2 Abbreviated Japanese journal names.

journal names	abbreviated names
Advances in Software Science and Technology	*Advances Softw. Sci. Tech.*
bit	*bit*
Computer Software	*Comput. Softw.*
Denki Gakkai Ronbunshi	*Trans. Inst. Electrical Eng. Japan*
Denshi Joho Tsushin Gakkaishi	*J. Inst. Electronics, Inf. & Comm. Eng. Japan*
Denshi Joho Tsushin Gakkai Ronbunshi	*Trans. Inst. Electronics, Inf. & Comm. Eng. Japan, Part ∗∗*
Denshi Joho Tsushin Gakkai ∗∗Bumon Zenkoku Taikai Kouen Ronbunshu	*Papers Annual Meet. on ∗∗ of the Inst. Electronics, Inf. & Comm. Eng. Japan*
Gazo Denshi Gakkaishi	*J. Inst. Image Electronics Eng. Japan*
Jinko Chino Gakkaishi	*J. Japan Soc. Artif. Intell.*
Joho Shori	*J. Inf. Proc. Soc. Japan*
Joho Shori Gakkai Ronbunshi	*Trans. Inf. Proc. Soc. Japan*
Joho Shori Gakkai Oubunshi (Journal of Information Processing)	*J. Inf. Process.*
Joho Shori Gakkai Eibunshi (Old) (Information Processing in Japan)	*Information Processing in Japan*
Joho Shori Gakkai ∗∗Kenkyukai Shiryo	*Preprints Work. Gr. for ∗∗, IPSJ*
Joho Shori Gakkai Zenkoku Taikai Kouen Ronbunshu	*Proc. ∗∗th Annual Convention IPS Japan*
Kyouto Daigaku Suri Kaiseki Kenkyusho Koukyuroku	*Papers Res. Inst. Math. Sci., Kyoto Univ.*
Nihon Software Kagakukai Dai∗∗kai Taikai Ronbunshu	*∗∗th Conf. Proc. Japan Soc. Softw. Sc. Tech*
Dai∗∗kai Programming Symposium Houkokushu	*Proc. ∗∗th Program. Symp.*
Suri Kagaku	*Math. Sciences*

Author's Guide

1 Introduction

Authors whose articles have been accepted for publication in "Advances in Software Science & Technology" have been requested to prepare the final form of their accepted papers based on this guide.

2 Sending an Article

When a paper is accepted by the Society, the author of the paper should send the final manuscript to the editor in chief.[1] The final manuscript should consist of two printed copies **and** an electronically recorded copy. If some figures are difficult to record electronically, those figures can be omitted from the electronically recorded copy.

The Society can accept the following media:

- a 5-inch or 3.5-inch floppy disk which is formatted by MS-DOS or PC-DOS (2HD or 2DD), or a compatible disk. The submitted floppy disk is not returned to the author.
- a 5-inch floppy disk written by Xerox Star or JStar. The submitted floppy disk is not returned to the author.
- a quarter-inch streamer cartridge tape in Unix tar format written by a SUN workstation or a compatible tape. Specify "`/dev/rst0`" or "`/dev/rst8`" and the block size. The tape will be returned to the author as a collect parcel.

If you prefer a medium not specified in this list, consult the editorial board[2] in advance.

The author is requested to write the paper on disk or tape as a LaTeX text file using the style file prepared by the Society. If the author has difficulty preparing such a text file, one that includes only text information is also acceptable (any control information must be removed). In this case, the print format for the mathematical formulas should be specified clearly using red ink on the printed copy.

The style file for "Advances in Software Science & Technology" is available from the Society[3] at cost as a 2HD or 2DD 5-inch floppy disk in MS-DOS format. The

[1] Send to: The Japan Society for Software Science and Technology, P. O. Box 104, World Trade Center Building, 4–1 Hamamatsu-cho 2-chome, Minato-ku, Tokyo, 105 Japan.

[2] The Editorial Board, The Japan Society for Software Science and Technology, P. O. Box 104, World Trade Center Building, 4–1 Hamamatsu-cho 2-chome, Minato-ku, Tokyo, 105 Japan. Or write to: Dr. Ikuo Nakata, Institute of Information Sciences and Electronics, University of Tsukuba, Tennodai, Tsukuba-shi, 305 Japan. E-mail `nakata@is.tsukuba.ac.jp`, Facsimile +298–53–5206.

[3] The Society for Software Science and Technology, P. O. Box 104, World Trade Center Building, 4–1 Hamamatsu-cho 2-chome, Minato-ku, Tokyo, 105 Japan.

ISBN 0–12–037103–0

floppy disk contains not only the style file but also this guide itself and a sample paper in LaTeX format.

3 Offprints

The author must purchase at least 100 offprints. Additional offprints can be ordered from the Editor-in-Chief at cost when the author sends the final manuscript. The order must be in units of 100 copies.

The price of the offprints is 2,500yen $\times p +$ 100yen $\times (n - 100)$, where p denotes the number of pages, and n denotes the number of copies.

	8 pages	16 pages	24 pages
100 copies	20,000 yen	40,000 yen	60,000yen
200 copies	30,000 yen	50,000 yen	70,000yen

If the final manuscript is not in LaTeX format, the author must pay 30,000yen for the conversion into LaTeX.

The unabridged edition of the Author's Guide contains instructions on how to use the LaTeX style files, a print sample, a sample of a text file, and instructions on how to specify the print format for the text file. The Author's Guide is available from the Society.

Japan Society for Software Science and Technology Membership Application Form

- Instructions:

  1. Fill in your name, address, and signature.
  2. Indicate desired membership status.
  3. When applying for a regular or student membership, fill in the requested sponsor's signature column.
  4. Send this application to the following address:

     Membership Committee
     Japan Society for Software Science and Technology
     Business Center for Academic Societies Japan
     2–4–16 Yayoi, Bunkyo-ku
     Tokyo, 113 Japan

  5. When membership is granted, an invoice for the membership fee will be sent. Please pay by bank check. After the membership fee is received, the subscription to the Society journal will begin.

Name: ________________________________

Address: ________________________________

city/state/zip/country: ________________________

I guarantee that the information provided for membership in the Japan Society for Software Science and Technology is correct.

Signature: ________________________________

Desired membership status (check one):

(   ) Regular member: Entitles the member to one vote in Society proceedings. Limited to university graduates or those with equivalent education, and who are sponsored by another regular member.

(   ) Student member: Limited to currently matriculated graduate or undergradute students, and requires the sponsorship by a regular member.

(   ) Associate member: Readers of the Society journal, with no right to address Society meetings or submit articles to the Society journal.

· Signature of sponsoring major professor:

University: ______________________________

Department: ______________________________

· Signatures of sponsoring regular members:[1]

Membership number: ______________________

Signature: ______________________________

Membership number: ______________________

Signature: ______________________________

- Publications
  - Society journal: Computer software (in Japanese), bimonthly (January, March, May, July, September, November)
  - English Journal: Advances in Software Science and Technology, annual (October)
  - Newsletter: monthly

  The Society journals and the Newsletters will be sent automatically to members. The journals will be sent to overseas members by surface, or by airmail to those who have paid the airmail fee.

- Conventions: A convention is held annually in the spring. Regular and student members can apply to present papers concerning the results of their research.
- Aims of the Society:
  1. To advance research related to computer software science and technology, to plan its diffusion, and contribute to the development of the technological culture by cooperating in many related areas.
  2. In order to carry out the items in 1, to do the following:
     (a) Convene academic meetings
     (b) Publish journals and books
     (c) Other work deemed necessary

Japan Society for Software Science and Technology
World Trade Center Building, P. O. Box 104
4–1 Hamamatsu-cho 2-chome, Minato-ku
Tokyo, 105 Japan
phone +3–3456–4536

[1] Leave blank if there is no regular member available.

- Membership fees:

Regular member:	14,000 yen (entry fee 2,000 yen + annual membership fee 12,000 yen)
Student	8,000 yen (entry fee 2,000 yen + annual membership fee 6,000 yen)
Associate member	9,000 yen
Airmail fee	3,800 yen

- Signature of Sponsor:

  – Regular member: To apply as a regular member, please indicate your most recent educational history:

  · Most recent university:

  University: ______________________________

  Bachelor of: ______________________________

  Year Graduated: __________________

  University: ______________________________

  Master of: ______________________________

  Year Graduated: __________________

  University: ______________________________

  Doctor of: ______________________________

  Year Graduated: __________________

  · Signature of sponsor:

  Membership number: ______________________

  Signature: ______________________________

  – Student member:

  · Present university

  University: ______________________________

  Department: ______________________________